QUEEN VICTORIA'S Youngest Son

THE UNTOLD STORY OF PRINCE LEOPOLD

CHARLOTTE ZEEPVAT

SUTTON PUBLISHING

British Library Cataloguing in Publication Data
A catalogue record for this book is available from the British
library.

ISBN 0 7509 3791 2

Typeset in 10/12pt sabon.
Typesetting and origination by
Sutton Publishing Limited.
Printed and bound in Great Britain by
J.H. Haynes & Co., Ltd, Sparkford.

CONTENTS

ACKNOWLEDGEMENTS

I wish to thank Her Majesty The Queen for graciously allowing access to documents in the Royal Archives at Windsor, and for permitting extracts from these documents to be published. I also wish to thank the Landgraf Moritz of Hesse for making available Prince Leopold's letters to his sister and brother-in-law from the Hesse Family Archive in Darmstadt. I am grateful to Colonel Richard Abel Smith, The Rt Hon. Lord Ponsonby of Shulbrede, Comte Frédéric de Mensdorff-Pouilly, The Hon. Mrs Crispin Gascoigne, Major Charles Liddell and Mrs Mary Jean St Clair, for allowing the use of material relating to their families, for providing information, or simply for knowing about the project and looking kindly on it.

This book has been like a jigsaw puzzle, without a guiding picture, and I am grateful to the staff of a number of libraries and archives for helping me to find the pieces. First, and above all, I wish to thank everybody at the Royal Archives for their friendliness, knowledge, encouragement and patience (and biscuits!), and especially the Registrar, Sheila de Bellaigue, for unravelling the mysteries of nineteenth-century German handwriting, Jill Kelsey and Allison Derrett for spending hours bringing out documents and putting them away afterwards, and for fielding all sorts of obscure questions, and Frances Dimond, Curator of the Photograph Collection, and her assistant Helen Gray, for their invaluable help with the illustrations.

I would also like to thank Dr E.G. Franz of the Hesse Family Archive, the Director of the Koninklijk Huisarchief in the Netherlands, Colin Harris and the staff of Room 132 at the Bodleian Library, Janet McMullin of Christ Church Library, the staffs of the British Library, the London Library, Oxford City Library and Hampshire Record Office; the National Trust, for use of material from the Hughenden Papers, Geoffrey Davenport, Librarian of the Royal College of Physicians, Dr Christine A. Lee of the Haemophilia Centre at the Royal Free Hospital, Beata Kloska, Librarian of the Royal Society of Medicine, the Archivists of the Royal Society of Arts and the Royal Society of Literature, Anne Clark Amor of the Lewis Carroll Society, and J.S. Dearden, Curator of the Ruskin Gallery. Barbara Williamson, Deputy Director of the Oxford University Careers Service, gave me an unexpected and fascinating tour of the Careers Centre, once Leopold's beloved little house.

Many people have shown an interest in the Prince's story, and come up with interesting material. I am particularly grateful to Sue and Mike Woolmans for following his footsteps around Cannes and Wiltshire (sorry, Mike) and to Sue for chasing up so many vital pieces of information, to Arthur Addington, David Horbury, Dr Denis Gibbs, Paul Minet, Geoffrey Swindells, Steve Webbe, Elizabeth Cuthbert, Christopher Moncrieff, Radmila Slabakova, Clive Linklater, Yvette Dalal, Gil Martin, Robert Golden, Harold Brown, and John Wimbles – and to my mother for patiently reading through the first draft as it happened, and assuring me that it was really quite interesting. Thank you, too, to my agent, Sheila Watson, and my editors, Jane Crompton and Anne Bennett: without all of these people, there would simply be no book.

Charlotte Zeepvat
October 1997

ONE

'OUR FOURTH YOUNG GENTLEMAN'

Oxford. Christ Church Cathedral on a February afternoon when the sun hangs low in the sky, already casting the long shadows of evening. A guide leads a small party into St Michael's Chapel, and, pointing to the stained glass window, begins to tell the sad story of Edith Liddell, whose face was used for St Catherine when Burne-Jones designed the window in her memory. 'She was the younger sister of Alice Liddell, the child who inspired *Alice in Wonderland*,' he says. 'She died very suddenly, only days after becoming engaged. Her family was heartbroken.' The visitors shuffle and sound sympathetic. Someone sits down, and a chair leg scrapes across the floor. 'There are several interesting memorials here. That is Prince Leopold, Queen Victoria's son, who came to Oxford in the 1870s. He fell in love with Alice Liddell – it didn't go very far, of course, but when the Prince married, years later, he called his daughter Alice.' The guide turns and walks away, explaining to anyone who cares to listen that Prince Leopold died of haemophilia, which was hereditary in the royal family. His last audible word is 'Romanov'.

As the footsteps fade into silence, the faintest glow of coloured light from Edith's window touches the pale grey marble of the Prince's memorial. Two people, remembered now for the part they played in someone else's story. Half-known fragments of their lives have been treasured and repeated until they are woven into the folklore of a place, containing truth, and yet removed from it. Edith, sister of Alice . . . Leopold, the man Alice didn't marry. Leopold the Queen's son, Leopold the haemophilic prince, whose suffering set the royal family on the long road leading to Russia, and the tragic illness of the last Tsarevich. Geneticists and

1

haematologists, students of royalty and lovers of *Alice in Wonderland* remember Prince Leopold for these things. But he had his own story, fuller and richer than the sum of these fragments. He lived, laughed, argued, and danced, and endured bouts of illness and depression, coming to terms with the difficult inheritance of haemophilia – and of being royal. He struggled for the right to lead a normal life, throwing enormous energy into every day, because he realised how brief his days could be. He tried to make a difference. To his 'inner circle' of friends, most of whom had some connection with Oxford, he seemed to have immense potential, and his death left an enduring blank. 'Life', one of them told him as his years at Christ Church drew to an end, 'life is precious, and we must try to make the best use of it we can.' He did.

The Prince made his first contribution to medical science unconsciously, on the day he was born. Thirteen years and seven children had not reconciled Queen Victoria to the business of giving birth. She dreaded the ordeal, and when she went into labour early on the morning of 7 April 1853, her doctor, Sir James Clark, called Dr John Snow to Buckingham Palace. Snow was one of the country's few skilled anaesthetists. 'At twenty minutes past twelve by a clock in the Queen's apartment', he wrote, 'I commenced to give a little chloroform with each pain, by pouring about 15 minims by measure upon a folded handkerchief.'[1] Soothed and relaxed, the Queen gave birth to Leopold, her fourth son, at a quarter past one that afternoon.

The use of anaesthetics, particularly in childbirth, was a new technique which raised moral and ethical questions. Many attacked the work of pioneers like Snow, arguing that it was wrong to interfere with the Divinely appointed order which made pain a natural part of giving birth: they predicted serious consequences for mother and baby. But the Queen was not afraid to provoke controversy. She was delighted with the chloroform's effects, and pleased to give the drug her blessing. The editor of *The Lancet* voiced his alarm that a technique which was still experimental had been used on so important a patient: chloroform was known to have caused several deaths. The *British Medical Journal* disagreed, approving of Dr Snow's work, and while the men argued, women knew exactly what to think. Expectant mothers all over the country began to demand chloroform when their time came. The use of anaesthetics in childbirth had come to stay.

The Duchess of Kent, Queen Victoria's mother, was at Clarence House when a messenger brought news that the birth was imminent. She walked to the Palace and arrived in time to see the new baby being carried through to the ministers in the Audience Room. She noticed that he was small – Leopold was the smallest of the Queen's babies at birth – and a vague uneasiness troubled her through the night, which she could not explain. The next day she braved bad weather and went back to the Palace 'to inquire after Victoria, & to see the Baby, the poor thing appeared to be delicate, which made me anxious.'[2] She was the first to sense that there might be a problem with Leopold. The letters that went out announcing his birth to the palaces of Europe were cheerful. The Queen wrote from her bed on 9 April to her uncle, King Leopold I of the Belgians, with news that the baby was to share his name. 'It is a mark of love and affection which I hope you will not disapprove. It is a name which is dearest to me after Albert, and one which recalls the almost only happy days of my sad childhood.'[3] 'I am proud and happy', the King replied, 'that the dear little Gentleman will bear the name of <u>one who has loved You most tenderly since you came into this somewhat confused world</u>.'[4] He would always be especially fond of Leopold.

Another of the baby's names had a very personal association for his mother. In April 1853, Queen Victoria was in the first flush of her long love affair with Scotland: the cornerstone of Balmoral was laid that autumn. She dedicated her baby to Scotland, giving him the name 'Duncan', after 'George', for his godfather, the King of Hanover, and before the inevitable 'Albert'. She even sent to Scotland for a wet-nurse; when Mrs Mackintosh arrived at Buckingham Palace in her bonnet and plaid shawl, speaking barely a word of English, the Queen was pleased to think that her baby would be nourished with the pure milk of the Highlands.

On the second or third day the doctors noticed a problem with the baby's digestion. His mother was told; she was still in bed herself, and would remain there for a little over two weeks. When she saw Leopold on 23 April she found it hard to believe that anything was wrong, and described him in her journal: 'a pretty child with large blue eyes, a very marked nose, a small mouth, & nicely shaped head with more, & darker hair than Arthur had. He fills out daily.'[5]

It was in the Queen's nature to be optimistic about illness, but the baby was not filling out, and his penetrating screams echoed down the palace corridors. He hardly ever slept. On 1 May the family moved to Osborne, where the local physician, Dr Hoffmeister, offered reassurance, but his medicine gave only temporary relief. The screaming went on. The Queen was touched to learn that her second son, eight-year-old Alfred, had visited the nursery twice to ask after his baby brother; the whole family was on edge, and Sir James Clark was sent for from London. It was Dr Hoffmeister, however, who found the answer. The pure milk of the Highlands was disagreeing with the baby, and on 9 May, Hoffmeister brought in Mrs Francis, a shipwright's wife from Cowes. Little Leopold suckled and slept.

In between the diagnosis of the problem and its resolution, the Queen and Prince Albert were working together on their collection of prints when a chance remark from the Prince provoked an outburst of hysterical anger from his wife. She continued in the same state through the next day, critical and tearful, with the Prince trying to calm her by letter. Only when Leopold was peaceful did the truth emerge. Victoria was afraid that she would be held responsible for his suffering, because of her fanciful choice of wet-nurse. In her journal she blamed the doctors for not seeing the problem sooner; at heart, she blamed herself, and she had even started to fear for her baby's life.[6]

This was the first crisis in an emotionally tangled relationship between mother and son. The simple delight the Queen felt in Leopold at first had become complicated by anxiety and an underlying whisper of guilt, which she was unwilling to face. His birth came at the beginning of a period of tension in the life of the royal family. The Queen had entered the year 1853 feeling, regretfully, that time was passing more quickly at thirty-three than it did at twenty-three. She resented her husband's increasing workload, and felt ill-at-ease with her elder children as they entered their teens.

These feelings were only a shadow beside the happier events of family life, but they were real, and each added its own strain.

For the moment, though, the anxiety about Leopold was over, and the Queen was delighted to see him putting on weight and taking notice of his surroundings. On 24 May, her thirty-fourth birthday, he joined the row of excited children waiting to greet her at the foot of the stairs, held in his nurse's arms with a posy of spring flowers balanced on his long gown.[7] But in the first stressful weeks no-one had thought to register his birth, and a late registration fee of seven shillings and sixpence would have to be paid to the Registrar for the Belgravia district.[8] The date of his christening was set for 28 June, the anniversary of the Queen's coronation, and as the royal family returned to Buckingham Palace an impressive list of relatives, friends and dignitaries came together from across Europe for the occasion.

The ceremony was held in the evening. Foreign ministers, Cabinet ministers and guests were shown to their places in the chapel, and the clergy stood beside the communion table, among them the Reverend Henry Liddell, Alice's father, who was one of Prince Albert's chaplains. Then the processions began. First the godparents: King George V of Hanover, Augusta, Princess of Prussia ('my august but intolerably tiresome Godmother', Leopold would later call her[9]), Princess Mary Adelaide of Cambridge and Prince Ernst of Hohenlohe-Langenburg, followed by their attendants. Next, heralds and officers of the Household led in the Queen's procession: Victoria herself, walking with Wilhelm, Prince of Prussia, and holding seven-year-old Princess Helena by the hand, then Prince Albert, leading five-year-old Princess Louise, with the Queen of Hanover. Behind them came Prince Alfred and his elder sisters, the Princesses Victoria and Alice, with Princess Luise of Prussia. At three, Prince Arthur was too young for ceremonies, and the Prince of Wales was confined to his bed with measles. The children were followed by royal guests and members of the Household, and when all had taken their places the music began.

With immense solemnity the Lord Chamberlain and the Lord of the Bedchamber to Prince Albert led the infant Prince into the chapel, carried by the head nurse, with Lady Caroline Barrington in attendance. She it was who took the baby gently from the nurse's arms and handed him to the Archbishop of Canterbury. Leopold screamed. But later, the Queen said, he was good and quiet. At eight o'clock the adult guests sat down to a banquet in the Picture Gallery while the hero of the hour was whisked away to the warmth and security of the nursery.[10]

The nursery would be his world for the next six years, with its regular progressions from Windsor, where the family spent Christmas, to Osborne, then to Buckingham Palace, and again to Osborne for the spring and the Queen's birthday. Then it was back to Buckingham Palace or Windsor until the summer, when Osborne beckoned once more, with its promise of sea bathing and games on the beach. In August and September the nursery remained at Osborne while the Queen and Prince took their elder children north to the Highlands; October would see them all reunited at Windsor, and there would be one more visit to Osborne in early December. In 1853 the nursery was in the capable hands of the Lady Superintendent, Lady Caroline Barrington. 'Lady Car' was the sister of General Grey, Prince Albert's private secretary, and had been one of the Queen's ladies before taking over the nursery. She had also been married with a family, and to Leopold she became like a second mother.

Lady Caroline was responsible for the overall management of the nursery, and for the children's earliest lessons. 'I have got a counting book', Leopold told his father in the summer of 1858, 'and Lady Ca learns me to count in my counting book.'[11] But the daily care of the children fell to the head nurse, Mrs Mary Anne Thurston. A widow in her forties with a grown-up daughter, Mrs Thurston had looked after the royal children since the spring of 1845. They were devoted to her, and she to them; she nursed them through childhood illnesses, heard their troubles and slept in their night nursery; even when they moved to the 'governess class' in the daytime, they went back to her at night. Leopold was especially close to 'Turton', because he needed a nurse so much longer than the other children. He would never forget how much he owed her.

Baby 'Leo' joined two other children in the nursery. Early in their married life the Queen and Prince Albert had devised a plan which divided their family into groups, with timetables and teachers appropriate to their age. At five, Louise was almost old enough for a governess and would soon leave the nursery. Louise was the prettiest of the Queen's daughters and became a gifted artist, but she could be moody, and she felt overshadowed by the older children. She was fiercely attached to her younger brothers, and the three formed a close group within the family.

Arthur, who was nearly three when Leopold was born, seems to have been an almost perfect child. He was attractive and good natured, and had a way of making quaint remarks which sent every adult around him rushing for a pen. He was never in trouble. Folk tales attach a special significance to the seventh child, and the magic certainly clung to Arthur. Everyone at Court adored him. Lady Caroline captured a typical moment in a report sent to the Queen in September 1853: 'I was nursing little Prince Leopold, when Prince Arthur brought me a great napkin & said I had better have it for when he spits! Prince Arthur is very fond of his "little Brother" & it is very pretty seeing him talk to "My Baby" like a little old woman.'[12]

The Queen made no secret of the fact that Arthur meant more to her emotionally than her other children; she loved them all, of course, in the good, practical way of caring about their well-being and wanting the best for them, but she *felt* more for Arthur. In 1858 she wrote a memorandum about him for her husband: 'This child is dear, dearer than any of the others put together, thus after you he is the dearest and most precious object to me on Earth.'[13]

The eighth child had no corresponding magic. From the start, Leopold was less eye-catching and less appealing than his brother, and the Queen was not the only one to make comparisons. His aunt, the Queen's half-sister Feodora of Hohenlohe-Langenburg, commented in 1854 that she hoped Leopold would not come to outshine his brother, and, after a visit to England the following summer, she remarked that she loved Leopold, 'although certainly not like darling Arthur'.[14] The Queen, leaving the nursery at Osborne in the summer of 1856, remarked to her uncle: 'To leave Arthur behind . . . gives me a great pang, for he is not only so lovely & engaging, but so sensible and so clever & such a very good little Child – that it is a delight to have him with you – wch I am sorry to say – is quite the reverse with your poor little name's Sake – tho' he is very clever & (when amiably disposed) amusing enough.'[15]

Shortly after Leopold's second birthday Augusta, Princess of Prussia, remarked to the Queen, 'Arthur is the favourite, and my poor godchild will not be so favourably judged by you as he deserves.'[16] She was teasing, but there was a truth in what she said which the Queen never saw. In time Leopold came to sense the difference and, not unnaturally, to resent it, and even when he was small it probably affected his behaviour. He was an affectionate child who attached himself to anyone who was kind, and he longed for attention. When the King of the Belgians visited England in November 1853, the baby stretched out his arms eagerly to the old man whose long, melancholy face and imposing manner would have scared most children. 'There is something so pleasing', the King remarked, 'in these marks of kindness from a little baby.'[17]

Haemophilia is often detected for the first time when a baby starts to crawl, and large bruises appear on his knees. Arthur's nursery nickname for Leopold was 'Little Neezie', but there are no surviving references to bruising: Victorian babies wore a great many clothes and were often carried, and this may have given protection. Leopold's teeth came slowly, and he was slow to speak, but no-one seemed aware of his condition. He was lively, responsive and intelligent, and his grandmother detected a passion for music in him; later years would show how right she was.

Only one piece of evidence sets Leopold apart in the early years, and it is found in the Queen's sketchbook. Victoria enjoyed drawing her children, as babies, as toddlers, playing, or being held, or bathed, but she seemed to shy away from Leopold. In 1854 she painted a back view of him and made one pretty drawing of him playing with Arthur. But then something changed. The following summer she tried to capture his attempts to walk, and produced a sketch with a disturbing hint of the grotesque about it: there is no softness, and no sense that the artist enjoyed watching her subject. While the surrounding pages of the book are full of pretty drawings of Arthur and Beatrice, Leopold does not feature again until 1857, when the Queen drew his head in profile. He was not a good-looking child, but the drawing is a caricature, and not a kind one. There would be no more sketches of him for four years, and then only one tiny back view, holding Beatrice's hand.

It would be wrong to make too much of this. Leopold may simply have been too fidgety, or too uncooperative to make a good model; the surviving attempts may have been failures (though the Queen still chose to preserve them). But it is the absence of drawings of Leopold, compared with the other children, which is striking. Like the comparisons with Arthur, the sketchbook may point to a vague uneasiness about the little boy, which had yet to crystallise into clear recognition of a problem.

His first recorded attack of bleeding occurred in the summer of 1855. On 2 July the Duchess of Kent was walking in the gardens of Buckingham Palace, when she met her grandchildren, without Leopold. She was told that he had been confined to the nursery by a bad fall. He was still in bed six days later: 'We had hoped he was getting much better, but today he is less well again, which is very sad', the Queen remarked.[18] When the royal family left for Osborne on 10 July, with the King of the Belgians, Leopold had a high fever and had to stay at the Palace with Lady Caroline and Mrs Thurston, and it was noted in the Court Circular that he had suffered 'a slight accident'.

The Queen told the Duchess of Sutherland that Leopold had had 'an accident to his lip'.[19] He must have fallen on his face, and was likely to have suffered bruising, swelling and intense pain, then the fever. Then, a few days after arriving at Osborne, his brothers and sisters came down with a temperature, a sore throat and a rash, and Dr Hoffmeister diagnosed scarlet fever; news from Buckingham Palace that Leopold also had a rash convinced everyone that he too had scarlet fever, so the fall was forgotten. But Lady Caroline was puzzled by this diagnosis in Leopold's case, because unlike the older children, who had been to the zoo, he had not been exposed to possible infection, and his throat was not sore. By 14 July he was eating heartily. She tried to convince herself that his skin was peeling – an after-effect of scarlet fever – but really could find little sign of it.

The good news was that he was recovering. He missed his family. 'The dear child often asks to have his curls made to go down to "Mama" – & constantly talks of "Arter" – & says all gone "poor Lee",' Lady Caroline told the Queen. (She kept one of the curls herself among her papers: a strand of fine, darkish blond hair, carefully preserved in a tiny envelope.)[20] Hearing that the Queen was consumed with worry for the scarlet fever patients, still quarantined in their nursery, the Duchess of Kent offered to take Leopold, and on 30 July Lady Caroline and Sir Edward Bowater, one of the grooms-in-waiting, delivered the little boy to Frogmore and left him there, with Mrs Thurston to nurse him.

The Duchess had a particularly soft spot for Leopold and he loved her, though he could be difficult. 'He is not always over gracious with me but I do not mind it', she said.[21] He must have reminded her very much of her daughter: in looks and temperament Leopold was becoming terribly like the Queen. He was well, apart from 'a slight derangement', on 2 August, and Mrs Thurston reported to his mother that he was very happy at Frogmore, 'singing about the rooms & seems quite at home, HRH spends a good portion of his time in the Colonnade playing at ball'.[22]

After ten days, Leopold and his grandmother joined the family at Osborne. He would continue to look pale for some time, but was well and active, and it was his behaviour, not his health, which bothered the Queen. Like most intelligent toddlers, Leopold became angry and frustrated when the older children did things he could not. When they teased him, he screamed. He was too adventurous, running and climbing without any sense of danger; his brother Alfred had been just the same. Lady Augusta Bruce, one of the Duchess of Kent's ladies, commented to her sister that 'Leo absorbs and engages my attention, holding me fast during the games . . . while he screamed at every new feat, "Look, look, hurrah", and clapped his hands. He is a dear, but passionate and always frightfully naughty in the presence of his parents, who think him quite a Turk!. . . I do not think they know how to manage him . . . however it is very difficult, for the battles are usually to avert some danger. He is perfectly reckless and fearless.' It was during the summer of 1855 that the famous scene took place between the Duchess and the Queen, when the Queen suggested that a whipping might be the answer and, to her mother's observation that it was painful to hear a child cry, remarked, 'Not when you have 8, Mama – that wears off.'[23] She and the Prince had begun to consider a naval career for Leopold; there must have been times when sending him to sea seemed an attractive option.

His third birthday, in April 1856, was celebrated with a Punch and Judy show on the Lower Terrace at Windsor, which caused great excitement. The Queen was beginning to suspect that he was wilful because somebody was spoiling him. She was not sure of her mother, and had grave doubts about Lady Caroline: 'I know Your Majesty thinks I am too indulgent to His Royal Highness & will not quite trust to what I say', the Lady Superintendent wrote, very frankly, that October, 'but I do assure Your Majesty that he has been very amiable – & really screams very little – Your Majesty must remember that he is like an only child upstairs, & being so much alone he does not learn to give & take as other children do. . . . I do not spoil him & he is very good with me. His Royal Highness is very intelligent & never forgets anything.'[24]

The Queen listened, and on her return to Windsor that autumn she found Leopold 'greatly improved'.[25] The year 1856 had been good for him, with only one minor accident in September, which left him with a badly bruised face.[26] He was well at Christmas, and shared the royal children's first encounter with St Nicholas, arranged by their father, who dressed a tall huntsman from the estate in black, with a long white beard and red nose, and covered him with 'snow'. St Nicholas made a dramatic entrance and asked the children if they had been good, handing out gingerbread and apples; according to their mother they were 'somewhat awed & alarmed', though they had fun guessing the true identity of their visitor.[27]

For his fourth birthday, Leopold went to the Coliseum theatre as a treat, with Arthur, Louise and Helena, and later in the day five little boys were invited in to play. A few weeks later he began to make daily visits to his mother's room, and to attend family breakfast and lunch, and the Queen, who was still recovering from the birth of Princess Beatrice, was pleased to find him 'very good & tractable'. She praised his appearance: 'He is a fine, chubby boy, with fine complexion, figure & limbs.'[28] But the unease was still present, and would soon find a voice; Queen Victoria liked children who were pretty, appealing and well-behaved, and she found it hard to see these things in Leopold for any length of time. He was fidgety, difficult, and annoying, though he could be amusing too, and so clever. At four years old he penned his first letter to his parents, in ink, in a large and wobbly hand: 'My dearest Parents – I hope you wont stay long at Scotland I send my love to my sisters and Arthur – from dear Leopold.'[29]

All the royal children were taught to write long and detailed accounts of what they were doing, thinking and feeling: it kept the Queen in touch with them when duty or pleasure took her away, and taught them to express themselves with confidence. So after this first letter, Leopold did not write for himself again for several years. It was an impressive effort for a four-year-old, but it was an effort, and at four he could not produce the long, full letters his mother expected. Instead, he dictated his thoughts to Mrs Thurston or the governesses, or to one of his elder sisters – in the summer of 1858 Helena told their father that Alice had been dealing with her little brother's correspondence.[30]

As the family began to fragment, letters became more important. The Prince of Wales and Prince Alfred had been educated away from home since 1856, and in January 1858 seventeen-year-old Victoria, the Princess Royal, was married to Prince Friedrich of Prussia. Leopold was at the wedding: he and his brothers wore full Highland dress, and Baron von Moltke described the scene to his wife in awed admiration. The Queen, he said, 'wore a tiara of diamonds in the shape of strawberry leaves, and a single diamond on her breast, which must . . . be one of the largest in the world. But far more handsome than this jewel even were her four young sons, who, dressed in Scottish costume, walked on either side of her. The little fellows with bare knees, their caps ornamented with eagles' feathers, their dirks, all studded with opals, in their stockings, and their kilts of royal Stuart tartan, looked splendid.'[31]

In June the Prince Consort went to Germany to see his daughter in her new home, and from Osborne the children wrote to say how much they missed him, and to tell him of their adventures. They described outings to Carisbrooke, walks and cowslip hunts, and afternoon sails on the *Fairy*, the tender to the royal yacht. Sometimes they went to Alverbank, near Gosport, where Alfred was preparing for a naval career with his tutor, the Reverend William Jolley. Shortly after Alfred's fourteenth birthday, Louise, Arthur and Leopold were taken to see him. They 'returned in high glee having amused themselves so much', Alice wrote; 'they told us a long story about Mr Jolly's dog Ginger, who played so many tricks.' Once, sailing on the *Fairy* with the Queen and Louise, Leopold watched his brother climb the mast of a nearby ship. He must have longed to join in.[32]

He was five, and his letters, faithfully written out by his sister, have a quirky originality. 'Dear Papa I am so unhappy because you are not here', ran one offering, written on 3 June. 'When will Vicky come back? Everything what I think, when I want to tell, I forget it. Baby makes such a noise, and when I am sitting opposite to Baby on the left side of the carriage, she kicks me, and she goes on saying oogly oogly. I have nothing else to say, but I send a Kiss & my love as well.' Several weeks later he wrote again, and Beatrice was still kicking, but he was pleased to report that she had started to walk. The Queen had joined her husband in Germany for his birthday, and Leopold was trying to fathom the implications of this: 'I hope Papa will be very happy, and I hope Mama will be very happy because Mama will be happy because it is Papa's birthday. I hope you will have very pretty presents and every thing what you like. Is Vicky and Fritz kind to Papa and Mama? and is Vicky grown?' He went on to ask after each of his sister's ladies-in-waiting by name.[33]

The children spoke and wrote instinctively in English, but Leopold could already dictate a letter in German.[34] His parents were considering his education, and in July the Queen asked Lady Caroline to make discreet enquiries about a French or Swiss governess for him, but it was Lady Augusta who found the right person, a widow named Madame Hocédé. The new governess would be expected to work with the other children, and the Queen was pleased with her musical skills, but her first duty was to teach Leopold.[35] Victoria was disappointed in her youngest son, and pinned all her hopes on Madame Hocédé. Writing about Leopold to her eldest daughter that November, she listed his failings: 'He is tall, but holds himself worse than ever, and is a very common looking child, very plain in the face, clever but an oddity – and not an engaging child though amusing. I hope the new governess will be able to make him more like other children.'[36]

The unease was becoming more apparent now, and the Queen would repeat the same criticisms time and again. Leopold was ugly, he was awkward, he was odd, he asked too many questions. Shortly after the birth of her first grandson she told her daughter,

'I hope, dear, he won't be like the ugliest and least pleasing of the whole family. Leopold was not an ugly little baby, only as he grew older he grew plainer, and so excessively quizzical, that is so vexacious.'[37] She was also impatient with his speech. In September 1858 she wrote to him from the cottage at Allt na Giuthasach near Balmoral, and the letter began in a friendly way, telling him what she and his father had been doing, and sending news of his brothers. 'Dear Arthur', she said, 'is very good & very funny, & calls Major Teesdale Major <u>Teezling</u> & Mr Walpole – Lord <u>Whirlpool</u>. This will make Lady Car laugh.' Then came the instruction: 'I hope Lady Car makes you speak <u>plain</u>, so that you will be improved in speaking when we come back.' A few months later she remarked on 'that unfortunate defect in his throat and speech which are much against him'.[38]

This gives the impression that Leopold had a serious speech impediment, but he grew up to be a highly praised public speaker with a fine tenor singing voice. His problem cannot have been so severe, and the Queen provides the clue to its nature herself. After the remark about Lady Caroline in her September letter, she went on to send her wishes to baby Beatrice, deliberately mis-spelt 'Beatruth' and underlined twice. There was no other reason for this, so she must have been teasing the little boy about his pronunciation. A year later she complained to the Princess Royal that his speech 'is so provoking as he learns so well and reads quite fluently; but his French is more like Chinese than anything else'.[39] Leopold had a childish lisp, with perhaps a weakness in pronouncing his 'r's; that was all, and it was soon outgrown.

Of course, the Queen's position was not easy. All parents want their children to do well, and to be approved of, and most feel that their children's behaviour reflects on them; Victoria had the added burden of knowing that everyone was watching her family and expecting a great deal from them. Her own expectations were correspondingly high, and she had no understanding of a child's capabilities. To her eldest daughter she once remarked, 'you all have always been so undutiful when babies', as if a dutiful baby were a real possibility.[40] But she does seem to have found Leopold particularly difficult, and for him, coming between Arthur, who could do no wrong in his mother's eyes, and Beatrice, who was rapidly becoming the family pet, the constant criticism must have been demoralising.

Fortunately, he was surrounded by affection. King Leopold was especially fond of him, and praised him for his achievements in the schoolroom, and for his original and amusing letters. With his godmother, Princess Mary Adelaide of Cambridge, Leopold could be more playful. He sent her a funny letter in November 1859 describing a comedy in St George's Hall given by the Haymarket theatre company: 'On Wednesday I went to a play and it was very funny and Buckstone amused me the most. And after I went to bed Mr Robson came and he broke everything, and afterwards Mr Robson became good. . . . And Mr Buckstone took Mr Walensky's hat and he hid behind a newspaper. And Mrs Montgomery was tipped out of the carriage. And I'm rubbing my hands together now because I'm happy to have written to you.'[41]

Leopold was always close to the Cambridges. His early letters also contain many references to his Leiningen cousins, the family of his mother's half-brother. Within the Household he loved Lady Caroline and Mrs Thurston, and was so attached to Lady Augusta Bruce that she began to worry that his grandmother might think it inappropriate. 'I am rather afraid of the Duchess being scandalized at our tenderness,' Lady Augusta told her sister, 'and do not speak much of Him. These are passages of a very tender nature. . . . he explained that he did not kiss Lady Gainsborough "or any of Mama's Ladies, only Lady A., she is Gd.Mama's Lady!" This of course makes it more proper!'[42]

Leopold was a very loving child. With his brothers and sisters, he cried when Madame Rollande, their French governess, left, but he took an instant liking to Madame Hocédé, who acquired the nickname 'Lina', and he was soon dictating letters to her in French. She was good fun. In one letter to Madame Rollande he wrote: 'I have just been running with Lina and Baby and afterwards Lina and Baby caught me.'[43] Despite the differences in the way they were treated, Leopold was affectionate to Beatrice, and he enjoyed being with Arthur and longed to follow him out of the nursery. He worshipped his elder brothers from afar, and his sisters were kind. When he was four, Alice wrote to Lady Caroline from Balmoral: 'What a little pickle Leo is getting and what funny things he says. . .

I shall be so glad to see him again for he is such a darling.'[44] For their parents' wedding anniversary in February 1859, she organised a musical performance: 'Helena, Louise and myself on the piano, Arthur on the drum, and Leopold on the triangle.'[45]

Then there was his father. The children's letters to Prince Albert are more than dutiful. They obviously loved him and felt his absences; he was affectionate when they were small, and parenthood came naturally to him. An increasing workload left him less time for the younger children, but he still enjoyed their company: one March morning at Osborne in 1858, the Queen found him making a snowman with the children, including four-year-old Leopold.[46] The Prince seems to have been especially attentive to his youngest son and, busy though he was, he would have delighted in the little boy's dawning intelligence and questioning mind. He is said to have given Leopold his first drawing lessons, and to have guided his interests towards art and music. One touching letter, which Leopold treasured, was written by his father in the summer of 1861, when he and the Queen were in Ireland. Prince Albert had just celebrated his birthday, and told Leopold how much he missed him and the other children, calling them his 'dear little Balmoral Division'. The words echo his tenderness and pride.[47]

TWO

FACING THE TRUTH

It took several years to recognise that Leopold had a serious problem. His first worrying symptom would have been bruises, more severe and more frequent than those of the other children. In the autumn of 1856, for example, Lady Caroline reported: 'Prince Leopold's cheek still looks very bad, but His Royal Highness does not appear to mind it at all.'[1] Then, a trivial fall could leave him lame for days, and sometimes the lameness came on without warning. In October 1857, the Queen and Prince Albert returned from Balmoral with the older children to find four-year-old Leopold waiting alone by the door at Windsor to welcome them home, 'looking very well', the Queen commented, 'but sadly lame, from having fallen yesterday'.[2] This is the first dated reference to lameness, but undated notes by Lady Caroline and Mrs Thurston inform the Queen of similar incidents, and these may have contributed to the little boy's awkward stance which annoyed his mother so much; he was probably beginning to experience stiffness and pain in his joints, and some of his screaming, which was put down to temper, could have been related to his illness.

The unease was there, but it was natural for parents and nurses to reassure one another, and to try not to make too much of his symptoms. Bruises are normal. Sprained ankles are normal. For long periods Leopold appeared perfectly healthy, and he was a tall, well-built, boisterous child, with boundless energy. In March 1858 he was allowed to stay up for his sister Louise's birthday ball, and he danced enthusiastically. The adults around him clung to the hope that he was just clumsier than the other children, and he was told off for falling over. When he was five, Leopold wrote to Princess Mary Adelaide, 'I fell down this afternoon and knocked my knee. . . . I am afraid you will say I am a very stupid little boy to fall down so often. But I never fall down with you' – a clear appeal for more sympathy than he was used to at home.[3]

The Queen cannot possibly have been aware of his condition when she made the remark about whipping him, in the summer of 1855, and for the next two years her only apparent worries were his behaviour and temper, but the deeper anxiety was always there, and the Princess Royal's wedding in 1858 provided a sympathetic correspondent with whom she could be open about her feelings. Then, her disappointment in Leopold was given full voice.

The remarks the Queen made about her youngest son at this time sound heartless. She even complained about his bruises, but impatience is a common reaction in mothers struggling to come to terms with serious illness in a child, or with the fear that their child may have a problem: how much easier, after all, to believe that a child is clumsy and badly behaved and can be normal if he tries, than to accept that something is fundamentally wrong with him. Returning in the autumn of 1857 to find Leopold unable to walk properly, she and Prince Albert would have discussed his accidents with the doctors if they had not done so already. The following April, Leopold fell during a family walk and cut his knee so badly that he had to be carried back to the Palace, and concern rises noticeably from this time.[4]

Even the royal doctors may not have realised what they were dealing with at first. Sir James Clark was the Queen's physician until his retirement in 1860, and other senior physicians and surgeons 'in Ordinary' were always attached to the Household. Then there were 'Extraordinaries' – doctors who had retired or were on probationary appointments – and specialists who could be called in as needed. Faced with Leopold's recurring symptoms, Clark is likely to have consulted his colleagues, and then more widely, and it may have taken him some time to find the answer.

In a monograph published in 1872, some thirteen or fourteen years after Leopold's haemophilia was first diagnosed, Dr John Wickham Legg stated that haemophilia 'has only recently become known'.[5] The Royal College of Physicians did not recognise the condition by name until the mid-1870s, but it did attract earlier attention in the medical press, particularly in Germany, as Legg went on to describe. His account is valuable because in 1866 he became Leopold's doctor, and his book gives important clues to what the royal family would have been told. He traced the developing understanding of haemophilia from medieval times, stressing that the earliest known examples were only individual case histories: the first scientific description of the condition did not appear until 1820.

The author of this pioneering work, Nasse, was a German, and from this date the study of haemophilia was concentrated in Germany. The condition came to be seen as a specifically German problem; Legg thought this himself, and suggested that marriage between first cousins, which was common in Germany, was a possible cause. Could this perception of haemophilia explain, at least in part, why Queen Victoria began to expect her doctors to be able to speak German? There was very little literature on the subject in English. In April 1859 Sir James Clark's replacement, Dr William Baly, was asked about his understanding of the language by the Queen when she and Prince Albert interviewed him at Buckingham Palace.[6] Dr Theodore Günther, Leopold's first medical attendant, was German, and Dr Poore, who followed Legg as Leopold's doctor, was sent to Germany by the Queen before he took up his appointment.[7]

Legg believed that the word 'haemophilia' was first used in Germany in about 1828; in England the term 'haemorrhagic diathesis' was more common. There were several new studies in the 1830s and '40s, and in 1840 an English doctor performed a blood transfusion on a patient with haemophilia. The operation was described in *The Lancet*, but English experiments were rare. In 1855, the year of Leopold's first recorded attack, J.L. Grandidier's *Die Hämophilia, oder die Bluterkrankheit* ('Haemophilia, or the sickness of the blood') was published in Leipzig. This was to be the standard work on the condition for the rest of the century, and its conclusions would have made disturbing reading for any parent.

Grandidier observed that half of all boys with haemophilia did not live to be eight, and a further three-quarters of those who survived their eighth birthday died before they were twenty-two. The lucky few who survived stood a chance of a normal lifespan, but there was no treatment for them beyond vigilance and care. Bleeding from a scratch or cut could be controlled with tight bandages; a worse symptom was bleeding from the internal organs. Nothing could be done to control it. Either the bleeding stopped, leaving the patient exhausted but alive, or it did not stop, and attacks were often accompanied by high fever and intense pain. Bleeding from the mouth or nose might be painless but equally dangerous, while bleeding into a joint, particularly the knee or elbow, could be extremely painful and carried the risk of permanent disability: the swelling distorted the limb, which might then take months to regain its natural position. Repeated attacks would lead eventually to a form of arthritis. Leopold had continual trouble with his knees, and photographs often show him with one leg bent. By 1861 he had started to wear a protective knee-pad.

But haemophilia is capricious, making it impossible to predict with certainty what would bring on an attack. Bleeding from the gum was often fatal, yet in 1865 Leopold had two teeth removed without ill effects. When he was twenty he fell from a horse, got up, and walked away. To add to the confusion, periods of illness were interspersed with months of apparently perfect health, when it was only natural to hope that the doctors were wrong, or that some miracle had effected a cure.

The implications for the sufferer were bad enough, but this would not have been the only worry for the Queen and Prince Albert, if they had been told the whole truth. In the 1850s no doctor could explain haemophilia in genetic terms, but they knew from experience that the condition was hereditary. They had seen that a woman from an affected family could pass haemophilia to her sons, though she had no symptoms herself.[8] By the 1870s Legg had come to believe that the *sisters* of haemophilic patients should never be allowed to marry, and said so in print. In the context of nineteenth-century royalty this advice would have been dynamite. When realisation of Leopold's illness was dawning on his parents, their eldest daughter had just married into the Prussian royal family and produced her first son. They had great hopes for the political future of the marriage, and their second daughter was approaching marriageable age. It was not the moment to discover hereditary illness in the family.

It is most likely that the doctors kept the hereditary nature of haemophilia to themselves, or broke it to Prince Albert alone. They, and he, always worried about the strength of the Queen's reactions. There is some evidence that he thought of improving the family bloodline, but the Queen never showed the slightest awareness that Leopold's condition had implications for the whole family. The second haemophilic boy in the family, her grandson Friedrich Wilhelm of Hesse, was born in 1870, and it took his mother Princess Alice little more than two years to realise what was wrong. Discussing the child with her eldest daughter, the Queen wrote: 'This peculiarity of poor little Fritz, like Leopold's which is such a rare thing and not in the family, is most extraordinary.' She put it down to 'the state of anxiety and distress she [Alice] was in before and after he was born'.[9] Either she had not been told that the condition was hereditary, or she refused to believe it.

But where did the illness come from? A man with haemophilia who has children automatically passes the gene to his daughters, making them carriers of the disease. The Queen's father Prince Edward, Duke of Kent, did not have haemophilia. Her mother could have carried the gene from her mother, and she from hers; haemophilia can pass unseen down the female line for generations. But the generally accepted view is that the illness occurred because of a spontaneous change in the cells passed from the Duke of Kent to his daughter, making Queen Victoria the first person in the family to carry the gene, though she suffered no symptoms. In *In the Blood*, Professor Steve Jones explains how the appearance of haemophilia in the royal family has helped scientists to discover the mechanism by which DNA is damaged – Leopold's second contribution to medical science.

Briefly, the body reproduces its cells continually by copying existing cells. Over time the risk of error in the copying increases, causing the gradual disintegration that is seen in old age. A woman's egg cells are all produced in her ovaries before birth, but a man produces sperm throughout life, and as he grows older the risk of mistakes – genetic mutations – in these sperm cells increases. The Duke of Kent was fifty when his daughter was conceived: much older than the average father, and old enough for the risk of mutation to be high.

Spontaneous mutation is seen as the most likely cause of Queen Victoria's damaged gene. But there is a possibility that the true route of the disease still lies hidden in the Queen's female ancestry. Her mother was a Saxe-Coburg by birth, and *her* mother a Reuss-Ebersdorf. Tracing the family tree back in the female line to the Queen's great-great-grandmother Ferdinande, Countess of Stolberg, and out along its branches, an interesting picture starts to emerge.

Ferdinande, who was born at the end of the seventeenth century, had eight children. One of her sons died unmarried at twenty-three, and three of her four daughters lost sons at an early age; the fourth had no children. Her daughter Karoline of Erbach-Schönberg was the Queen's great-grandmother. By her marriage Karoline had seven children, including two sons who died under the age of eight. Her third son, Heinrich LI Reuss-Ebersdorf, grew up, married and had children. He died as the result of a convulsive fit, the same apparent cause of death as Leopold. Only one of his children had a family, his daughter Adelheid, and four of her five sons died in childhood. His sister Henriette married Emich Karl of Leiningen, and they had one son, who died at the age of six. When Emich Karl married for a second time, he chose his wife's niece, her sister's daughter Viktoria of Saxe-Coburg, and by *her* second marriage Viktoria became the Duchess of Kent, Queen Victoria's mother.

In 1804, Viktoria's eldest sister Sophie married Count Emanuel Mensdorff-Pouilly. Genealogies always state that they had four sons: in fact they had six. The third, Alfred, was born on 23 January 1812, and at first he seemed bright, cheerful and normal. At two he became withdrawn: the doctors put this down to an over-long teething, but his grandmother feared the presence of a more serious illness. On 14 April 1814 her diary notes: 'Early today Alfred frightened us out of our wits. Suddenly he developed a weakness in the left leg, and he crawled, and for some time could not get about at all. . . . The doctor blames it all on the teeth.'[10] The weakness passed but the child did not recover, remaining listless and miserable though he had no fever and no obvious sign of illness; the doctor was baffled. On 22 April the weakness returned, and two days later his father returned home 'and found the poor little one already unconscious with inward convulsions in his little head. No remedy worked, Death already clung fast to his lovely prey.'[11] Alfred died on 28 April 1814.

Alfred may not have been haemophilic, though the sudden lameness in his leg is reminiscent of Leopold. A younger brother, Leo Emanuel, was born on 16 March 1815, and he too seemed healthy, though his mother was extremely ill during and after the birth. On 4 May 1821, six-year-old Leo was running about outdoors with friends until seven in the evening, but during the early hours of the next morning he was suddenly seized with stomach pains and convulsions: 'they held me back in the next room,' his mother wrote, 'his screams rent my heart, he had more convulsions, struggled and suffered until half past three! Then the dear blue eyes grew blind in everlasting night!'[12] He had been shivery some time before, and she believed that he caught a chill while playing, but that seems a slight cause for so terrible an end.[13]

Children in the nineteenth century were at risk from all manner of illness, but the striking thing about this entire family is the fragility of its sons. The case may never be proven, but the existence of Alfred and Leo Mensdorff demonstrates how unwise it is to be dogmatic about the family tree; other early deaths may have gone unrecorded, and in any case, before the 1820s doctors would not have been in a position to recognise haemophilia. A sufferer could die of some other illness, or live to adulthood, complicating the picture still further, but if even one of the many short-lived boys in Queen Victoria's female ancestry could be shown to have died as the result of an accident, or of bleeding, the defective gene would be apparent in the family long before it affected Leopold. Even Dr Legg raised the possibility of royal haemophilia. Too discreet to mention Leopold in writing, he commented that the condition was no respecter of persons and named the sixteenth-century King Charles IX of France as a haemophilia sufferer.

But in the 1850s, all that mattered was the illness of one small boy. Leopold was six in April 1859, and his birthday was celebrated with a children's costume ball at Buckingham Palace. The Queen and Prince Albert collected him from the schoolroom in the morning and took him to see his presents; 'He is thank God! much stronger & more robust, & a clever, honest & well intentioned boy', Victoria confided to her journal, always more positive than her letters to her daughter.[14] The excitement rose in the evening as the children put on their costumes. Leopold and Arthur appeared as the sons of Henry IV, in tights and short doublets, while their sisters Helena and Louise became Swiss peasants for the night. Two Saxe-Coburg cousins, Philipp and August, dressed in eighteenth-century uniforms, and were fifteen minutes late because no-one could be found to powder their hair. Writing to her daughter, the Queen remarked, 'those 2 fat boys – looked well enough – but really they are monstrous in size – poor Philippe's thighs and legs looked as if they were stuffed! Your sisters and little brothers looked very pretty, particularly Arthur and Louise.'[15]

The evening was a triumph, described in the pages of the *Illustrated London News* and other society journals. The Queen and Prince Albert, the Duchess of Kent, and a select gathering of royal parents, stood on a dais to watch just over two hundred guests, all between the ages of six and fourteen, dance a polonaise, a quadrille, waltzes and galops, until supper was served at midnight. 'The Children all enjoyed it so much,' said the Queen, 'no one more than little Leopold.'[16]

Madame Hocédé had started her lessons with him in January 1859, and his progress was rapid. Prince Alfred teased him about this in a letter from Jaffa, written on 22 March: 'I am glad to hear how nicely you are getting on with your French & when I come home I expect you will speak nothing else.'[17] In May Sergeant-Major Edwards was appointed to work with the little boy, perhaps in an attempt to improve his awkward posture. The family went to Balmoral in May and Leopold was left with his governess, but his sisters promised to write. Helena obliged, though she had little to say. 'Have you been sitting to Mr Winterhalter since we left?' she asked Leopold. 'I suppose your picture will soon be finished.'[18]

Leopold was ill in June, and in August he fell at Osborne, and injured his knee. A letter from his mother to the King of the Belgians at this time gives the first clear evidence that she and Prince Albert had been told about their son's condition. She did not give the illness a name, but on 2 August 1859, when Leopold was lying immobile on the schoolroom sofa, she wrote, 'Your poor little namesake is again laid up with a bad knee from a fall – w^h appeared to be of no consequence. It is very sad for the poor Child – for really I fear he will never be <u>able</u> to enter any active service. This unfortunate defect . . . is <u>often not</u> outgrown – & no remedy or medicine does it any good.'[19]

Leopold was unable to walk for just over a week, and the Queen praised his patience. Lady Caroline sent him a book and a toy tower and he wrote to thank her, in French, describing games in the Swiss Cottage, and the excitement of watching a battleship fire all its guns in salute to his mother. Two days later he wrote to Mme Rollande, telling her about a rural fête held in the grounds of Osborne to celebrate his grandmother's birthday. Letters are poor company for a six-year-old, but after the birthday celebrations the rest of the family had gone to Scotland, leaving him with Beatrice and the ladies. 'Leopold still has such constant bad accidents that it would be very troublesome indeed to have him here', the Queen told the Princess Royal on 2 September. 'He walks shockingly – and is dreadfully awkward – holds himself as badly as ever and his manners are despairing, as well as his speech – which is quite dreadful.'[20]

Even though she had spoken to the doctors, she seemed not to accept that Leopold did not walk and stand well because he was ill, and often in pain. She still blamed him. She sent him a letter from Balmoral, in French, urging him to be good and obedient, to improve his manners, and always to sign his letters 'your <u>respectful</u> and affectionate son'.[21] Letters from his brother and sisters must have been more fun: Arthur sent a gift of 'Scotch bread' which Leopold shared with Lady Caroline and his grandmother, and his beloved Lady Augusta. Louise told him all about the Highland games and sent sugar plums.[22]

The weeks passed, with sea-bathing, drives, and trips on the *Fairy*. Once, Leopold was taken to Norris Castle to hear the band of the Rifle Brigade, and he spent the afternoon dancing to the music. But on 18 September he fell on the gravel walk by the Swiss Cottage and scratched his knee, and four days later it became inflamed; this may have been a simple infection, as Lady Caroline and Dr Hoffmeister believed, but Lady Caroline's report to the Queen suggests that they were not aware of the possibility of bleeding into the joint.[23] 'Poor little Leopold again laid up with a bad knee', the Queen commented. 'Very vexatious.' Helena sent him 'a little indiarubber ball, to amuse you, whilst you are not able to walk'.[24] A few weeks later the knee was bad again, and had to be supported with a splint.

Leopold's haemophilia could not be ignored, and as the year drew to an end, his parents were thinking hard about his future. Since January 1859 Arthur had had a male governor, Major Howard Elphinstone, who was still in his twenties and had been awarded the Victoria Cross for his service in the Crimea. He was finding his charge naughty and unwilling to learn, and after discussing Arthur with the Queen at Balmoral in September, he noted in his diary that Leopold was brought into the conversation. The Queen laughed that her youngest son's love of learning had certainly not come from her, for 'she hated lessons, the Prince Consort on the contrary liked them above all else'.[25]

The remark is a clue to the way in which the Queen's attitude to Leopold was changing, probably with Prince Albert's help. At times he did feel that she was unnecessarily severe with the children: 'It is not possible to be on happy friendly terms with people you have just been scolding', he told her, in October 1856.[26] Now, her attention was drawn gently to Leopold's intelligence and pleasure in his lessons, and her feelings began to soften. The idea that the little boy could grow into a replica of his father seems to have been planted at about this time, and after the autumn of 1859 the Queen made no more complaints about Leopold's clumsiness, awkwardness and ugliness. She praised and pitied him, and accepted the reality of his condition.

A letter to the King of the Belgians in January 1860 gives the first clear indication of the way haemophilia had been explained to the Queen. The family always celebrated New Year's Day with a party in which the children recited, played musical instruments, and gave their parents drawings and poems. Leopold's contribution in 1860 was a German hymn, and a French poem six pages long which he recited without faltering – no mean achievement for a six-year-old. 'Poor Child', the Queen told her uncle, 'he is so very studious & so very clever but <u>always</u> meeting with accidents, which with another child would not be <u>mentioned</u> even, but which from the peculiar constitution of his bloodvessels which have no adhesiveness become dreadful. He has now a bump on his forehead which is as big as a nut from the slightest touch against a press 3 weeks ago! And unfortunately all the "faculty" say <u>nothing</u> whatever can be done for it, – he may & it is to be hoped, <u>will</u> outgrow it – but since June he has been debarred from <u>every active</u> amusement & has had a succession of (totally unavoidable) accidents! He is very patient and fortunately very studious & fond of reading.'[27]

In haemophilia the blood lacks one of the necessary clotting factors, but nineteenth-century doctors did not understand the clotting mechanisms of blood, and there were all manner of theories about the cause of the condition. Dr Legg believed that it resulted from imperfectly developed blood vessels, so it is not surprising to find the Queen voicing the same idea, and Leopold's illness was described to the family and to some members of the Court in these terms. Prince Albert sent an explanation to his eldest daughter in May 1861, and a month later, Lady Augusta told her sister, 'His veins are too weak and he is subject for the least thing to bleeding, sometimes from the nose, sometimes internal. It is doubtful whether he may grow up, but they fear never to be a strong man.'[28] A few months later, Leopold's aunt Feodora sent the Queen a remedy for staunching the flow of blood.[29] The Queen's hope that her son would outgrow his illness was probably an optimistic view of advice that the most dangerous years would be childhood and adolescence.

In December 1859 Prince Albert had confirmed Major Elphinstone's appointment, and let him know that in time Leopold's education would be entrusted to him also, and one day in January 1860, the Queen called Elphinstone out on to the terrace at Windsor to discuss the best way to treat Leopold. She listened to his ideas, and asked him to pass them on to Madame Hocédé. A few days later the Major went to watch Leopold drilling in the Oak Room and was called over to discuss him with the Queen and the governess. Walking away down the corridor, the Queen confided her fears that the little boy was growing weaker, and Elphinstone suggested that running and outdoor exercise would be more stimulating for a lively boy than sedate walks with a governess.

The advice was accepted. On 29 February Colonel Dudley de Ros, the Prince Consort's equerry, photographed Leopold on the terrace at Buckingham Palace clutching a hoop and stick, the outdoor toy beloved of small Victorians. His health improved, and on his seventh birthday his mother praised his intelligence and devotion to lessons. He spent the day at Virginia Water with Arthur, and in the evening the two little boys and their sisters were taken to hear Haydn's *Passion* performed in St George's Hall.[30] From Berlin the Princess Royal sent Leopold a book, with an affectionate letter: 'I wish I was there to give you a kiss – wch I do in thought don't forget.'[31] The family was closing ranks around him. In May Alfred wrote from his ship HMS *Euryalus*, docked at Plymouth: 'I hope that your leg is quite well again & that you have had no more accidents since I left. I suppose you will dance a great deal at the ball in a few days whilst our ship is dancing on the waves.'[32]

But there would be more accidents. The ball Alfred mentioned was probably the country dance held on the evening of the Queen's birthday. Leopold joined in gleefully, and was lame for the next few weeks, with pain in his ankle. Before the ankle had been able to heal, he sprained it again, and could not walk at all, but his disability was no longer allowed to separate him from the family. In the autumn he was taken to Balmoral for the first time, and was well enough to explore the countryside. He rode Topsy the pony, with John Brown holding the bridle; this was his first meeting with a man he would come to detest, but in 1860 that storm was far away. He went for morning drives with his mother, and walks with Arthur and the Major, and saw the Highland games at Braemar. Once, the family climbed Allt Craigie; 'Leopold walked part of the time at Grant's hand,' the Queen wrote, 'being delighted with everything.'[33]

But as 1860 drew to an end, the bleeding attacks became more frequent. Leopold often had to be carried, and could only join the family outdoors by riding in a 'little carriage'. He had nosebleeds too, but at seven he was too old to stay in the nursery, and he longed to join Arthur with Major Elphinstone: growing out of women's care was an important step for a boy. In January 1861 the Queen drafted a memorandum: 'As Prince Leopold is sometimes attacked with nose-bleeding in the night, (& tho Major Elphinstone's door w^ld be open – he might be unable to call) there ought to be a bell w^h he c^ld easily ring to enable him to have assistance immediately.' She chose Herr Ruland, the German Librarian, to deputise for Elphinstone during any absences, and if illness or accident prevented Leopold from walking 'he s^hld either remain in the Bedroom or be carried, <u>for</u> the <u>day</u>, upstairs to the Governess.' His right to sleep in his brother's rooms was to be respected.[34]

Elphinstone submitted a detailed schedule for his new charge. Leopold was to get up at 7.45 a.m., be dressed, and spend the rest of the first hour learning some French by heart. Then he could go outside with Arthur before breakfast – though Elphinstone wondered if he should be allowed to eat first, 'as he is delicate'. One of the governesses, Madame Hocédé or Mademoiselle Bauer, was expected to amuse him until lunch, at 11.15. Lessons followed: an hour's German (or French on Saturday), and half an hour's writing with the Reverend Jolley. Then Leopold was to stay indoors with a governess 'and amuse himself as best he can', though if bad weather kept Arthur indoors, the two boys could play. At three the governess would take Leopold outside again, at 4.30 he would get undressed, and have a final hour of French before supper in Arthur's room. When ill, he would spend the whole day with the governess and a maid from the nursery.[35]

The Major could be forgiven if he felt uneasy about this: Leopold was a huge responsibility for a young man with limited experience of children. But just over a week after the document was written, the little Prince was moved into his brother's rooms, and the Queen was pleased to see how much happier he was with this arrangement, which confirmed his status as a boy and not a baby. Then, on 16 March, the Duchess of Kent died, plunging the whole family into grief, and the Queen into an emotional state which alarmed her family and the Court. Nobody seems to have thought of the children's reactions. For the younger ones the most tangible effect of their grandmother's death was the pall of gloom cast over every family event for months. On 1 May, Arthur's birthday, Elphinstone kept the two younger boys at Buckingham Palace while the rest of the family went to White Lodge, where they stayed for several days.

On 16 May the Queen returned to Buckingham Palace, and after two days the whole family left for Osborne. Suddenly, a week later, Leopold began bleeding from the kidneys and passing blood. He was kept in bed all day, and the next day was moved back to the nursery where Mrs Thurston could look after him. Three days passed without improvement. Dr Baly had been killed in a railway accident in January and the new doctor, William Jenner, advised the nurse to keep him absolutely still and quiet. He told the Queen there was no danger; clearly there was, but Prince Albert had decided for her own sake and for Leopold's to take her back to Buckingham Palace, and Lady Caroline was called to Osborne to take charge. The Queen tried to be reassured, but complained to her eldest daughter, 'I think it both cruel and wrong to leave a sick child behind. . . . I am very much annoyed and distressed at being forced to leave him by the very person who ought to wish me to stay. But men have not the sympathy and anxiety of women.'[36] It was probably this very anxiety which prompted the Prince's decision.

On 1 June, she reluctantly said goodbye to Leopold, 'who is so good & patient, & occupies himself in working & plaiting &c – Ly Caroline B, Thurston, & a gentleman remain with him & the Doctor will sleep every night in the house'.[37] As soon as she arrived at the Palace, she gave a note to Dr Jenner to take back to Osborne, praising the little boy's patience and assuring him he would soon be well. But the treatment was not pleasant. Fearful of the effects of 'straining', Jenner had prescribed regular doses of a strong laxative, to be given at intervals even during the night. On 3 June, Lady Caroline reported that 'Prince Leopold would have had a good night had he not been so often woke to take the medicine. The aperient medicine has acted very much, & tired His Royal Highness very much – & his appetite is not good, owing to the medicine – There was decided improvement during the early part of the day – but this afternoon there has been a return of the bad symptom tho' I trust not to the same extent as before.'[38]

Worse was to follow. Some weeks before, Princess Alice's fiancé, Prince Louis of Hesse, had come down with measles while staying with the royal family. During the night of 4 June, Leopold began sneezing, and this brought on a nosebleed. By morning he was feverish; an anxious telegram was despatched to the Palace, and Jenner, who had returned to the Queen, set out again for Osborne.

The journey took the best part of the day, and Lady Caroline could only watch anxiously as the bleeding and sneezing continued. In the evening she drafted a lengthy telegram describing the little boy's state. He had lost a considerable amount of blood, and the first spots were appearing on his face: 'He is extremely restless weaker and paler than he was – The bleeding from the other part has not returned. Unless he is decidedly better in the morning Dr Jenner will not leave.' To this Jenner added a reassuring message, to calm the Queen.[39]

The crisis passed, and by the next evening Jenner felt able to return to Buckingham Palace, where Beatrice had come down with measles. Dr Cass was left to attend to Leopold. The little boy's eyes were very painful, but he seemed more concerned to protect his mother, and pleaded with Lady Caroline not to send too alarming a report. The Queen was touched, and told the Princess Royal how affectionate and thoughtful he was. She sent him a miniature tea set, which seems an unlikely gift for an eight-year-old boy, but its arrival coincided with another crisis.

On 7 June Leopold had developed a cough, which bothered him all day. At ten that night, during a coughing fit, his nose began to bleed and Dr Cass applied a cauterising solution with a paintbrush. 'This caused very great annoyance to the poor Child & from that time till near three he went on in the same way, dozing, coughing & the nose beginning to bleed. The poor Child's Head & Hands had to be held when it was necessary to apply the solution!', Lady Caroline reported, '& I was most thankful Your Majesty was not here.' Gradually the coughing and bleeding died away, and Leopold was able to slide into real sleep. A fire was lit in the day nursery and the bed was wheeled through, without waking him, so that the bedroom could be aired. In the afternoon Lady Caroline settled down to write a long and detailed letter to the Queen. 'I own I have been <u>very much alarmed</u> perhaps more so than there was any reason to be. . . . but thank God! I <u>think</u> all will be well now.'[40]

When Leopold woke, he was shown the tea set and persuaded to have some tea and a bread crust – the first solid food he had taken for days. Perhaps the china was not such an odd gift after all. 'Words cannot say how happy I feel at seeing darling Prince Leopold so much better, & able to talk cheerfully again', Lady

Caroline told the Queen. She requested a miniature spoon and sugar tongs, which were duly sent.[41] For the next few days he was kept very quiet, and ate a little more each day. On 11 June he began to work on a screen he had started to make before the illness, and he was allowed out of bed for the first time. The next day he dressed. 'He is certainly very thin & very weak', Lady Caroline reported, 'it is all he can do to walk across the room, but as his appetite is now good he will soon regain his strength.'[42]

The relief was enormous. Alice sent him some presents from the Crystal Palace: 'poor love, such a sad tiresome time for you, I wish I could have been with you'. Helena bought him a French book from a bazaar, and Louise had already sent flowers from his garden at Buckingham Palace.[43] By 14 June he was well enough to sit outside for a little while, and four days later he was playing in the Swiss Cottage with Lady Caroline's niece Louisa. On 19 June he arrived home, still looking very pale. Dr Cass had accompanied him all the way, and his sea-sickness on the boat had given Lady Caroline a great deal of anxiety. 'I feared the straining might have brought on an attack of bleeding', she said, but all was well, and Leopold was just happy to be home.[44]

THREE

CHÂTEAU LEADER

Leopold was still very weak, and the doctors suggested that he should spend the winter in a warmer climate where he could exercise outdoors. As they considered attendants to send with him, the Queen and Prince Albert remembered a German doctor they had met at Balmoral the previous autumn. Then, Theodore Günther had been nearing the end of a two-year appointment as tutor to Lord John Russell's sons. He was twenty-six, and the royal couple were impressed with his manner. On 16 July 1861 Herr Ruland, the Prince Consort's German librarian, wrote to ask Günther if he would take charge of Leopold for six to seven months, from October until his return to England.

Günther's principal duty would be constant supervision of the little boy, whose problem was explained as 'a certain general weakness of the constitution which manifests itself particularly through a tendency towards haemorrhages, (from the nose, the gums etc.)'. Lessons would take second place to the real object of their stay, which was to build up Leopold's strength. Günther was to work in association with a local doctor, and responsibility for the economic and domestic management of the household would be given to an English gentleman, or perhaps to a family. The doctor was offered all expenses and an honorarium of £200 and, to the Prince Consort's delight, he accepted.[1]

It was Sir Charles Phipps, Keeper of the Privy Purse, who suggested a suitable family to send. Sir Edward Bowater was a Waterloo veteran in his seventies, a married man with a nineteen-year-old daughter. He became an equerry at Court while the Queen was still a child, and before that had followed Wellington through the Peninsular Campaign, which provided him with a wealth of exciting stories. Trusted to escort Leopold to Frogmore in 1855, Sir Edward was absolutely reliable, and this new request came at an opportune moment for, as Phipps undoubtedly knew, he had just lost his country home. The request from the Prince Consort reached him on 11 August, and it lifted his family from their depression: they were told that their destination would be the south of France.

Dr Günther was invited to Balmoral early in October to get to know Leopold, and the little boy took to him straight away, as he took to each new person who came into his life. August had been an easy month for him, with only a few days of lameness: 'Prince Leopold has been out in the little carriage as H.R.H. is <u>rather</u> lame', Lady Caroline told the Queen one day, 'he complains of one of his feet, but there is no bruize & nothing to be seen.'[2] In September news of his journey reached the papers. The duchesse d'Aumale offered her villa in Palermo, but a lease had already been taken on the Château Leader at Cannes. Leopold was looking forward to the winter. On 25 September he wrote to Madame Rollande, in French, telling her that he was delighted to be going to France and hoped to see her. In Scotland, he said, the weather was terrible.[3]

When the royal family returned to Windsor, the Bowaters were invited to the Castle, and their daughter Louisa described the visit in her journal. After a panic because she had no suitable bonnet – she had to buy one on the way – they arrived on the morning of 28 October and were taken to meet Lady Caroline, who explained all they would need to know about Leopold. They lunched with the Household, and then met the royal family 'and very pretty it was to see them all together. . . . The little ones, including Prince Leo, played about and amused themselves by trying to make the dear little Princess Beatrice, who is evidently the pet of the family, say French words.' The next day Elphinstone and Günther took the younger Princes to the Bowaters' rooms. 'Two such darling boys I have not seen for a long while', was Louisa's reaction, though she could not escape the special charms of the seventh child: 'They were full of fun and merriment, and seemed greatly to enjoy croquet and hide-and-seek. Prince Arthur especially, with his handsome face and courteous manners, has carried all our hearts away.'[4] Poor Leopold could never escape the comparison.

Leopold left Windsor at eight o'clock on the morning of 2 November. 'He cried when I kissed him – and wished him goodbye', the Queen told the Princess Royal, 'but he was in good spirits otherwise.'[5] Prince Albert followed them out on to the Castle steps. 'You'll take care of the boy, won't you?' he asked Sir Edward, and the old soldier replied, 'I will sir, as if he were my own.'[6] The Prince's words to his son are not recorded, but the scene haunted Leopold. In 1871, after parting from his newly married sister Louise, he told her: 'When I stood on the steps watching you go, I could not but remember when I myself said goodbye to dear Papa on those very steps, nine years ago, & never saw him again; & it added greatly to my sorrow.'[7]

At the last moment, Drs Clark and Jenner wrote detailed instructions for Günther. Leopold was to spend as much time as possible outdoors, warmly wrapped. He could walk and ride a pony, but it was important not to let him trip over, and he was to avoid violent exercise. Constipation was the doctors' greatest fear, and Günther was to watch carefully for this and administer laxatives if necessary. There was 'grey powder', a mixture of mercury and chalk used as a purgative for children, and 'sulphate of soda' to be given 'if the lips and gums should be particularly full and red as sometimes happens before an attack of bleeding', and care was to be taken with any injury.[8]

The party sailed from Dover to Boulogne on 4 November, under the guidance of the Queen's courier Joseph Kanné. They watched in amazement as tough women dock workers at Boulogne carried their heavy luggage off the ship and transported it to the hotel. The next day they took the train to Paris; it was dark when they arrived, and an attaché from the British Embassy was waiting at the station with two carriages. The Embassy would be their base for several days; Günther took his pupil around the city, and they visited the theatre to see the opera *Don Pasquale*. It sounds rather advanced for an eight-year-old, but Leopold loved it. He wrote to his mother, and Elphinstone remarked to Günther that it was a nice letter, but in future the Prince should write on black-edged paper, and it might be as well to correct his spelling.[9]

The Queen had sent a letter herself, timed to reach her son in Paris, urging him to make the most of his experiences: 'we think with pleasure of the great interest & amusement of the journey for you. Do not the people & soldiers & everything look so different to England, & does it not sound droll to hear everyone speaking French?', she wrote, but it must all have been overwhelming for so young a child.[10] Leopold hardly knew his companions. For the first few days he was stiff and quiet, hiding his feelings behind a front of rigid self-control. It was not until the party had left Paris and was on its way by train to Dijon that he felt able to relax. 'The Prince began to be much more sociable', Louisa wrote, 'and in the evening he came and laid his head on my shoulder.'[11]

By 10 November they had reached Avignon, where they stayed at the Hotel d'Europe. Sir Edward, whom Leopold had begun to call 'Grandfather', had been taken ill, and Lady Bowater was too anxious to leave him, so Dr Günther took Louisa and Leopold for a walk in the town. They were followed by a mysterious beggar, covered from head to foot in black robes with a slit for his eyes. 'The Prince shrank up to me', Louisa wrote, 'and even I felt glad when the doctor dropped a few sous into his box, and so got rid of him.'[12] It was a fine, clear day, and in the afternoon the doctor took the youngsters to see the cathedral and the old convent. Their driver was delighted with them: he had been awarded an English medal for his service in the Crimea, and proudly showed it to 'the son of the English Queen'. He drove to the heights above the Rhône, where they could see the whole of Avignon spread out in the valley in bright autumn sunshine, below the grey olive groves, and the snow-capped peak of Mont Ventoux. 'Not a sound was to be heard', Louisa remembered, 'save the distant tinkling of a bell.'[13]

From Avignon their journey became more of an adventure. The railway stopped at Toulon, some seventy miles to the west of Cannes along the coast, so on the morning of 13 November the party divided into two groups; Leopold with Dr Günther and Lady Bowater, and Louisa with her father, and each was settled into a carriage with their luggage while an excited crowd of local people gathered to see them off.

They rattled eastwards over rough country roads, where the only living things were flocks of sheep and goats. Once they passed an old woman riding a mule, perched comfortably between two loaded panniers. She was wearing an enormous hat, and knitting as she went. A team of road menders shouted jokes to their postilion, and occasionally they saw another carriage, or a donkey cart loaded with wine casks, but when they stopped for a change of horses whole villages turned out to stare. By the end of the first day they reached the Hotel d'Eléphant at Vidauban. Feeling grimy and stiff, their first thought was 'to get out of the village as quickly as possible, and scramble up the rocky terraces of the olive gardens on the hillside'.

At 9.30 the next morning they set off again, heading east and slightly south, towards the little coastal town of Fréjus, where, as they passed the ruined arches of the Roman aqueduct, the travellers caught their first glimpse of the Mediterranean, blue and gleaming in the sunlight. From Fréjus the old coach road climbed up into the Esterel mountains which shield Cannes to the west, passing close to the base of Mont Vinaigre, the highest point on the massif. In the eighteenth century the road was notorious for highwaymen, and convicts still hid in the impenetrable hills, but after climbing for two hours Leopold and his companions came to the highest point of the road unscathed, 'and saw the sunny peaks of the Basses Alpes clearly defined against the deep blue sky, towering over the lower ranges of hills, while far below, basking in the Southern sun, lay the white houses of Cannes'.

After a final change of horses near the summit, 'we began a long descent through stone pines and juniper and arbutus scrub', Louisa wrote, '. . . until we reached the Château Leader, one of the finest villas on the Toulon road, and as far as I can see, one of the nicest in Cannes. All the rooms are large and airy, and the drawing-room opens on to a terrace commanding a lovely view of the Mediterranean, the Îles Lérins, and the Esterelles jutting out into the sea.'[14]

Leopold was homesick at first, and had a swelling on his knee caused by a bump in the railway carriage some days before. The doctor reported that he was not happy about eating meat, and Prince Albert replied that he had not been fond of meat for some time, but it was important to make him eat it.[15] The Queen did her best to jolly the little boy along, though she was determined that he should not forget his family. That autumn all the news reaching Windsor was bad news. She wrote on 15 November: 'I am so glad to see you enjoy your journey which I quite envy you to have taken, for you have seen so much which I have never seen! . . . You must send me a print or a photograph of it as soon as you can. – Here we have been in such sorrow since you went! – We have lost 2 dear Nephews, (your dear Cousins) – of typhus fever; first, Ferdinand (Louis Oporto's 4th brother) & then dreadful to say – four days after – Pedro, the young King of Portugal, husband to dear Stéphanie, whom you will remember & who died 2 years ago – (who you were so fond of – & whose photograph you have got) died of the same! . . . We loved him as a Son & his loss is a great grief to us. . . . We hope that you are a good, obedient & well mannered little Boy.'[16]

Four days after arriving in Cannes, Leopold's arm began to hurt, but he tried to keep it quiet. He told his sister Louise in a letter, appealing to her to tell no-one but 'Lina' Hocédé and Arthur.[17] But the problem could not be hidden for long. Louise replied on 28 November: 'I hope your poor arm is better and that it does not pain you so much: we often think of, and talk about you dear Leo', and Major Elphinstone and the Queen both wrote to ask how he had injured the arm.[18]

Sir Edward's illness was a greater anxiety. Dr Günther observed a steady decline after their arrival in Cannes; soon the old man could hardly summon up strength to go beyond the garden. His wife would not leave him, and the news caught the Prince Consort when he too was at a low ebb physically and mentally, shaken by the deaths in Portugal, and worried by his eldest son's encounter with an actress. The plight of his youngest son, miles away in France with a sick guardian, preyed on his mind, and he wrote to the British Embassy in Paris, asking for a gentleman to be ready to assist Günther. To the doctor, he suggested that it might be necessary to warn Lady Bowater gently of the seriousness of her husband's condition.[19]

On 23 November Major Elphinstone wrote privately to Günther to tell him that Lord Rokeby, 'in whose judgement & discretion the Prince has entire confidence', had been alerted to their situation and was prepared to take charge of Leopold should the need arise, but had been told to communicate with the doctor alone. Prince Albert was afraid of upsetting Lady Bowater at a difficult and sensitive time.[20] But a few days later, Sir Edward reported his own state to the Prince. He wrote 'in so straightforward, but so sad and resigned a tone that His Royal Highness could not fail but to anticipate the worst'. Prince Albert therefore advised the old soldier to call on Lord Rokeby directly if he felt the need. But if Günther believed that Sir Edward was about to die, he was to move Leopold into the hotel at Cannes, for the Bowaters' sake, and the child's.[21]

Briefly, Sir Edward's health seemed to improve. Leopold was better too, and Elphinstone sent instructions that he was to start lessons. A timetable was to be sent to the Queen, with occasional reports 'of the lessons he has done each day, and "<u>how</u>"', and Günther was to look for suitable boys for him to play with.[22] So far Louisa had been the little boy's constant companion, reading to him, playing chess, and doing her best to divert him 'when fits of home-sickness came over him, on receiving letters from Windsor'. Once he was well, they went outside, and on fine mornings rode their favourite donkeys, Jacques and Catherine, up to the olive groves and vineyards. They played croquet, and sometimes Dr Günther took them further afield, on picnic expeditions into the mountains.[23]

But events were about to take a turn no-one could have foreseen. On 2 December Prince Albert sat down with Princess Alice to write to his son. It was the last letter he would ever send:

My dear Leopold,

Although very unwell, with general depression and therefore not able to hold a pen myself, I dictate this to Alice, to thank you for your dear little letter. I am glad you like your games at croquet and have such beautiful weather. Here it is cold, damp, and detestable. . . .

I trust you had your pocket money, which I have fixed at 2 nap:[n] a month.

> Goodbye dear boy,
> Ever
> Your affectionate Papa.[24]

Leopold was young, but he knew more than most eight-year-olds about illness, and by the time news of his father's state was sent officially to Günther – couched in the most hopeful terms – he may already have guessed the truth from this sad little letter, and from Louise. On 8 December she wrote to tell him that their father was still ill 'but he does not like any body to know it so I only tell you because I thought you would like to know what is going on here'.[25]

Understandably, the adults on both sides tried to be positive. Plans were afoot for Leopold's first Christmas away from the family. Günther consulted Elphinstone, and was told to spend about £10 on presents; the little Prince's most frequent wish was for a dog, which he could have, but the Major also suggested a list of toys: building bricks, lead soldiers, a ball, a kite, a pocket compass, a 'set of battle door & shuttle cock' and books, with some more unusual items, like flower vases, and 'pretty table ornaments'. The family were sending opera glasses, a set of table croquet and a miniature violin. A second letter instructed Günther to buy a good Christmas tree, and a present from Alice. He used Elphinstone's first letter to work out his plans, and its margins are covered with pencilled comments and lists – 'bow & arrow; Princess Alice present; Carpentry things', and so on, with meticulous calculations of prices.[26]

Elphinstone's second letter warned the doctor not to address anything to the Prince Consort for the next ten days, though it still gave no hint of anxiety. The letter was dated 9 December, and would have taken two or three days to arrive. Short bulletins about the Prince's condition followed, and Louisa and her mother began to suspect the truth; meanwhile, their own anxiety was intense. At 4 p.m. on 14 December, Sir Edward suffered a stroke, and he died peacefully two hours later. When it became clear that death was imminent, Leopold was moved to the hotel with Dr Günther, but news that Sir Edward was dead had barely had the chance to register when a telegram arrived from Windsor: 'Pray break to Prince Leopold that the Prince is very ill and that we are in great anxiety about him.' It was 8 p.m. Prince Albert died at ten minutes to eleven.[27]

The next day was a Sunday. Lord Rokeby arrived from Nice at midday, carrying the telegram with news of the Prince's death. Günther had already warned Leopold that his father was very ill;

now both men agreed that under the circumstances a hotel was not the best place for the little boy to be, and he was taken back to the Château Leader. 'After we had returned to our old apartment', the doctor told the Queen, 'I conveyed the terrible news to the poor dear Prince. He was naturally extremely distressed. He said he had thought about such a sad occurrence and prayed the dear Lord to prevent it, but in general he conducted himself with great fortitude.'[28]

In Windsor, Major Elphinstone sat down to write to Günther, and his thoughts were with Leopold: 'Poor child, little can he conceive the awful loss he has sustained in the sudden death of his natural protector.'[29] Louisa had her own loss to cope with, but she clung to Leopold. Their fathers had died within hours of each other, and this created a natural bond which she and her mother felt so strongly that they opted to stay with Leopold when Sir Edward's body was taken to England for burial, following what they felt would have been the old soldier's wish. They became especially close to their charge: 'Prince Leopold's pretty, winning ways greatly endeared him to us both', Louisa wrote, 'and during the next few weeks he helped to cheer my poor mother, and would coax her to go out when no-one else could do this.'[30]

But at first there were no outings. Three days after the news came, Leopold sent a letter to Arthur. He wanted his family, and in the next few weeks he would write often to Arthur and to Louise. 'I am very very much greived to hear of poor dear Papa's death,' he told Arthur. 'I got a letter from Major this morning, in which he sent me a photographe of poor dear Papa, to be put in a frame like poor dear Grandmama's.'[31] To Louise he wrote of his love for his father, and of the changed atmosphere at the Château Leader: 'Poor Lady and Miss Bowater are very very unhappy, I take my meals with them and Dr Günther takes his meals with Lord Rokeby. Poor Lady Bowater and Miss Bowater have not gone out since the death of poor Sir Edward.'[32]

Leopold worried terribly about his mother, and even the weather seemed full of foreboding. Writing to his brother on 22 December, he said, 'I got a letter from you and from Major this morning, in your letter, I was glad to see, you said a great deal of dear Mama, of whom I wanted so very much to hear, I hope dear Mama is quite well. There is a great wind today, and the sea is very rough, the slaming of the doors made a great noise in the night.'[33] But by the end of the month his spirits had rallied. Lady Bowater and Louisa felt ready to face the world and took him with them, on short walks first and then longer outings, and he sent Christmas presents for his sisters and brothers.

Leopold was more fortunate than the other children because he was so far from home, with adults who helped him through the bereavement. His mother's first letter to him after the deaths, which he mentioned to his sister, has not survived; the second shows only too clearly the continuing pressure which her children faced.[34] On 16 January she took up her pen. 'My wretched, miserable existence is not one to write about!' she told Leopold. 'You are an affectionate little Boy – & you will remember <u>how</u> happy <u>we all</u> were – you will therefore sorrow when you know & think that poor Mama is more wretched, more miserable – than any being in this World <u>can</u> be! I pine & long for your dearly beloved precious Papa so dreadfully!' She sent him '<u>2</u> Photographs of beloved Papa, w^h you can have framed – but <u>not in</u> black, – a Locket with beloved Papa's hair & a photograph – w^h I wish you to wear <u>attached</u> to a string or chain round your neck & a <u>dear</u> pocket handkerchief of beloved Papa's, which you ought to keep constantly with you.'[35]

No-one would doubt the depth of the Queen's grief, or the enormity of the shock she had suffered, but it was an extraordinary way to write to a little boy who had just lost his father. She never seemed to understand that her children had feelings of their own for Prince Albert, which they needed to express in their own way. Instead all were drawn into the vortex of her mourning – except Leopold. He still felt a vague anxiety for home, expressed in requests for photographs of Arthur and locks of his hair, but he was enjoying life again. At the end of January he told his brother, 'This morning I played at croquêt with Dr Günther, Miss Bowater, and Mrs Long who is a great friend of Miss Bowater, Mrs Long and Miss Bowater played against Dr Günther and me, and Dr Günther and me won the game.'[36] The morning croquet became a ritual, creating a fashion in Cannes where the game was unknown, and a croquet lawn was laid out for Leopold in Mr Woolfield's famous garden at the Villa Victoria.

In February the Queen reproached Leopold for not noticing 'the dear 10th', her wedding anniversary, but his mind was full of outings to nearby villages, and the need to win at croquet at least once a day.[37] This was not from any lack of feeling – his later comments about the parting from his father show that he did feel the loss – but he was young, and protected by people who did not share the Queen's need to prolong the first shock of grief. He was also in perfect health. Shortly after his father's death, Leopold complained of pains in the joints, and in his hands, but Elphinstone advised Günther that this was a normal symptom of his condition. Once it passed, he had no further problem.

Günther was a good teacher. Faced with a pupil who must spend most of his time outdoors, the doctor encouraged Leopold to observe the natural world. Together they searched for lizards among the rocks, and scrambled up the side of waterfalls looking for different species of fern. They studied insects: Günther's enthusiasm was genuine and his knowledge broad. With Lord Charles Fitzroy, heir to the Duke of Grafton, who had been sent from England in February, Günther took his pupil on expeditions around Cannes and into the mountains. They visited Le Cannet and the medieval town of Vallauris, and took a carriage drive to Antibes. A longer excursion took them back over the Esterels to explore the densely wooded Maures massif to the south-west of Fréjus, and once, after climbing a gorge near Napoule, they caught a distant glimpse of Italy on the skyline.

The contrast between this life and home was deepening all the time. The Queen had taken refuge at Osborne after her husband's death, and in March she returned to Windsor. This was bound to revive painful memories, but her description to Leopold left nothing to the imagination – 'A dreadful, dreadful return! Here everything is even more dreadfully harrowing.' Only a few weeks were left of her son's stay at Cannes, as she reminded him: 'You will, my poor little Darling, find Mama old – & thin – & grown weak – & you must try & be a comfort (tho that none can be – for none can replace the All in All I have lost).' She described the consolation she found in spreading flowers on the deathbed, and in her plans for the Mausoleum 'where beloved Papa will rest, & I too – & all of you in time'.[38]

The effect of all this on a child can easily be imagined, and Dr Günther wrote to Windsor immediately asking to keep Leopold longer at Cannes, or to change the plans for his first months at home. Physically the little boy was fine, so the doctor must have been thinking about his emotional state, and his fears would have been reinforced by the next letter from Windsor, in which Louise warned her brother how different things would be: 'there will be no dear Papa to tell you pretty stories and amuse us as he used to do; it will be very sad for you when you come home.' She described the mournful rituals around the deathbed, in the room where the children had once had their Christmas trees. 'We went to St Georges', she added, 'and put wreaths where dear Papa lies only we cannot see the coffin because the floor covers it.'[39] But Günther's request fell on deaf ears. Dr Jenner replied by return: the arrangements for Leopold had made by the Prince Consort and the doctors – the arrangements would stand.[40]

No-one looked forward to going home. 'We left Cannes with a pang of regret at the break-up of our pleasant party', Louisa wrote, 'after a last drive along the Happy Valley, a last visit to Mr. Woolfield's pretty garden, and a last game of croquet!' Lord Charles Fitzroy planned a different route home, to spare the Bowater ladies any painful memories, and the party travelled west to Marseilles, and then north by Lyons, Paris and Amiens.[41]

Meanwhile, Major Elphinstone and Arthur were sent to the 'Lord Warden' at Dover to meet them, with ominous instructions. Elphinstone was 'to take care and make poor little Leopold understand that his return will be a very sad one, that he comes back to a House of Mourning and that his poor broken-hearted Mother cannot bear noise, excitement, etc.'[42] The travellers arrived at the 'Lord Warden' on 3 April, and the Major reported that Leopold 'has grown, not only in height but much stouter. His shoulders & chest are much broader; his face, neck and hands are quite bronzed, and he has altogether a much more healthy and a far stronger appearance than formerly. In comparing him to Prince Arthur, one would at first sight say that he was the stronger of the two.'[43] He impressed the little boy with the solemnity of his return, and the next day the whole party made their way to Portsmouth, and crossed the Solent on the barge *Victoria and Albert*. Alfred was waiting for them at Osborne pier.

Lady Bowater and Louisa stayed at Osborne until after Leopold's birthday. Louisa's first impression was of overwhelming sadness, but she found the Queen as kind as ever, and there was an unquenchable life in the royal children. On his birthday, Leopold went for a drive with Alfred and Arthur. 'In the afternoon', Louisa wrote, 'we had an interminable game at croquet with all the Princes, and after tea had immense fun in the corridor playing with their little theatre.' The next day she and her mother left, after a final walk with Dr Günther and Leopold. The two younger Princes were allowed to go as far as the mainland on the *Fairy*, and Leopold 'cried bitterly' when the time came to say goodbye.[44]

Five months is a long time in a child's life. Leopold had grown away from home and its ways, and the readjustment would be hard. He had been the only child in a house of sympathetic adults; now he returned to the pig-in-the-middle position between Arthur and Beatrice, who both received more attention than he did. Having a little sister again was especially frustrating, and there were squabbles. In May, Helena reproved him, 'Beatrice is quite well and so good . . . she is not a "stupid little thing" as you call her'.[45]

Prince Albert's plan had been to place Leopold with Arthur under Major Elphinstone, and by the end of the year the two boys were to move into a separate house for their education. This was what Leopold wanted, but it was looking increasingly unlikely. Emotional trauma is thought to increase the frequency and severity of haemophilia attacks, and it is striking that the little boy who had spent three months scrambling up rocks, riding donkeys and playing games of croquet in Cannes was ill within weeks of returning home. Arthur bumped into him during the croquet on his birthday and his arm had to be put in a sling.[46] Then he sprained his ankle, and his knee and foot hurt. Dr Jenner ordered that instead of going with his brother on a sea cruise in the Admiralty yacht *Vivid*, Leopold should be sent to Balmoral, but a swelling on his thigh delayed the departure for some days.

After some disquiet about Günther – the Queen toyed with the idea of keeping him on permanently, but Elphinstone persuaded her against it – the doctor was asked to look after Leopold at Osborne, with Colonel Du Plat. Lady Caroline's nephew was there too, and Leopold settled happily. 'Yesterday afternoon', he told his brother, 'Albert Grey came to play with me, and we played at spinning some beautiful tops of silver which spin for twenty minutes without stopping, when Albert was gone I went out driving in the phaeton . . . there was a great storm and the outrider's horse ran away with him, there was nothing but lightening and thunder the whole evening.'[47]

By 8 May he was well enough to travel to London. He had been writing regularly to Louisa since their parting, and now he invited her to Buckingham Palace with her mother; the letter was so mischievous, offering to order a carriage, sherry, 'and some gout stuff for you', that Louisa consulted Günther to ask if he really had permission. 'My darling Miss', Leopold had written, '. . . I hope to have a quarrel with you on Friday. Please come, I quite forgot to invite also Lady Bowater; but I thought "naturally" she would come . . . . If you don't come on Friday you will get a tremendgous "scolding", Dr Günther will give it you, and I will call you the most <u>unkind</u> person in the whole world, it would <u>indeed</u> be very very very unkind and naughty . . . it would be very very hard upon me, and would make me "really" very unhappy because I shall not see you for a very very very long time.'[48] Reassured by the doctor, the ladies were pleased to accept.[49]

On the evening of 14 May, Colonel Du Plat and Dr Günther took Leopold to the Euston Square terminus of the London and North Western Railway, on the first stage of their journey to Balmoral, which would take four days. Leopold was still feeling playful, and told his brother: 'On monday evening I am going to frighten Dr Gunter in my Goast's dress, but I wont show myself to Beatrice because Major does not allow me. Give my love to dear Major . . .'.[50]

But the Major had reached an important decision. For some months he had been unwilling to leave Arthur and Leopold together without supervision, in case of accidents, and in June 1862 he wrote in confidence to Sir Charles Phipps about their future. He did not want to take Leopold away from home as planned, because he thought the child had been spoilt at Cannes: 'The Rebuffs which he met with at home, were wanting to keep down his self esteem, and, I am sorry to say, the result is clearly traceable in his character.' Arthur, on the other hand, needed to leave home as a matter of urgency: without his father he was becoming hard to control. 'I need not tell you that Prince Arthur is a favourite, a great favourite, and as such it is but natural that he should be exempt from the scoldings which fall to the share of his brother.'[51] There could be no clearer evidence of the difference in the way the boys were treated.

Officially, there was no immediate response to this. Ranger's House in Greenwich was still being prepared for Leopold in August, and a German tutor, Adolf Buff, was employed for both boys at a salary of £300 a year.[52] In November the Queen confirmed her husband's intention to appoint Elphinstone governor to both her sons, but by then the Major and Arthur had moved into Ranger's House. Leopold was at home, where he would stay.

FOUR

'THE ILLNESS OF A GOOD CHILD'

In the autumn of 1862, Leopold and Arthur and their sisters accompanied the Queen to Coburg, but the journey came to a sudden halt in Reinhardtsbrunn, the Gothic hunting lodge built for their grandfather on the edge of the Thüringer Wald, when Leopold accidentally pierced the roof of his mouth with a steel pen. The bleeding could not be controlled because it was such an awkward place to cauterise, and after several days Dr Jenner lost his nerve and telegraphed to Berlin for a surgeon. It must have been a terrifying experience for the little boy, poised between life and death with adults panicking around him. He was cared for by Rudolf Löhlein, his father's valet, and on 1 October the surgeon, Professor Wilms, painted a strong cauterising solution on to the roof of his mouth and ordered finger pressure on the wound at the first sign of bleeding, no matter what the difficulty.

The Queen wrote to Princess Alice in great anxiety: 'He has not lost near as much blood as frequently before – but the fear was – the bleeding c^ld not be stopped & <u>then</u> – you know he c^ld <u>not</u> have lived. On Tuesday night I went in at ½ p 11 & there he was – nursed by Löhlein – very sick – bringing up blood – & it was an anxious – <u>sad sight</u>.'[1] But the Professor had encountered haemophilia before, and his treatment worked. He accompanied the royal party when they moved on to Coburg on 3 October, and there was no further bleeding.

Leopold's strength returned quickly, and he was soon well enough to explore his father's old home. He met Baron Stockmar, Prince Albert's trusted adviser, but the meeting which stayed in his mind long after the holiday was over had happened on the way to Reinhardtsbrunn. In Brussels at the beginning of September, the Queen was introduced to Princess Alexandra of Denmark, the future Princess of Wales. Leopold was impressed, and for months after the engagement was announced he praised Alexandra in his letters. But he was alarmed to hear that he must welcome her on her arrival at Osborne pier that November; the Queen pointed out that with Arthur's removal to Greenwich, he had become 'the only Prince in our poor house!'[2]

At 7.45 p.m. on Wednesday, 5 November, the Princess's ship, the *Black Eagle*, fired a signal to announce her arrival off the Isle of Wight. Helena accompanied Leopold to the pier, and old friends were close by: Lady Caroline went with her brother General Grey, Lady Augusta Bruce and Lord Charles Fitzroy, who had shared the last month at Cannes. 'The night was perfectly still', Lady Augusta told her sister, 'the moon shining brightly, and making the waves as they broke on the beach look like silver. The two steamers and the Frigate had lights burning, there were lights also on the Pier, and the band of the *Emerald* played from time to time. All this, however, had no power to still the impatience of our Royal Brother and Sister, and greatly had I to struggle to be allowed to sit in the comfortable carriage, instead of standing on the wet stones.' At last the national anthems sounded, and Lady Augusta took Leopold to the landing place.

He was terrified, and quizzed her about how she would introduce him, what he should say, what he should do with the bouquet he was clutching, but he need not have worried. There was no chance to do anything as 'the pretty graceful Princess stepped lightly on shore, took the great representative of the House of England in Her arms and kissed him'.[3] From this moment Leopold worshipped Alexandra and took her part in everything.

Soon after her husband's death, the Queen had written to Elphinstone about Leopold. She expected to die herself from the shock of grief before her youngest son grew to manhood, but found comfort in thinking, 'if he is spared <u>how much</u> he may resemble his precious father in character – in many of the qualities at least and . . . may go on with His work. The Queen's precious Prince surely sees his dear little boy whom he was anxious for, and blesses and loves him.'[4] Modelling her younger sons on their father had become a favourite notion, particularly when she reflected on the Prince of Wales's fall from grace, which had caused his father so much anxiety. In September 1862 Prince Alfred shocked her by following his brother's example: 'to have to bear alone what dear Papa could not bear alone is too much!'.[5]

So, although she did not announce that Leopold was to stay with her permanently, he was drifting into that position. When it seemed that he might die at Reinhardtsbrunn, 'the ugliest and least pleasing of the whole family' was finally transformed into 'our cleverest and best boy', whose mother would protect him – and in her mind the danger to his health was inseparable from the danger to his moral well-being.[6] Her elder sons had 'fallen', she had not been happy about letting Arthur go to Greenwich, but Leopold was still a child, whose character could be moulded and controlled. In December Herr Buff was told that the little boy must not visit the Prince of Wales in his room without special permission.[7]

Leopold marked time with his sisters, becoming especially close to Louise, who encouraged him to draw, and gave him clay to experiment with – 'when it is soft enough take it out of the water and keep it damp by putting wet towels round it, you can pinch it into any shape you like.'[8] But he longed for other boys. Sometimes Albert Grey visited, and when Albert went to Harrow different boys were invited in his place. On a fine, windy day in May 1863, Hallam Tennyson, the elder son of the poet and a boy of Leopold's own age, visited Osborne with his family, and Leopold took to him instantly. They went to the beach, to a quiet corner where Leopold showed Hallam a favourite and rather dangerous game: he liked to make ships out of paper, set light to them with a match, and watch them sail away.[9]

He was increasingly lonely at home, living for the occasions which reunited the family, and always longing for Arthur and Major Elphinstone. Just before the Prince of Wales's wedding in March 1863, Louisa Bowater met him on the green by St George's Chapel at Windsor with his brother and the Major, 'and great was the laughing and talking with me and my two little chaperons'.[10] The Princess Royal and her husband, now Crown Prince and Princess of Prussia, came from Berlin with their four-year-old son

Wilhelm, who disgraced himself during the ceremony by throwing the stone from the head of his dirk across the floor of the chapel and biting Leopold's knee.[11] Alice, who had married Louis of Hesse in July 1862, came home for the wedding; only Alfred was missing, recovering from typhoid in the naval hospital in Malta. His return, and the birth and christening of Alice's first baby, prolonged the reunion for several weeks; the baby was born two days before Leopold's tenth birthday. But life was closing in around Leopold. In June he began bleeding internally, and the Queen, believing that riding had brought on the attack, decided that it would be too dangerous for him to ride, 'except at a foot's pace', for the next year. In fact, she would never be willing to let him ride again, and this was just the first in a long series of deprivations.

The Queen felt sorry for him, but found comfort in a thought which strikes a chill into any modern reader. 'But oh!' she told her eldest daughter, 'the illness of a good child is so far less trying than the sinfulness of one's sons – like your two elder brothers. Oh! Then one feels that death in purity is so far preferable to life in sin and degradation!'[12] Leopold, in pain and facing more and more restrictions, did not want to die – in purity, or any other state. His mother was trying to cast him into a role beloved of sentimental Victorians: the saintly invalid child, sweet-natured, patient, and close to Heaven, selflessly bringing enlightenment to those around him. Nothing could have been further from the real Leopold. Full of spirit, he resented his illness and wanted to fight against it, and no amount of parental wishful thinking would change him.

He was still bleeding when he found himself on the edge of a storm affecting two of his favourite people. The Queen had been uneasy about Madame Hocédé for some months, suspecting her of being a bad influence on the Princesses. Helena and Louise had been reading books which were not thought 'suitable', probably novels; when Louise claimed that she had found the books, the Queen was certain that the governess was encouraging her daughter to lie, and dismissed her. Madame Hocédé was given a pension, and told that as the children were older there was no longer need for three governesses, but she added to the Queen's anger by telling the children that she had been dismissed.[13]

Often there is an unbridgeable gulf between the perspectives of parents and children. The Queen believed she had taken the only action possible. Entrusting her children to other people was inevitable in her position, but she was always wary of those she appointed, and quick to suspect that they were not reliable. She cared about her children. But to Louise and Leopold, Madame Hocédé was 'Lina', and their friend. She was Leopold's own governess; while he was at Cannes she wrote to him regularly and his letters home included messages for her. He would continue to write to her occasionally, and she to him, for the rest of his life, and her dismissal left a hint of resentment, on which later events would build.

Lady Caroline watched Leopold sadly, remembering his illness of 1861. To Lady Augusta's sister-in-law she commented, 'How I wish I could hear of his being stronger!' – and she sent him some notepaper with embossed ciphers created from his initials. He was delighted: 'they are both so pretty, lilac and silver are two such beautiful colours, I like also the forms very much. . . . I am a great deal better today', he assured her, 'and I am allowed to go up and downstairs, but then I have to be led by somebody. Mr Buff wishes me to remember him to you.'[14]

Buff had stayed with Leopold when Arthur went to Ranger's House. He was a desperately shy man, and the Household did not take to him. Louisa Bowater met him at Osborne in January 1864, and at dinner one evening she was told to speak to him in German. 'I got on capitally with him, to everyone's surprise', she wrote, 'and I think he is an ill-used little man. His extreme shyness makes him unpopular here, and they take so little notice of him, I think it makes him worse.'[15] Leopold also liked Buff, but he was missing his brother more with every day that passed. He sent sad letters to Ranger's House appealing for news, with messages for the Major, who was still supposed to be his governor, and he tried desperately to keep up Arthur's interest in the hobbies they had shared. In the Swiss Cottage at Osborne, the Princes had a collection of insects: 'I caught the other day a very big fine white moth of which we have only got very small ones', Leopold told Arthur in July 1863, 'it is called a Gold-tail.'[16]

A month later, the Queen took him to Coburg again. He had a bad leg on the journey but soon recovered, and Arthur was never far from his thoughts. Herr Buff and Alfred took him butterfly hunting, and he told Arthur that they had caught 'a great many butterflies, of which many we had not got in our collection'.[17] They stayed at the Rosenau, Prince Albert's birthplace, which had become very special to Leopold. 'I am very glad to hear that you liked the "Rosenau",' he commented to Arthur a year later, 'because you would not believe me when I told you that it was such a nice place.'[18] With Buff and Sir Thomas Biddulph he explored Coburg, and afterwards he and Buff called on Herr Florschütz, Prince Albert's tutor. Leopold owned a letter written by his father to Florschütz in 1840; the tutor probably gave it to him at this time.

The stay in Coburg brought him relief from one of the Queen's more unwelcome fancies. She often insisted that her sons should wear kilts, to emphasise her allegiance to Scotland, but in Germany? 'It is dreadfully hot today', Leopold told Arthur on 16 August, 'I am wearing today for the first time ever since 1860 white trousers on which I have made ink blots in writing to you, and Mama said that I need not wear a kilt even on Sundays because she thought I would astonish the natives too much.'[19] He sounded surprised, and he probably was, for this was a rule which was seldom relaxed. A few months later when one of his legs became swollen, Louise reported to Arthur that 'the doctors say it comes from wearing the kilt in such cold weather, but dear Mama does not think so, poor little boy he says it hurts him very much'.[20]

The 1863 visit to Coburg brought another welcome change. At the Rosenau Leopold acquired the dog he had wanted for so long, forgotten in the dramas of December 1861 – a dachshund which he named 'Waldmann' or 'Waldi'. Waldmann became his constant companion, and only to please Arthur would he occasionally leave his pet behind: 'I take Max out very often,' he told Arthur the following summer (Max was Arthur's dog), 'but I can never take him out with Waldmann because they will fight; Mamma says both your dogs can go to Osborne.'[21] Pets were another thing the brothers had in common, and Leopold was determined that in his new life, Arthur would not forget. In the same letter he told him, 'We put the guinea-pig with the other guinea-pigs, and it went into some of their holes, but the next day we found it lying dead on the road.'

Leopold was fascinated by the natural world. He loved cats, and as a small boy had been given his own white cat, named Snowdrop. At Osborne he found an injured bird which he nursed in his room, and he tended his own gardens at Osborne and at Buckingham Palace. When Arthur and the Major went to Switzerland in 1864, he appealed for 'some of those big "Demoiselles" (a sort of "dragonfly" with a blue body)', and for 'a "rose des Alpes" dried from Mont Blanc I should so much like to have one.'[22] This last may have had a sentimental association, as there was a dried 'rose des Alpes' in an album Prince Albert made when he visited Switzerland as a young man, which the Queen treasured.

By the start of 1866, both brothers were collecting stamps. 'I thank you very much for the letter you wrote to me and for the envelope and stamp you sent me for my book', Leopold told Arthur, '. . . P.S. My stamps number 191.'[23] For four years, his sights were fixed constantly on Arthur. When a baby was born, or a sister ill, when there were cricket matches, or accidents or outings, Arthur had to know, and Leopold always added greetings to the Major, and appeals for letters from him. Letters and gifts from Arthur were gleefully and gratefully received. If the Prince Consort had lived, the two boys would almost certainly have stayed together. This could not have cured Leopold, but it would have made him happier, which might, in turn, have had an effect on his health.

But it was not to be, and the Queen saw his loneliness as a sad but inevitable result of his condition. She reprimanded her other children if they seemed to be neglecting him. When the Crown Princess forgot his birthday in 1864, but sent a present for Beatrice, her mother was quick to let her know that 'poor, good Leopold ought not to have been quite forgotten. He suffers so often, and leads so sad and solitary a life. A pretty classical German book would give him such pleasure and if you would ask the Queen to send him her print, he would be delighted.'[24] In the summer of 1864 the Hesse family stayed at Osborne, and Louis carried Leopold everywhere because he could not walk. Arthur sent him a walking stick, and he was well enough in August to perform his first official duty, laying an infirmary foundation stone. He sent his brother an account of the event from the local paper, adding '<u>and</u> you can be sure what is written in it is perfectly true, which is not always the case in those newspapers', a perceptive comment from an eleven-year-old.[25]

Decisions about his future had to be reached, and in 1864 an unexpected event made the Queen think. On New Year's Day, Alfred announced that he did not want to be heir to the duchy of Saxe-Coburg, a position he had been groomed for since childhood. This was a shock, but his mother and her advisers were shrewd enough not to pressurise him, in the hope that he might change his mind. Meanwhile, they had to consider the alternatives. The Prince of Wales's suggestion that Leopold might be made heir, leaving Arthur free for a career in the army, was very firmly stamped on by the Queen – Leopold was far too frail. Elphinstone agreed. Arthur, he said, with his love of all things military, was essentially German in character, whereas Leopold 'will hereafter become of far greater use in England than Prince Arthur could possibly become . . . by patronizing the sciences, for which he has a decided taste, & which must otherwise receive but little encouragement'.[26]

He was right, but a very different idea was taking shape in the Queen's mind. Alfred had said that he wished to remain in England to help her with her work. He was warned that this would require immense dedication: Sir Charles Phipps told him that attendance on the Queen must become his first duty, overshadowing his profession and his pleasures.[27] Even the Queen issued warnings. She wanted Alfred to change his mind, until he did, and then the realisation of what he had offered suddenly hit her. Indignantly, she told her uncle, 'the idea of living <u>only</u> to assist me did <u>not</u> I believe please him, <u>painful</u> as the feeling is to me'.[28] In the midst of this disappointment, she turned to Leopold. He was clever enough to assist her one day, and so sweet, so affectionate, and so innocent, that given the right upbringing he would never want to leave her. Alfred's waverings had more far-reaching implications for his brother than he could have imagined.

That summer the Queen drafted a lengthy memorandum about Leopold. Because of his condition he was not to play active games with other boys, '& all the <u>essentially</u> English <u>notions</u> of "<u>manliness</u>", must be put out of the question. He must be constantly watched by his Tutor & treated with firmness but with tenderness & affection & <u>not</u> with severity. . . . I <u>do not</u> wish that any attempt sh^d be made to remove him <u>from me</u>, & <u>from his own Home</u>, for he learns very well <u>wherever</u> he is, & he can no where be so well treated & cared for than when he is with me.'[29] She was happy with Buff, but he had only been engaged till the summer of 1865, and was keen to leave. Her first instinct had been to look for a replacement: Professor Max Müller at Oxford was asked to suggest 'a young man of about 24 to 28 – of great intelligence, with plenty of observation & knowledge of character & a good deal of learning & especially good knowledge of different countries and languages. He sh^d have a very even temper & like children – but plenty of firmness – He sh^d either be a German or Swiss of good manners & deportment – who had complete knowledge of England & the English language – or an Englishman, devoid of all prejudices and peculiarities of his nation & of the young men of the present day.'[30]

On reflection, though, the Queen had decided against this: 'to take a complete Stranger, w^d for the next 2 or 3 years be a very dangerous experiment on account of the Child's health & the poor Child, who is of a very clinging disposition & extremely fond of Mr Buff w^d feel his leaving him very painful.'[31] Buff must be persuaded to stay for at least two years. If he would not, the Queen hoped that Sir John Cowell, whose appointment as Alfred's governor would end in 1865, would accept the position, while masters from Eton could continue to teach Leopold when the Court was at Windsor. In the event, Buff stayed until January 1866, and Cowell became acting governor after Alfred's coming of age.

More sensitive decisions had to be made about Leopold's personal attendants. He was tall and of normal build, and carrying him would become more difficult as he grew older. He needed a strong manservant who could be trusted with the full truth about his condition – and the Queen was less willing to talk about this than she and Prince Albert had been in the early days.[32] It was unfortunate for Leopold that his need for a servant coincided with a significant change in the domestic staff of the palaces. At the end of 1864, Dr Jenner and Sir Charles Phipps recommended that the Queen should bring John Brown to Osborne for the winter, to hold the reins of her pony and enable her to keep up her riding. By February 1865 she had decided to make the appointment permanent, calling Brown 'The Queen's Highland Servant'.

Other Highlanders followed: the Queen delighted in their self-esteem and independence, and found them superior in every way to English servants. She trusted absolutely in their loyalty. But the qualities which she valued so highly came across to others as arrogance and rudeness. When complaints were made, the Queen defended the Highlanders, and the more unpopular they became, the more defiantly she stood by them. Brown was the most important; to the Queen he was outspoken, helpful, and reliable, and while he was around the others were safe. They took advantage of her favour in small ways: petty, but intensely annoying to those who knew that complaints against the Highland servants would never be heard. In July 1865 John Brown's 22-year-old brother Archibald was appointed 'Brusher' (a sort of junior valet) to Leopold.

Archie Brown was chosen because he was strong enough to carry Leopold. The Queen wanted 'a faithful, steady, trustworthy, intelligent servant <u>without any</u> vulgarity, & with plenty of <u>self respect</u>' to be placed close to her son, and her first choice had been Alexander Grant, who was more intelligent than Archie, but smaller.[33] Now she was so certain that Archie was the right man that she allowed everything about Leopold's illness to be explained to him.[34] His appointment coincided with another attack of internal bleeding, and his presence was invaluable in August when Leopold slipped on board the *Alberta* in mid-Channel and injured his knee very badly. Walking was impossible; for the rest of the voyage Louise kept him amused with her drawings, and when the ship docked, Archie had to carry him to land. Louise found it 'rather alarming seeing poor Leo carried down the ladder from the ship but Archy managed it very well'.[35]

They were on their way to Coburg, for the first complete reunion of the Queen's nine children since 1858. On 26 August 1865 the whole family attended the unveiling of a statue of Prince Albert in the market square. Photographs were taken of them together, which show Leopold looking very drawn and tired, and obviously unable to stand without support. But the pain did not stop him from thinking of his friends: he bought two crystal hairpins in Coburg for Louisa Bowater, and an amethyst bracelet for Lady Caroline; it cheered him to hear that when the family went to Balmoral on their return, her nephew Albert would go with them.[36] Loneliness had made him desperate to please. Lady Macclesfield visited Windsor at the end of 1864, and while she was critical of the way Beatrice was spoilt and petted, she had nothing but praise for Leopold, 'a charming boy, so gentle & courteous, and considerate for others'.[37]

The Queen was sure that he was becoming happier at home, and growing into the future she planned. In February 1866, she was persuaded to open Parliament for the first time since the death of her husband. Leopold's knee was bad and he had to be left at Windsor, but as soon as the ceremony was over, she sent him a note: 'if _ever_ I go again I hope _you_ will be able to go with me. I seemed as _in_ a _dream_, & hardly saw or heard anything. – Great crowds of people very loyal. – I still shake so much I can hardly hold my pen. . . . I am going back to Windsor almost immediately. – I rejoice to see you soon again darling.'[38]

Satisfied with the arrangements she had made for her son, the Queen wanted to confirm Sir John Cowell as his governor, but this was not to be. In March, Leopold told Louisa Bowater of an unforeseen change: 'unfortunately on account of the death of poor Sir Charles Phipps, Sir John has been made master of the household, and so he is looking out for another person to succeed him, it is very tiresome to change so often'.[39]

There was more: before leaving, Cowell made it clear that he had reservations about Archie Brown, who was about to be promoted to valet. Complaining about any of the Highland servants required superhuman tact, but he suggested that Archie was slow, had a bad memory, and could not spell. If he made other complaints, the Queen did not repeat them when she asked Elphinstone to help sort the matter out – by telling Cowell that he was wrong. 'Good Archie Brown' could not be faulted on anything that mattered, she was sure: 'in a little time he will become a very good servant, & whether he is a little slow, & not an _accomplished_ valet signifies _very little_. He has had no trial in a responsible position, & the Queen believes his want of memory applies entirely to his attendance on Sir J. Cowell – wʰ he had _as well_ as his very constant attendance on poor Leopᵈ in wʰ he really is desirable. The Queen cˡᵈ not and wˡᵈ not put another near his bed.' She decided to appoint another Highlander, Robertson, as valet to the new governor, and to arrange spelling lessons for Archie.[40]

Elphinstone had every sympathy with Cowell. He offered the services of Arthur's valet, Collins, who had cared for Leopold before, to spend a week training Archie, but his only reward was a swift rebuke: he was not even to speak to Cowell until he had seen the Queen, who was confident that Archie was vital to Leopold. 'The Queen does <u>not</u> think it advisable that Collins sh^ld come to teach Archie. He will learn things gradually better, as he does now.'[41]

For the new governor, Cowell approached the Deputy Adjutant-General, who suggested a young Lieutenant of the Royal Horse Artillery. Walter George Stirling was twenty-six, smart, personable and extremely popular, though rather reserved. The Prince Consort had chosen military governors for the elder Princes, and everyone spoke well of Stirling; the Queen allowed herself to be persuaded, though she felt unsure. She appealed to the Major to be present when Stirling arrived, as 'Major Elphinstone will easily understand <u>what</u> a trial it will be for the Queen to <u>begin</u> with a total stranger, unknown to the beloved Prince'.[42] In this remark, and the attitude it betrayed, lay the seeds of trouble.

Stirling was called to Windsor on 24 March to meet the Queen and be briefed about Leopold. His appointment began on 4 April; the written instructions given to him by Cowell show that the Queen's only response to complaints about Archie had been to give the servant a more central role. Archie had special duties from Dr Jenner relating to Leopold's health. If new clothes were needed for Leopold, Archie was to submit the patterns to the Queen. Stirling was to ensure 'that Prince Leopold behaves civilly to the servants, more especially to those constantly about him. Any attempt at the slightest rudeness should at once be reported and the Prince be made to beg pardon.' Leopold was said to be in the habit of contradicting people he was speaking to, a fault Stirling was to correct – which would appear to be a reasonable general requirement if it were not for the end of the sentence: 'Lieutenant Stirling should therefore be in and out of Prince Leopold's bedroom whilst he is dressing.' Only one person would be in the bedroom then for Leopold to contradict – Archie Brown.[43]

Somebody must have told the Queen that Leopold and his valet were not getting on well. Perhaps Leopold was being obstructive and difficult, as boys of twelve or thirteen can be, but it was unusual for him to take a dislike to a new person. He was always eager to please and grateful for any attention, and most people shared Lady Macclesfield's opinion. To Louisa Bowater, meeting him four years after Cannes, he was still 'my own boy . . . quite unchanged and to me very dear'.[44] He would never forget her, either: in his letter of March 1866 he complained, rather sadly, 'I do not know how it is that you always discover my valentines, I always try to disguise my handwriting.'[45] If he did resist Archie, and argue with him, then he probably had good reason, something the Queen seems not to have considered.

The key may lie in the special duties Archie had from Dr Jenner: Stirling was given a separate list of these, which has not survived. They may simply have involved caring for the Prince when he was ill, but the instructions given four years earlier to Günther show the importance the doctors attached to watching for signs that an attack was impending. If the valet had been told to make sure that Leopold was not constipated, or to see if he was passing blood, he was being given a task which could only be handled with great sensitivity, by someone Leopold liked and trusted. He had reached the age when a child becomes conscious of his own body, and the intervention of a thoughtless or unkind adult would be likely to make him difficult, and unhappy. By placing so much reliance on the valet, the Queen had left her son open to bullying and petty spitefulness of an unpleasant kind.

Some confirmation of this may be found in the Prince's growing dislike of Dr Jenner. Any suggestion that Leopold was building up to an attack of bleeding would lead to weeks of what the Queen called 'strict treatment', with doses of laxatives and a restricted diet. This was unlikely to have endeared the doctor to him. Leopold also felt that Jenner did not take his genuine complaints seriously. On 30 April 1866, he wrote from his bed to Louise: 'I may not leave my room, I had a very bad night and my cough is much worse, not quite "nonsense" as Dr Jenner told Mamma, I may not speak, in fact I can hardly speak, Sir James Clark said that if I did not take great care I would get the whooping-cough.'[46] It was whooping-cough. Arthur, Louise and Beatrice came down with it too, and they were still coughing nearly a month later when Louisa Bowater visited Windsor. A funny remark by Beatrice 'was received with shrieks of laughter, resulting in a simultaneous burst of whooping-cough from Princess Louise, Prince Arthur, and Prince Leopold. It was a horrid shame, but it was impossible to help laughing!'[47]

But Leopold was entirely delighted with his new governor. Stirling was only two years older than the Prince of Wales, and he came from that world of independent young men which Leopold eyed with longing. His elder brothers had reached it. Even Arthur was nearing the time when he would enter the Royal Military Academy. Leopold must have realised that he would never follow his brothers into uniform, but he still wanted to be accepted as a man, in a man's world. He took to Stirling instantly, and the Queen liked him too, at first, 'very much. He seems kind & sensible', she commented in her journal, '& I hope he will take real care of our poor dear Boy.'[48]

The governor was not expected to teach his charge. Stirling's instructions laid down that lessons should continue as before, with extra German tuition from the librarian Herr Sahl, who would stand in for him during any absences. His role was more parental, watching over the general well-being of his charge, making sure that he attended lessons on time, replied to letters, and behaved properly. Stirling would also select companions for Leopold, submitting their names to the Queen and asking her permission before sending invitations. He took his duties seriously and was quite strict, which Leopold never minded. Years afterwards he was still quoting Stirling's favourite saying, 'look slippy', at times when he was running late, or dragging his heels over something he should have done.[49]

On 26 May the Queen set off for Cliveden, taking Helena, Louise, Beatrice and Leopold, with Mademoiselle Bauer and Lieutenant Stirling. Louisa Bowater was with them, and she described their arrival, when 'our exclamations of delight were unbounded and we rushed about like wild things. Anything more beautiful than this place it would be hard to find.'[50] Leopold agreed. The next day he praised the house to Arthur as 'the most beautiful place I ever saw in all my life either here or abroad, it is a true paradise, it is a beautiful house, there is . . . a clock tower with chimes like at Westminster or Antwerp, and they play exactly the same time as at Westminster. Mamma and the sisters live in the main wing, but Mr Stirling and I and the gentlemen live in the east wing . . . I am living in the room in which General Garibaldi lived two years ago.'[51]

But beneath the surface of paradise, all was not well. Robertson, the Highlander attached to Stirling, had no idea of the duties of a valet. As an army officer, Stirling was not used to servants who had to be asked nicely before they did their job, and he had angry words with Robertson. Before their departure for Cliveden the Queen had hoped to discuss this with Elphinstone: 'it will never do to speak harshly and dictatorially to Highlanders;' she wrote, 'their independence and self-respect and proper spirit . . . makes them resent <u>that</u> . . . a young officer accustomed to order about soldiers may not understand the <u>peculiar</u> nature of these people.'[52] But Stirling was a Scot himself, from Faskine in Lanarkshire, and he did not share this indulgent view of the Highlanders. To the Queen's dismay, Elphinstone agreed. On 28 May she protested, 'It is not fair to take the part of the <u>stronger</u> agst the <u>weaker</u>', but in truth, it was the servant who was in the stronger position.[53] The 'total stranger, unknown to the beloved Prince' stood no chance against one of the Queen's Highlanders.

For the time being, the matter was allowed to drop, though the Queen made it clear that she would be watching Stirling. Then, as the holiday at Cliveden drew to an end, Louisa noticed a worrying little incident which would have serious repercussions for Stirling and his pupil. One hot afternoon, she and the Princesses joined Leopold for a game of croquet. 'Our pleasure, however, was sadly spoilt by the dear boy having an attack of faintness which alarmed us all. Happily he recovered quickly, and the Queen . . . did not know of it till her return.'[54]

Leopold had started to have fits. If this was one, it must have been about the first, since Elphinstone did not hear of them until May, and the Queen always turned to him immediately with any problem concerning Leopold.[55] A memorandum written by Dr Jenner in 1881, shortly before the Prince's engagement, gives a summary of the problem as it then appeared: 'Prince Leopold has from his boyhood suffered from attacks of an epileptic character – These attacks have always been of short duration, leaving the Prince after a few hours rest, as well as before. They were never frequent, rarely less than a year and sometimes more than two years intervening between them.'[56] But in 1866, no-one knew how serious the fits would become. The Queen was advised that her son's attacks were a mild form of epilepsy, 'tho' it is hoped they will never assume the really formidable character of <u>those</u> distressing attacks', she told Elphinstone. She also told him that Jenner had found a medical student to replace Stirling, for it was resolved in her mind that Stirling must go.

Victoria was using her son's illness to rid herself of a man she disliked, but she would never have seen it in these terms. She loved Leopold, and was sure that she was acting in his interests. The first reasons she gave for her decision were understandable and sincere – if only the doctors had warned her sooner about the fits, she said, she would never have thought of employing an army officer. She tried not to criticise Stirling, but was too honest to hide her true feelings. 'In strict <u>confidence</u> she may however tell Major Elphinstone, that she does <u>not</u> think that Mr Stirling was <u>suited</u> for that post; he has not enlarged views or knowledge, enough to lead & develop so clever a boy as Leop^d – <u>without</u> a <u>father</u>, – nor has he softness & kindness of manner & character . . . the Queen must likewise own – that there is <u>that</u> in M^r S's manner – w^h (& she <u>felt</u> it, tho she did not admit it – from the <u>very 1st</u>) w^n w^{ld} make it <u>very</u> difficult for <u>her</u> to get on with him.'[57]

As before, with Madame Hocédé, it was the parent's view against the child's. The Queen was convinced that Stirling was harsh and arrogant. She listened to the Highlanders – for it becomes apparent from later papers that Archie Brown was at odds with Stirling too – and completely misjudged the Lieutenant. She also failed to see how vital Stirling was to Leopold. For him, the governor represented hope that despite his problems he could be brought up as a normal boy, and grow to normal manhood. The Queen was rapidly coming to the conclusion that he could not. His increasing delicacy made her feel that he could only survive at home, and this fitted in rather well with her own need for companionship. The struggle for Leopold's future had begun.

FIVE

AFTER STIRLING

The last weeks of Lieutenant Stirling's brief appointment were miserable for all concerned. Sir John Cowell had to break the news of his dismissal, though he, like Elphinstone, had every sympathy with Stirling. The Queen instructed him to say only that Leopold needed a medical attendant, to spare the Lieutenant's feelings, but both Cowell and Elphinstone suggested a more tangible way of softening the blow: in a few months Prince Arthur would need a reliable young officer to guide him through the first stages of army training. If Stirling were offered that position, his 'retirement' could not reflect badly on him. But the Queen was adamant – and knowing that two men whom her husband had trusted believed she was wrong gave a defiant edge to her refusal. Stirling was *not* the sort of man she could tolerate near her younger sons. She complained of his 'hardness & harshness' of manner, and gave up all idea of having medical grounds for his dismissal, referring to this herself as 'the ostensible reason'.[1] The real reason was that she disliked Stirling's attitude to the Highland servants, and her feelings were hardening by the day.

But what was Leopold to be told? The Queen warned Elphinstone to be careful what he said about the new tutor: 'Leop^d is not however to know that he is a real medical man – but merely one versed in medical knowledge.'[2] There was a certain stigma attached to the idea of a medical attendant, and besides, the Queen was afraid that her elder sons might look down on the new man for being a civilian. Even Arthur was not to be told the truth, and by the end of July she had decided to prevent all contact between Arthur and his elder brothers at Balmoral, for fear that he might 'try to lower Mr Legg the <u>new tutor</u> in P^ce Leop^d's eyes'.³

In fact, Leopold was not even thinking of the new tutor. The prospect of losing Stirling made him miserable and angry, with all the intensity of adolescence. He blamed his mother. She felt terrible, confiding to Lady Biddulph on 27 July, 'to feel my Child is not open with his poor Mother, & is <u>evidently between</u> 2 fires – is <u>quite</u> dreadful to me. – <u>Today</u> he appeared with a <u>great</u> gold ring on his <u>finger</u> at luncheon, & on my asking him what it was & <u>who</u> had <u>given</u> it him; he said 1st "<u>Somebody</u>" had given it him, & on my asking him who? He grew very <u>red</u> & said "Mr Stirling."' The ring was not an unusual gift, and Leopold would have given Stirling something similar, as he and his brothers and sisters did to other departing attendants. It was his defiant loyalty which upset the Queen. 'I am sure the Child's feelings <u>are</u> being worked upon', she told Lady Biddulph.⁴

Inevitably there was more trouble with the Highlanders, who were triumphant about Stirling's dismissal. Leopold hated Archie Brown now and resisted his attention, and Stirling stood by him. Louise supported her brother too, and after the Lieutenant's departure she and Leopold sent him a comic letter, writing alternate lines, 'to our wellbeloved W.G!!! A very kind friend of ours in Scotch political troubles, but (thank God!) is out of it now.'⁵

There was an incident of some kind, probably an argument, between Stirling and Archie before the end, which the Queen was to mull over for months to come. She began to fear what Stirling might say about his dismissal outside the Household, where her own reliance on John Brown was arousing silly but damaging gossip. Elphinstone told her that Stirling could be trusted, and she reminded him of this five weeks after the Lieutenant had left: 'In speaking of Mr Stirling, the other day to the Queen, M. Elphinstone assured the Queen he <u>thought</u> there was no fear of his talking. The Queen trusts therefore there is no fear of his trying to throw blame on that excellent, devoted & trustworthy young man Archie B. whom he insulted and injured for the Queen w^ld deeply resent it. The Queen trusts that M. Elphinstone's good advice to him extended to <u>that</u>?'⁶ Stirling's name was still to appear on published lists of the Household as an 'Extra Groom', and it was made clear that his future would depend on his discretion.

The date for his departure was set at Saturday 4 August, four months to the day since his arrival. The Queen decided to give him the customary leaving present on the Friday afternoon, to make sure that he would be out of the house before Prince Alfred arrived on Saturday. 'I dread his indiscretion & thought to wound', she told Lady Biddulph, but it was a tragic misunderstanding.[7] Stirling was more loyal to her and her son than she would ever know. For the rest of his life Leopold wrote to him regularly, in secret, and until he achieved a degree of independence these letters were his safety valve, into which he poured his extremes of frustration, anger and anxiety. It was a secret Stirling never betrayed.[8]

The first letter was written less than twenty-four hours after the governor's departure. 'I cannot say how I miss you', Leopold wrote, 'I always expect to see you come in the morning as you always did, and as I was carried down to breakfast Louise and I missed you looking over the banister at the top of the staircase at us.' He was afraid to be alone now with 'the dreadful scotch servants', but escape was difficult because he had injured his leg again, soon after the visit to Cliveden. In constant pain and unable to walk, he relied on Herr Sahl and Sir John Cowell to stay with him, and they did their best to help. Stirling's replacement arrived on the afternoon of 5 August with Dr Jenner, and dined with his pupil; he was John Wickham Legg, who would go on to write the 1872 treatise on haemophilia.[9]

In 1866 Legg was a keen young doctor with a particular interest in bleeding disorders. Three years earlier, as a student, he had watched a haemophilic boy die slowly from a simple nosebleed. This aroused his pity and his curiosity, and he studied every case that came his way, collecting information on his patients' build, their families, colouring and intelligence, and on other diseases which seemed to affect them, in an attempt to understand their condition. It is easy to see why Jenner chose him; easy too to see why he accepted the appointment, though he was ambitious to succeed in medicine and would be unlikely to stay with the Household for long.

At first Leopold was wary. He wanted to like Legg, but the atmosphere around him was tense, and it was hard to be sure of anybody. The Queen was fighting hard to counteract what she saw as Stirling's bad influence, by separating her son from anyone who might reinforce his dislike of Archie Brown. On 19 August, Leopold told Stirling, 'What you predicted has at last come to pass, Sutherland tired of being under Archie will not stay here any longer and I expect he will soon go away. I feel really quite miserable now. Col Du Plat is no more allowed to come near me, and now Waldi is not allowed to come and stop with me in the house, I suppose because Brown does not like him. I am scolded from morning till night by Mamma although Mr Legg is very kind to me and I do not think has tried to get anything out of me concerning you, but it does not matter, for if he tries to do it he will not succeed as I take good care not to let anything out.'[10]

Sutherland was a servant, and Colonel Du Plat one of the Queen's gentlemen, and a close friend of Stirling. Losing their support, and even the company of his dog, was bad enough, but worse was to follow. On 27 August, Leopold wrote again, and his mood was bleak. 'I am no more allowed to stop with Louise as I used to do', he said, 'and this morning I got a message that I was never to ask anybody to come into the railway carriage in going to Scotland without first getting Mamma's permission.'[11] Ever since his return from Cannes, Leopold had been close to his sister, and her sitting-room was one of his favourite refuges. It would be hard not to see an element of jealousy in the Queen's action. Louise entertained, comforted and encouraged her brother and he turned to her instinctively. His troubles were hers. In December she told Louisa Bowater, 'I was stupid breaking down that day at Cliveden about Leo, but I am often anxious about him. . . . Poor little fellow he is never allowed to come to me now, it is a great grief to us both. He said to me one day "Lucy I dont know what would hapen to me if you ever went away all would be over for me then"; I dont know whether he has thought of this again, but I did not forget it.'[12]

The Queen's anxiety was natural, but her attempts to force Leopold to be happy in the restricted world she offered were adding misery to his physical illness. Far from weaning him off outside influences, she was increasing their attraction for him, and his hatred of the Browns deepened by the hour. There was a real danger that he might sink further and further into self-pity, because home offered no distraction from his sufferings; fortunately, he was blessed with an intense thirst for life, and there were still people close to him who understood his needs. If Dr Legg knew nothing of his letters to Stirling, others did, and kept the secret. Herr Sahl and Sir John Cowell were good friends to Leopold in the difficult summer of 1866, and he had found a new ally too, whose influence would change the whole course of his life.

In June Mr Shuldham, the young Eton master who had taught Leopold for two years, left to get married. The Reverend Robinson Duckworth joined the Household in his place, recommended by Dean Stanley of Westminster and his friend Henry Liddell, now the Dean of Christ Church. Arriving at Windsor to find his new pupil immobile, miserable, hardly speaking to his mother, and at the centre of an emotional storm between Stirling and the Highlanders, Duckworth could have been forgiven for turning tail and heading straight back to Oxford, but he stayed, and began to play a quietly constructive role in the whole sorry business.

Duckworth was one of those people whose awareness of others' feelings amounts almost to a sixth sense. He became one of the principal channels through which Leopold's letters went out to Stirling, and the Lieutenant's replies were returned, because he saw how much it mattered, even though the letters had to be carried behind the Queen's back. At first the Prince was writing every week, and apologising even for a day's delay. Duckworth was sympathetic to the Queen's anxieties, and she came to like and trust him, but he saw that the danger to Leopold's character inherent in her plans was as real as any risk to her son's physical health.

In the weeks following Stirling's departure, Duckworth and Legg arranged a series of outings, with Sahl or Cowell, to give Leopold a break from the claustrophobic atmosphere of home. First, they went to the fort at Sandown, on the Isle of Wight, where, 'we found an artillery-man in his shirtsleeves . . . he was very civil and immediately let us in, inside we saw heaps of conical bullets and a lot of breachloaders . . . we then went to a spot overlooking the cliffs we thought that we were not seen by anybody, but we were very much mistaken, for when we had finished our luncheon we saw Lord Ranillah standing just above us and looking at us, we were horrified but fortunately his Lordship departed'. It was a hot day, and Leopold and his friends laid down on the grass to watch the ships in the Cowes Regatta.[13]

At Alum Bay a week later, they encountered an Italian organ-grinder, 'who had been 24 years in England and could hardly speak a word of English; so we told him to stop and play to us at luncheon, afterwards we gave him something to eat and a halfcrown which he said he preferred to all the eatables'.[14] Leopold's letters to Stirling, otherwise full of unhappiness, lit up when he described these outings: he was only thirteen, and he needed stimulation and adventure.

At Balmoral in October, Duckworth began to introduce a new element, taking him to deliver toys to poor children at Aberarder. The moral lesson may or may not have sunk in; for Leopold, riding in a carriage with Sahl, the most exciting part of the day was the moment when a drunken rider crashed between the carriage and Duckworth's horse, and, falling 'caught hold of Mr Duckworth's leg and tried to pull him off his horse but at that minute Mr Duckworth's horse shyed and ran to the other side of the road so that saved him, but the drunken man was in an awful rage and sprung up swearing on his horse and galopped off again at a dreadful rate'.[15]

By mid-October, the Prince was finally able to walk again after four months. He needed a stick, but was glad to be free of restraining splints and bandages, and of his hated wheelchair, ordered the previous December: glad too to be free from enforced dependence on his valet. Renewed health enabled him to see and do much more. He was allowed to attend an evening concert at St James's Hall in London, and to play with selected Eton boys, and as he grew happier, his letters to Stirling became shorter and less frequent. His feelings about Archie Brown, however, were unchanged. Early in 1867, the Queen complained to her sister that Leopold was unkind to his attendants, and ungrateful, and Princess Feodora tried to explain how frustrating dependence could be for a boy of his age.[16]

Leopold was beginning to lead two lives, growing, learning and becoming more mature with his tutor and other friends at Court, but still trapped in a damaging cycle of emotions with his mother, the ordinary tensions of parent and teenage child intensified by his illness and by the Queen's widowhood. Cut off for much of the time from his brothers and elder sisters, except by letter, he nonetheless enjoyed better relationships with them. They understood his frustrations, and knew that, young as he was, they could talk to him about their feelings. Shortly before his birthday in 1866, the Crown Princess wrote to him of her homesickness in Berlin, as spring came and she remembered the primroses at Windsor: 'here we have nothing of the kind, as yet not even a green leaf or a little daisy to boast of, wch makes me quite melancholy. On market days I cannot resist buying pots of wall flowers and mignonettes, to stand in to my window and make the room look gay and spring like.'[17] Even at twelve, Leopold was a sympathetic listener.

As the 1860s drew to an end, he was finding a new interest in his growing list of nephews and nieces. He was only five when he first became an uncle, and the baby was born hundreds of miles away, so the experience is unlikely to have meant much to him. But soon the Queen had grandchildren in England as well as Germany, and Leopold was curious about them all, regularly demanding photographs and information. Writing to the Prince of Wales in 1866 to thank him for a Christmas present, he asked 'I suppose Albert-Victor can run very well now', and he was always eager to hear about the Princess Royal's children.[18] But Alice's family would come to mean most to him. By 1867 there were three little girls in the palace in Darmstadt. 'I wish you could see them when they play all together', Alice told him in April, 'Irène rolls about the floor over & over like a ball & enjoys the noise and fun of her sisters.'[19]

Outside the family circle, Duckworth had found a novel way of broadening Leopold's horizons and, at the same time, underlining the advantages of home. Autograph collecting was in fashion, and in 1865 Leopold was given an album of his own, handsomely bound in dark brown leather and stamped in gold with his name and a coronet.[20] He hardly used it at first, but how many boys could petition the Prime Minister, the Archbishops of Canterbury and York, and some of the country's most distinguished statesmen, artists and writers without stepping beyond their own front door? The Queen's son could, and from 1866 onwards the collection began to blossom – and if Leopold were to ask these great men for their autographs, he would also have to speak to them, and perhaps learn from them.

Charles Kingsley took the opportunity to be inspiring, writing 'What doth the Lord require of thee: but to do justly, & to love mercy, & to walk humbly with thy God?' on the proffered page. Sir Stafford Northcote, President of the Board of Trade, was a little more tongue-in-cheek: 'May Your Royal Highness always set a bright example; but may no one ever be tempted to take a leaf out of your book.' Charles Hallé contributed two staves of music, and at Balmoral in 1867, Landseer added a delightful pen-and-ink sketch of a scruffy little dog, lying curled up but not quite asleep. Tennyson, Winterhalter and Disraeli added their names to the album, Longfellow wrote out the first verse of his poem 'Excelsior', and even those who could not be asked in person could still be collected. Knowing the Prince's interest, several members of the Household gave him letters they had received with interesting signatures, and these too were mounted and treasured.

One contributor, though, outshone them all. Letters to 'My dear Duckworth' appear throughout the album, making it clear that the tutor's enthusiasm for the project was its driving force. And it was through Duckworth, quite incidentally, that a new window opened in Leopold's life. Before his appointment at Court, Robinson Duckworth was a Fellow of Trinity College, Oxford, and most of his friends and acquaintances, whose names appeared in the book, were Oxford men. He would not have given Leopold their letters without telling him something about them, and in this way the boy began to learn about a life from which his condition need not exclude him. University was the place for someone with his intellectual gifts and desire to learn, and it was a world where physical strength would be relatively unimportant.

Tucked away modestly among the letters pasted in Leopold's album, one cut-off signature could almost slip by unnoticed. 'Believe me, at 1.30 a.m., sleepily but sincerely yours, C.L. Dodgson.' It was an endearing reminder of Duckworth's friend the Reverend Charles Lutwidge Dodgson, Mathematical Lecturer at Christ Church, better known to history as Lewis Carroll. *Alice in Wonderland* caused quite a stir when it was first published in

1865, and Leopold, an avid reader, is likely to have known the book well, particularly as his sister Beatrice owned the second presentation copy (the first went to Alice Liddell), and he had 'the Duck' from the Pool of Tears, Robinson Duckworth, as his tutor. For Duckworth was there, rowing stroke, that July day in 1862 when Dodgson took the three Liddell sisters up the river from Folly Bridge to Godstow and a literary masterpiece was born. Duckworth was proud of his association with *Alice*, and could explain many of the book's mysteries and in-jokes to Leopold – and these stories would have pointed the boy once again towards Oxford.

Dodgson had an instinctive sympathy for the young, and was fascinated by royalty, and some time in 1867 Duckworth must have told him about his pupil's restricted life. The response was imaginative and generous. In November Dodgson sent Leopold a bundle of autograph letters for his collection, introducing him to some of the leading figures in contemporary art and literature – and Oxford. There were letters to Dodgson from the novelists George MacDonald and Charlotte M. Yonge, from the theologian H.P. Liddon, from Pre-Raphaelite painters Arthur Hughes and Holman Hunt; some discussed Dodgson's photographs, one his book, and there was even one from Sir John Tenniel about the original illustrations for *Alice in Wonderland* – 'Could you manage to let me have the text of "A Mad Tea-Party" for a day or two? There is much more in it than my copy contains. The subjects I have selected from it are – The Hatter asking the riddle . . . and – The March Hare and the Hatter, putting the Dormouse into the tea-pot.'[21] All these were added to Leopold's collection, and to his store of knowledge.

In July 1867 Dr Legg left the Household, and Duckworth was promoted to governor. Informing her eldest daughter of the change, the Queen described him as 'a really most talented and charming person . . . . The only objection I have to him is that he is a clergyman. However he is enlightened and so free from the usual prejudices of his profession that I feel I must get over my dislike to that. Mr. Duckworth is an excellent preacher and good-looking besides.'[22] A new tutor was appointed in August, on Duckworth's recommendation. So far Leopold's teachers had come and gone, but the new man, Robert Hawthorn Collins, would stay with him for the rest of his life.

For the moment, though, Leopold still missed Stirling. His life was much fuller, and his letters to his former governor described receptions and reviews, state visits, Japanese jugglers at St George's Hall, the birth of a new nephew and niece, and his concerns for his sister-in-law, the Princess of Wales, ill with rheumatic fever. He never mentioned the Browns once in 1867, or complained of his own unhappiness. But when 'the anniversary of our sad separation' came around, Leopold wrote to say how much he wished to see Stirling again, 'to speak of it; it is exactly the kind of day it was last year, very hot and very oppressive'.[23] The Lieutenant had returned to his regiment at Woolwich, and Arthur saw him often, but plans for meetings with Leopold had so far come to nothing.

Christmas at Osborne came and went, and it was fun: 'We are spending a very merry Christmas here', Leopold told Princess Alice, 'last night the tree was stripped & the Protheros were invited to come, and after the tree had been stripped we played at "Blind man's buff". We are going to act charades next week so we are very busy preparing for them.'[24] He told Stirling too: 'the words are "Homely" & "Final", we mean to act on Tuesday and Thursday.'[25] It sounded so innocent, but was almost the prelude to tragedy. These first charades went down so well that another performance was arranged: on 21 January the children acted 'Banditti', and the Queen was delighted. 'Leopold was inimitable as Dobbins', she wrote, '& again in the 2nd act as Mrs Anacrow Placid's wife. His acting and bye play in the last scene was excellent.'[26] But the fun was hardly over when he began bleeding from the bowel, lightly at first, but without relief. Dr Hoffmeister said he must be kept quiet in his room, and decided to stay in the house.

The crisis came a week later, when the haemorrhage increased and with it came pain and sickness. Through the night of 28/9 January the Queen sat by the bed waiting for the end, but when morning came, Leopold was still alive. Dr Paget, 'the only person in England who understood this peculiar complaint', was sent for from London, but before he arrived his patient appeared to be slipping away, and injections of ice and iron were tried as a last resort.[27] 'Dear Car we all but lost him last night & he is still in a very critical state', Louise told Lady Caroline. 'Jenner is most kind

& so is Paget, but they are very anxious. . . . I am fearfully anxious so is Mr Duckworth. Every thing is being done that can be thought of, but our darling is in the Almightys hands.'[28] For the next few days Leopold would be on the edge, with further bleeding and delirium, but somehow, painfully slowly, he found the strength to fight his way back.

As the news broke, anxious letters and telegrams poured in to Osborne. 'How very ill he must have been', Princess Feodora wrote from Milan to the Queen, 'and <u>what</u> anxiety you must have gone through on that dreadful night! I shudder to think of it . . . . It will take some time, I suppose, to get strong after so much loss of blood as he has had. Was he himself aware of his danger? And is he at all nervous about himself now?'[29] Lady Augusta Bruce, married to Dean Stanley now, but still one of Leopold's dearest friends, told her sister, 'I can not but hope, having seen him rally so often and from such severe attacks when all hope seemed gone. Darling Boy – God's will be done.'[30]

The Queen stayed with Leopold, postponing her return to Windsor until he could be moved. At the beginning of February, as she sat reading to him, she was moved by the near-miracle of his survival. 'I felt that henceforth this dear child, who as it were, has been given back to me from the brink of the grave, must be my chief object in life.'[31] Spring came round, and with it the sense that the unhappy aftermath of Stirling's dismissal had been put behind them. Not only was Leopold 'very clever, taking interest in and understanding everything', as she told the Crown Princess: 'He learns, besides French and German, Latin, Greek and Italian; is very fond of music and drawing, takes much interest in politics – in short in everything. His mind and head are far the most like of any of the boys to his dear Father.' But, more significantly, she added, 'I think he is happier now because he sees where his course lies, and does not think of what he cannot have.'[32] Her sister reinforced her hopes for Leopold's future: 'having him a good deal near you, must do him good, please him and bring more confidence between him and you, when you are together, his society will grow more and more agreeable . . . he must be a comfort and a pleasure to you as he will not have to leave you soon, nor ever for long, poor dear boy!'[33]

The Queen was certain that Leopold could never leave home, never ride, never act, never be involved in society's pleasures, certainly never marry, or lead an independent life, but these things mattered so little to her, in her widowed state, that she knew he would not miss them either. Watching his mind develop, she believed that he could grow into the role his father played by her side, sharing her work and eventually gaining the experience to advise her. He would be her assistant, Beatrice her companion, and the two young people, brother and sister, would be company enough for each other. She was sure, quite sure, that the three of them would be perfectly happy if other people did not interfere, and the prospect was a comfort and a delight. But in truth, the change she observed in Leopold was only depressed resignation, and his real mood emerges in a mournful little poem he wrote for Louise in March:

> I think of thee, my sister,
> In my sad and lonely hours;
> And the thought of thee comes o'er me
> Like the breath of morning flow'rs. . . .[34]

Illness had set him back again and tightened the circle of home life around him, and his spirits did not rally until a few weeks after his birthday in April, when he bumped into Stirling in London. 'It was really an unlooked for chance to meet you so wonderfully as we did', he wrote, 'it was the first time since two years that I had spoken to you, had there not been so many people there we might have talked for a little longer. I went to Aldershot for the first time the other day with Mamma, it was very nice. What are your own plans?'[35]

Leopold's plans, or rather his mother's, were for a summer holiday in Switzerland which had been under discussion for three years. This was supposed to be a closely guarded secret: the Queen's reluctance to perform official duties in person was causing so much resentment that she feared aggravating the public mood by announcing the idea too soon, and she insisted that the trip was being undertaken only on Dr Jenner's orders. She would travel incognito, taking a very small suite, and what she called her 'inseparables', Louise, Beatrice and Leopold (how he would have hated the word).[36] He gave the details to Stirling 'on the sly', finding great amusement in the incognito and all the fuss that surrounded it. First he was to be 'Count Leopold Kent', then 'the Hon. Leopold Kent'; there were squabbles at home about the names and he decided that if Stirling were to write to him, it would be safer to address all letters to Duckworth, who was to be one of the party.[37]

The tone and style of Leopold's letters were changing, and he sounded more like a young man, and a friend, and less like a little boy writing to a favourite teacher. He teased Stirling for taking holidays in 'that detestable Scotland', and for the extraordinary number of holidays he took, and soon after arriving at Lucerne, he ended one letter: 'P.S. "Somebody" says I ought to call you by some other name than cold "Mr Stirling", tell me what name I may call you!'[38] 'Somebody' must have been Louise or Duckworth, the only other holidaymakers who were in on the secret, and from this time onwards, Leopold's letters would go to 'My dear George Stirling'.

The party reached Switzerland on 7 August, and they stayed for a month. In many ways, it was a good time. Leopold was entranced by the view of the mountains from his window in their hotel, the Pension Wallis, which stood on a hillside overlooking Lucerne and the lake. It was very hot at first, which suited him, but even after the weather broke he enjoyed exploring. He shared his mother's admiration of the monument to Arnold von Winkelried, a local hero, at Stans, and visited Altorf with Duckworth to see the old clock tower and the statue of William Tell. On 22 August, the Queen took Louise, Lady Ely and Dr Jenner into the mountains for three days, and the rest of the party were left to their own devices. Colonel Ponsonby told his wife: 'Upon the "Cats away Mice will play" principle, we are going at it. . . . Today we went to Alpnacht & then drove to Lungern, had luncheon in a field & rambled in woods. Leopold and Beatrice quite delighted.'[39]

But there were shadows. Both John and Archie Brown had been chosen to go, and a remark in one of Leopold's letters suggests why he hated them so much, and at times feared them. 'I am rather in the grumps just now about everything', he commented on 3 September, 'the way in which I am treated is sometimes too bad (not Mr Duckworth, of course not, he is only too kind to me) but other people. Besides that "J.B." is fearfully insolent to me, so is his brother; hitting me on the face with spoons for fun, etc – you may laugh at me for all this; but you know I am so sensitive, I know you will feel for me – their impudence increases daily towards everybody.'[40] The Browns were loyal to the Queen, but the feeling did not extend to a resentful fifteen-year-old who could not hide the fact that he hated them, and was helpless to fight back. If the Queen had understood, she would certainly have put an end to it, but her trust in the Browns was so fixed that no-one could make her understand. They do not even seem to have tried.

After two years the Stirling affair was still an open wound. The Count of Flanders, King Leopold's younger son, visited Windsor in 1867, and when someone told him the story he deliberately asked the Queen about Stirling across the dinner table: 'She blushed & grew very confused', Leopold wrote, '& then said that "you had not been long with me", he burst at once into one of his usual fits of laughter.' Robert Collins, Leopold's new tutor, met Stirling and liked him, and according to Leopold, he expected to share the same fate, 'for his free & easy way of talking'.[41] Once the holiday in Switzerland was over, the Prince began to prepare for his confirmation, and hearing that people who had been with him in the past would be invited, he took his courage in both hands and asked his mother if he could invite Stirling. In 1866 she had said that the Lieutenant might be invited back to Court occasionally, but her reply this time was sadly predictable. 'I knew what the answer would be', Leopold told Stirling, 'but I considered it to be my duty to you to ask, I am very sorry about it.'[42]

SIX

SHADES OF THE PRISON HOUSE

Leopold was confirmed at Whippingham Church on the Isle of Wight on 30 January 1869, wearing Prince Arthur's black tailcoat. The Wales family stayed at Osborne afterwards, and he had fun playing with their children; the Queen was impressed by his skilful management of the mischievous little Wales Princes, Albert Victor and George. But the games ended before February was over. 'He was looking far too full and heated for several weeks past', she told her eldest daughter, 'and I lived in dread of something. Medicine was constantly given and he seemed well, but was very foolish in running and jumping about and in over-exciting himself with the children. On Thursday evening after dinner, when everything almost was packed, I was told that bleeding had again shown itself . . . and that on no account must he move.'[1]

The year 1869 was to be a bad one. This attack was not so serious as the previous one, but it was severe enough to reach the newspapers. In April Leopold was unable to walk, with swelling and pain in his thigh: 'he is growing so fast that we must expect things of this sort', the Queen told a friend.[2] He injured his thumb too: in May he remarked to Sir James Paget that it was 'almost quite well – but not very beautiful to look at yet'.[3] The Queen did her best to cheer him up, awarding him the Order of the Garter in May: 'He will be a year younger than his brothers were', she told the Prime Minister, 'but far older than the Queen's Uncles and Cousins were, when they got it; and the Queen thinks, as the poor Child is so often suffering – debarred from every profession and from almost every amusement of his age, and is the <u>cleverest</u> and most studious of Our

4 sons, that this would be a <u>great</u> gratification to him, and give him much pleasure, which he <u>fully deserves</u>.'[4] In the autumn she abandoned her self-imposed silence and began to play the piano again with Leopold and Beatrice, 'to please them as they read so well at sight and are very fond of it'.[5] But Leopold fretted against the unfairness of his lot. He was still tied to Archie Brown, whose position was unassailable; in May, the Queen raised Archie's status to 'upper servant', while Leopold felt completely hemmed in, believing that the Browns were watching him, and reporting him to his mother: he was convinced that anything he enjoyed, and anybody he cared for, would be taken away.

Comparisons between his life and his brothers' depressed him even more. In the autumn of 1868, Alfred sailed from Plymouth on a world voyage on HMS *Galatea*, which would last until 1870. In August 1869, Arthur left for Canada with the Rifle Brigade, while Leopold set off once again with his mother and sisters for Balmoral – 'we shall spend – <u>eleven</u> – weeks in horrid Scotland, till we are quite congealed'.[6] The Queen may have dedicated him to Scotland at birth, but he hated the country determinedly now, as determinedly as she loved it – though once he could escape from home, it was as interesting as anywhere else. Duckworth and Jenner took him on a tour of Perthshire in September, which he enjoyed, and he anticipated better things when he returned to England. He would be unlucky. There was one visit to the opera with Collins, then a pencilled note written from Leopold's sofa one grey morning in November broke bad news to Princess Louise: 'Dearest Loo . . . . I have got another internal bleeding, the same as I had in February at Osborne. I hope it may pass away soon. At present I am utterly wretched. You had perhaps better not come down.'[7]

Leopold was bedridden through Christmas, and into the New Year. In January 1870 his knee began to swell, and gave him a lot of pain, and splints were used to keep his leg straight and prevent the swelling from distorting the joint. 'I am altogether very low about myself', he told Stirling from Osborne, 'as no sooner had I recovered from my last tedious illness, & no sooner was I able to get about again, than here I am laid up again. I had so much hoped when we left this place to have been able to enjoy myself at Windsor & in town; but now no doubt I will be completely debarred from every amusement. This life here is becoming daily more odious & intolerable. Every inch of liberty is taken away from one, & one is watched, & every thing one says or does is reported. Of course Mr Duckworth and Mr Collins are kindness itself, but then I am sure that they are both very much disliked at headquarters. Oh! how I do wish I could escape from this detestable house!'[8]

His only distractions were music, letters and books, and the games of bezique he played with Duckworth, but in March he confided a new anxiety to Stirling: 'I greatly fear that Mr Duckworth is going to be treated in the same way as you were; but pray don't mention this to <u>anyone</u>, neither if you write to Mr Duckworth or Mr Collins, as it would bring me into great trouble, besides it is only a <u>suspicion</u>.'[9]

He was right, though. Soon Duckworth sensed it too, telling Leopold, 'The time will soon come when it will be seen what you are made of.'[10] He was probably thinking of the upsets surrounding Stirling's dismissal: at seventeen, Leopold could be expected to show more control. Duckworth may also have worried that without his support the Prince would lapse into self-pity, abandoning the fight to overcome his problems; they may have discussed the idea of university, which the Queen would never agree to without a struggle. If Leopold were to achieve that, or any other form of independence, he would have to be very cool and determined, and think how to argue his case: emotional outbursts would do no good at all.

But while they waited and worried, the Queen's decision was made, and a new man chosen. Dr George Vivian Poore was in his early twenties, and had served as surgeon on board the *Great Eastern*. Unlike Legg, he had no particular interest in bleeding disorders; his real concern was typhoid, and other diseases caused by poor drainage. The Queen accepted him on Dr Jenner's recommendation, and on 7 April 1870 Poore wrote to his mother and told her that he was to be sent to Paris and Berlin before he took up his appointment.[11]

Leopold tried appealing to the Queen, but it made no difference, and in misery he turned to Stirling, confiding his suspicion that the Browns were behind Duckworth's dismissal: 'you can't imagine how

L. [Louise] & I are tyrannised over by headquarters, it is quite unbearable.'[12] On 21 April, he explained his situation to Princess Alice: 'Mamma thinks that, on account of the bad state of my health, I require to have a doctor constantly about me & therefore Mr Duckworth, who has been with me for the last four years, will have to leave. He has ever been more like a brother to me than anything else, & I am, as you know, very fond, indeed, of him, so the separation will be very painful to both of us. The doctors themselves say that there is no real necessity for it, but Mamma wishes it, so it must be done, I have done everything I could to prevent it.'[13]

Louise complained angrily to Elphinstone that Poore would be nothing more than Leopold's keeper; she was upset on her brother's behalf, but also on her own. In sharing her anxiety for Leopold, the Princess had become very attached to Duckworth, who is said to have been her first love; he was an attractive man, and her life was as restricted as her brother's. She designed a gold ring as a leaving present from them both, commemorating the year Duckworth became Leopold's governor with the inscription: 'Forget us not. Le. Lo, '67'.[14]

That spring it felt as if the whole world was against them. General Grey, Prince Albert's private secretary, who had been a father figure to Louise and Leopold ever since the Prince's death, suffered a stroke on 26 March, and died within the week. Leopold grieved for him, and believed that a dangerous gap had opened in the Household. 'He was the <u>only</u> person who dared to say to H.M. what he thought was right & what she ought to do. . . . It is practically the end of the Queen's reign, as she will now retire always more from public life.'[15] He was becoming acutely aware of the mood in the country, where the Queen's reluctance to be seen in public was making her very unpopular. There was nothing he could do about this, but it added to his frustration. He was touched to receive some Japanese ornaments from Lady Caroline, the General's sister, for his birthday: 'I can't tell you how I value your kindness in writing to me & sending me such a nice present, when you have got so much else to engross your thoughts', he told her.[16]

April dragged into May and Leopold's health refused to improve. Louise sent him board games, he had several visitors, and the Queen allowed him to have Waldi brought indoors again. He took a lively interest in the news; there was a particularly gruesome series of murders that spring, and Irish terrorists were active. 'If the Fenian raid into Canada continues', he told his sister, 'Arthur will have an opportunity of sniffing powder, happy boy!'[17] Louise sent him copies of the *Graphic*, and he devoured the pages of *Punch* and *The Saturday Review*, but two shadows undermined every attempt to take his mind off his illness: the impending loss of Duckworth, and the fear that the Queen would insist on taking him to Balmoral, where he might become too ill to be moved. He wrote to her, begging for permission to stay at Windsor, and she agreed, leaving for her May visit without him.

By the end of the month, the internal bleeding had stopped, but the swelling returned to Leopold's knee, bringing intense pain. Collins developed a bad headache and Jenner, suspecting the onset of typhoid, sent him away to his lodgings and forbade all contact with Leopold for fear of infection. The Prince had become very fond of Collins, and knew how much he would rely on him once Duckworth had gone, so this new separation was more than he could bear. 'Mr Duckworth & I are left quite <u>alone</u> in this enormous house', he told his sister. 'We have just telegraphed to Dr Legg to ask him to come if he can, because it would be too much for D to be quite alone with me.'[18] His own head was aching, and his leg in agony. Morphine was used to give temporary relief, and when he was able to produce a letter, in pencil, lying on his back, it was Collins he wanted to write to. Duckworth carried the letters in defiance of the doctor's order, because he knew how much it mattered.

Through June and July Leopold's messages went out to 'My dearest Bob', and they must have made painful reading. 'I am so wretched, I lose all faith in God & man, why am I to be thus tortured?' 'I suffered on Tuesday more than I have ever suffered . . . I thought I would really go out of my mind. . . . I feel inclined to cry all day long, I am <u>so</u> wretched. All I can see out of my window is the dim grey castle wall, & the window of your dear old empty room.' 'I feel that my life is so empty and idiotic; I find no pleasure in living, but only pain.'[19] To his sister and to Collins, Leopold wrote of his longing for death, even at his own hands, to end the agony.[20] But he never forgot to ask about Collins' health, and he arranged for gifts of books and fruit to be sent.

It is hard now to imagine the pain of a haemophilia attack, at a time when no treatment was available but morphine, which could be used only sparingly and as a last resort. Leopold was just seventeen, and was describing an experience beyond most people's comprehension: incapacity and pain, stretching into weeks, then months – and he knew that there would be no cure. If the pain went away, it would return. Alick Yorke, Leopold's equerry and friend for the last ten years of his life, said that above all things the Prince dreaded a long and painful death.[21] The wonder is not that he sometimes suffered the bleakest depression, as these letters show, but that he ever managed to rise above it at all – yet his delight in life and in people never left him, and he could laugh even at the darkest times, mocking his own suffering and the physical indignities involved with grim black humour. On 20 June his first godchild, Prince Francis of Teck, was christened. Leopold was delighted to be a godparent, and he wanted to attend the service, but when the time came and he was still bedridden, he joked to Collins: '(bless its little bum! <u>heart</u> I mean) I am of course not present; I am so pleased, because I always laugh on such occasions.'[22] This combination of mischief and irreverence was becoming typical of him.

In mid-June the Queen returned, and spent as much time as she could by her son's bed. She must have been horrified by the state of him. Some days he lay screaming with pain; once chloroform was tried with the morphine, but it made him violently sick. 'I have now always to lie on an air cushion as my bones are coming through, on account of the thinness of my body', he wrote, and his mother longed to help him, but Leopold had not forgiven her for Duckworth and was in no mood to be friends.[23] He destroyed Collins' letters, fearing that he too might be dismissed, and muttered darkly about the Browns: for this, at least, he had good reason. On 3 July he complained to Collins of 'that <u>devil</u> Archie, he does nothing, but jeer at, & be impertinent to me every day, & in the night he won't do anything for me though I order it, not even give me my chamberpot, & he is so insolent before the other servants, the <u>infernal blackguard</u>. I could tear him limb from limb I loathe him so.'[24] He was completely at the valet's mercy.

In the tense weeks leading up to Duckworth's departure,

Leopold's anger deepened, and old resentments came to the surface. Ever since birth, he had been overshadowed by Arthur, the Queen's acknowledged favourite. Between themselves the brothers were good friends, but Leopold could not help feeling jealous, and from 1870 this became an issue between him and the Queen. Preparations were being made at the start of July for Arthur's return from Canada, and the difference between his life and Leopold's could not have been greater. 'Arthur the Happy & the Magnificent is on his way home;' Leopold remarked to Collins. 'I wonder if triumphal arches will be erected across the Atlantic, to celebrate the arrival of this great hero.'[25]

Duckworth finally left on 13 August, though unlike Stirling he would still be attached to the Household as a chaplain, and occasional tutor to Princess Beatrice. But this did not comfort Leopold, and even though his leg was slowly improving, he saw little to be cheerful about. He had been prepared to like Dr Poore, who arrived in June, until an incident took place which shook his confidence. Poore took exception to the local doctor who came in twice a day to see Leopold: as 'medical attendant' he expected sole responsibility, and his temper snapped. 'They say I must stand it. I say I won't. It remains to be seen who gives in', he fumed, in a letter to his mother, '– if they do not I leave – my mind is made up. The difficulty arises I think from a reluctance on Jenner's part (from feelings of jealousy) to give me any medical standing here.'[26]

Poore's ruffled feathers were quickly smoothed, but he had not made a good impression. Leopold was wary of him for months, and even the Queen had second thoughts about confirming him as Duckworth's replacement. Instead, she placed the doctor and Collins on an equal footing, with all decisions affecting Leopold to be referred directly to her; her intermediary and messenger was to be Archie Brown, 'on whose great discretion the Queen can implicitly rely'.[27]

By July Leopold was well enough to go to Osborne with his mother, though he still could not walk. In August they made the journey to Balmoral, covering seven hundred miles in twenty-three hours, as Dr Poore remarked in surprise. 'The luxury of it was something considerable – an enormous carriage provided for 3 people and good sofas to sleep upon.'[28] Throughout the autumn of

1870, Poore's letters home would provide a fascinating outsider's view of the Household; behind his temper lay a kind heart and a keen sense of humour. He was much more impressed with Balmoral than Leopold had ever been. 'This is apparently a very enjoyable place', he wrote, 'and much of the restriction and formality of Windsor & Osborne is dispensed with – the less clothes you wear the more OK you are considered. My colleague Collins is attired like a noble satyr but I intend to keep my knees and shin-bones to myself.'²⁹ He did, however, allow himself to be photographed in Highland dress to please Leopold, borrowing from various people to complete the outfit.

In the warm days of August and September they enjoyed outings and picnics, and Poore was amazed by the beauty of the scenery, especially the sky: 'Last night the whole vault of the sky seemed covered with lambent rose-coloured flames all converging to the zenith . . . . The colour was very brilliant but so thin and peculiar that all the stars shone through it. It was wonderfully beautiful.'³⁰ He was very taken with Louise – 'she is lively, clever and exceedingly good looking' – and impressed by the depth of the Queen's knowledge on a range of subjects. Early in September they discussed the care of the wounded in the war that had raged for some weeks between Germany and France: the Franco-Prussian war was on everyone's mind that autumn. The entire Household was fiercely pro-German, and Beatrice's French governess clung nervously to her room.³¹

At first Leopold shared the general feeling, and told Stirling off for taking the French side: 'Can you sympathise with the Emperor who made war for no reason but for his own aggrandizement', he asked.³² His thoughts were with Alice, whose husband had gone away to fight on the German side. Left alone in Darmstadt, the Princess was in the late stages of her fifth pregnancy, and it was not in her nature to be idle. 'I hear that you are exerting yourself very much in making bandages & shirts etc', Leopold wrote, '& I hope we may be able to help you, by sending linen and lint to you.'³³ But within months his wider sympathies were changing, in line with the general feeling in the country: 'It seems as if the war would never end;' he commented in December. 'I think Bismarck is a clever but wicked scoundrel . . . . I have been slowly veering round to the French side out of pity for them, & out of dislike to Prussia's behaviour towards England.'[34]

At last there was a real improvement in his health. 'I am glad to say that my charge has begun to walk about again with the aid of crutchy sort of walking sticks', Poore wrote to his mother, at the end of September, '– this is the first time for more than 5 months.'[35] Leopold was feeling a lot more hopeful too, though it was infuriating for him to learn that Stirling was in Scotland, but still out of reach: 'the rage against you has never cooled down, nor ever will, I think', he told him. 'I have not made my mind up yet whether I like the newcomer (Dr Poore) or not; but he does pretty well [Poore had actually been with him for four months: as long as Stirling's entire appointment]; I like Collins every day better; so you can still consider <u>him</u> as a link between us.'[36]

That autumn saw Louise's engagement, which Leopold was bound to receive with mixed feelings. He was delighted for her and liked Lord Lorne, her fiancé, but he knew that the marriage would take away one of his closest allies. The Queen's attempt to restrict contacts between him and Louise had only made them closer, and their parting would be hard. But at least the engagement brought a new liveliness to Balmoral at the close of the season. On 9 November Poore wrote to a friend describing the festivities, from a castle already veiled in seven inches of snow. A few days earlier a beacon had been lit on the summit of Craig Gowan, and 'Collins & I with the help of 2 servants managed to get our Royal Youth to the top of the hill (in a wheelbarrow) to see the fire lighted. It was an enormous bonfire and there was much piping and dancing and cheering and drinking of whiskey beside it till we all felt ready to burst with loyalty.'[37]

Since Princess Helena's marriage in 1866, Louise had acted as her mother's informal secretary, writing many of her personal letters. Now the Queen began to prepare Leopold to take over, entrusting him with a few letters and simple arrangements. This was a first step on the career she planned for him, and with the end of the holidays she began to assert her interest in his education, asking Collins to draw up a detailed timetable. Leopold seemed not to mind. He was ready to put the last, terrible year behind him and make up for lost time, and his only worry was the loss of Louise. He wrote to Stirling from Osborne, wishing him 'a merry Christmas and a 'appy New Year . . . . I suspect this year <u>we</u> are going to spend an uncommonly dull Christmas, however I shall try to be as happy as I can, as it is the last time dear Louise will spend Christmas with us, at least in her unmarried state.' But another separation had turned out to be less final than he expected: after a few months' absence Duckworth was back. 'I saw the Reverend Duck about four times whilst we were at Windsor', he told Stirling.[38]

Leopold had an unfailing ability to bounce back from depression and illness. When he was well, even home did not seem so bad, and he seized every chance to play host. Towards the end of 1870 the Empress Eugénie and her son arrived at Windsor, and he had 'great fun' acting as guide to the young Prince Imperial ('& some lovely Spanish ladies').[39] An old friend visited Osborne at the start of 1871: Louisa Bowater had recently married, and Leopold was pleased to see her, and to meet her husband, Sir Rainald Knightley. Together they went out after breakfast one morning and spent two hours exploring the grounds and examining the curiosities in the Swiss Cottage museum, collected by Leopold and his brothers and sisters in the distant summers of childhood. In the evening they played the Christmas game, 'Snapdragon', which involved plucking raisins from a dish of burning brandy. 'It was an immense treat to see my own dear little Prince so comfortable', Louisa wrote in her diary, 'more comfortable than I have ever seen him since we left Cannes. He has come out wonderfully, grown quite into a man. . . . Certainly he is a singularly pleasant companion.'[40]

With this new maturity, Leopold was finding new interests. He still collected autographs, but by the start of 1871 had discovered something more exciting. For about ten years it had been possible to buy card-mounted photographs of celebrities, and collecting them was all the rage. Stirling responded willingly to his requests for photos of society figures, particularly ladies; in January 1871 Leopold wrote to thank him 'for the photo of Lady Clifden; though that was not the one I wanted, as I have already got it . . . the one I was anxious to possess, was one of Ly Clifden dressed for a "tableau vivant", with a pendant of Lady Spencer.'[41] Poore joined in, finding several photographs of the singer Adelina Patti, whom Leopold heard for the first time in May. He was thrilled with them, and asked, 'there is a very charming <u>cabinet</u> likeness of her as "Marguerite" in "Faust", kneeling with her hair falling down her shoulders, which I should immensely like to possess, do you think you could get it? You must send me the bill for them or I will ruin myself in photos.'[42]

This collection signalled a growing interest in the opposite sex, and Leopold's letters began to include comments on the ladies he saw at Court, made with great charm and obvious innocence. Lady Clifden was one of his favourites – 'how charming and lovely she is!' – and he was troubled by the illness of Lady Caroline Cavendish, one of the maids-of-honour: 'she is a great friend of mine, & if anything happens to her it will be a <u>great</u> loss to the Household.'[43] Louise's wedding in March 1871 nearly broke his heart, but he still kept his eyes open at the wedding supper, and sent her a spirited critique of the female guests: 'Your sister-in-law, Lady Percy, looked remarkably handsome, I think, & very well dressed, I can't say the same as to Lady A. Campbell, who was rather oddly dressed, but looked very pretty all the same. Arthur flirted the whole evening with one of your bridesmaids, Florence Montagu, (who in my opinion is as ugly as her brothers are handsome), whilst I devoted myself to Mrs Earle who looked <u>lovely</u> last night.'[44] At a dance held for Arthur's birthday in May, he felt a first, fleeting passion of his own: 'I danced six dances & had a most charming partner for 3 of them, namely Miss Fitzroy (Lord Charles's only daughter), who is as pretty as she is simple & unaffected, she is a sweet girl, strikingly like her brother who was at Balmoral last year, & I can't help telling you though this is strictly between ourselves that I have fallen over my ears in l*** with her.'[45]

The Household took note. Colonel Ponsonby was amused, and remarked to his wife, 'We have sayings of Leopolds now cropping up. He is beginning to have an eye for beauty, & his remarks on the coffee room girl are repeated and how he persisted in dancing opposite to her as often as he could.' He went on to say how frustrated Leopold was because his mother still invited boys for him to play with.[46] Parents are often the last to notice how grown-up their children have become, and this was one development the Queen did not want to see; Leopold started to smoke at Balmoral in the spring, but was banned from the smoking room, and his mother gave orders that he was not to go fishing with Alfred, home from HMS *Galatea* and sporting his first beard; at all costs, Leopold must be protected from the corrupting conversations of men, even his own brothers.[47]

From the spring of 1871, Leopold faced a number of extra restrictions like these, which had nothing to do with his health, and everything to do with his mother's wish to keep him at home. She would justify them on health grounds, believing that his only possible future lay with her, but it would have been hard to make him see this. At heart the Queen must have known that he had to grow up, but she tried to cling to him, dismissing his every independent idea as the result of someone else's bad influence. Ironically, she was trying to cling to the most independent of her sons. She had never found it easy to relate to Leopold, and he, from infancy, had turned to others for affection and understanding. As an eight-year-old at Cannes he had learned to live apart from the family: it was too late to pull him back, and attempts to manipulate his feelings could only lead to resentment.

So, through 1871 and onwards, predictable clashes occurred. Leopold hated Balmoral, 'that <u>most vile</u> & <u>most abominable</u> of Places', but he was well, and so had to go twice, in the spring and the autumn.[48] His awareness that the government, the Household, and his brothers and sisters, would all have liked to curtail these visits made the imposition harder to bear; he seethed, and longed for Windsor and London, where it was possible to enjoy some freedom. Early in May he went to hear Patti in *Don Juan*, and managed, with Arthur's help, to arrange a meeting with Stirling, whom he had not seen for several years. He spent two hours at the Academy, attended a reception at the Palace, and visited Duckworth in his new parish. On a few occasions Poore took him out in the city, and they explored the Embankment and the new fruit market.

Leopold was warming to Poore. When Stirling worried that his letters were being intercepted, early in 1871, the Prince was quick to say that 'Dr Poore, whatever his faults may be, would sooner leave at once than do anything of that kind.'[49] But in May, the Queen decided that the doctor was no longer needed. He would be replaced by a Scotsman, Dr Marshall, who was not to be attached specifically to Leopold. 'Put not your trust in Princes', Poore raged dramatically to his mother, seeing dismissal as a very poor reward for his patient's recovery.[50] It was Leopold who tried to pacify him, in his own way, by reminding him of the awkward start to his appointment: 'I think we both of us thought it possible if not probable, after the explosion which took place last July, that there would be a change sooner or later . . . . I shall always remember with gratitude your kindness & attention to me during my illness last summer. However I can't understand your being sorry to leave such a place as this, as I have always envied those who have done so.'[51]

He found it much harder to be reconciled to the loss of his sister. Their parting revived memories of their father, and for the first few weeks Leopold was thoroughly miserable, caring for Louise's canary with bemused loyalty, and counting the days until her return. But the separation did bring about a gradual change in him, and, from being emotionally dependent on one elder sister, he began to draw closer to the others. The Crown Princess visited Osborne in the summer with her children, and Leopold took her sons on long expeditions around the island. But he was not only occupied with the children. Republican feeling was growing throughout the country, and in August immense pressure was brought on the Queen to postpone her departure to Balmoral. The Crown Princess had come home worried by the way her mother's seclusion was interpreted in Germany, and determined to mobilise her brothers and sisters into action; at eighteen, Leopold was old enough to be included.

There must have been many excited discussions in the summer of 1871, before the Crown Princess drafted a long and carefully worded appeal to the Queen, which all the children and children-in-law except Beatrice signed. '<u>No-one</u> has prompted us to write,' it ran, 'no-one knows that we are doing so – except we ourselves. . . . It is we your children, whose position in the world had been made so good by the wisdom and forethought, and the untiring care of yourself and dear Papa, who now feel how utterly changed things are, and who would humbly entreat you to enquire into the state of public feeling, which appears to us so very alarming.'[52] But the letter would never be handed over. The Queen, sensing herself to be under siege, lashed out in anger at her ministers and insisted on

Balmoral. She claimed to be ill, though many doubted her word, and on 15 August she waved goodbye to her eldest daughter with less regret than usual, before her own departure for the north.

The emotional repercussions of the affair rebounded particularly harshly on Leopold. Any change to the Queen's routine would have been good news for him, and he must have hoped that with the others behind him, a breakthrough might have been achieved. But all the plotting and planning had given way to complete anti-climax. Ponsonby noticed how Leopold cried on parting with his sister and her sons. They could go away, but he had to stay with the Queen whatever mood she was in, and she was well aware that her family was critical of her. She was genuinely ill too, with a throat infection, an abscess on her arm, and worsening rheumatism. The autumn would be difficult for them all, but it brought Leopold one real consolation: Princess Alice and her family arrived at Balmoral. Temperamentally, as he was beginning to discover, he and Alice were very much alike, and no-one in the family understood him quite so well as she did.

They were almost ten years apart in age, so there was no chance for them to know one another well in the early days; Leopold was only nine when Alice left England as a bride. She helped to teach him; his earliest letter to her future husband was written in March 1861, during one of her lessons: 'today I have read about Darius III or Cordoman, and about Alexander, and about the Colossus of Rhodes', Leopold wrote. 'I like my lesson with Alice so much, because she is always so good to me.' He added a shy little message, which surely came from the Princess herself: 'I hope you will come back soon because I love you very much.'[53] It was a sign of the understanding that would grow between the three of them.

Like Leopold, Alice inherited her father's questioning mind and intense seriousness of purpose. They shared a love of music too, and art, and as Alice did not always get on well with her mother, she could understand the difficulties Leopold had. Their friendship grew slowly, on the Hesse family's visits to England and Leopold's travels with the Queen, and Leopold was just as comfortable with Louis, who was kind, straightforward and sociable. In November 1870 the Hesses tried to draw Leopold closer to their family by inviting him to be godfather to their baby son, the child Alice was expecting when the Franco-Prussian war was at its height. 'We have added dear Leopold's name to the others', Alice told the Queen when the baby was christened, 'as his sad life, and the anxiety his health has so often caused us all, endear him particularly.'[54] No novelist could have devised so sharp an irony as this, for, unknown to them all, little Friedrich Wilhelm of Hesse was the second member of the family to have haemophilia. This, too, would deepen the bonds between Leopold and his sister.

When Alice arrived at Balmoral in the autumn of 1871 to find her mother ill and emotionally overwrought, she took charge, easing the situation with the quiet efficiency of a born nurse. Every evening she played the piano to the Queen, sometimes alone, and sometimes with Leopold, though he was just getting over an injury to one of his fingers. He wrote letters for his sister during the day, and played with her children, becoming particularly attached to his little godson; at a year old, 'Fritzie' was round, pretty and very bright, showing no more sign of bleeding than his uncle had done at a similar age, and Leopold delighted in making a pet of him.

By November the Queen was much better, but Leopold had fallen on the stairs and hurt his knee, and was walking with two sticks. At first he was terrified that the accident would lead to another year of immobility, but the swelling soon went down; even so, neither he nor his mother was in a particularly good mood. Alice, sensing that the Queen was tiring of her presence, had taken her children to stay with the Prince of Wales, and this did not help Leopold. 'H.M. has grown more tyrannical over me & indeed over everybody than ever, since her illness, so that one feels more savage & morose than ever;' he told Stirling. 'I must say that I am getting heartily tired of my bondage & am looking forward to the day when I shall be able to burst the bars of my iron cage & fly away for ever' – but disenchantment had not made a republican of him. In response to the MP Sir Charles Dilke's public demand that the Queen should be deposed and a republic established, he remarked, 'I wish somebody would horsewhip him.'[55]

This was the tragedy of Leopold's situation: under the skin, he and the Queen were very much mother and son. She longed for a loving, confiding relationship with him, he longed to get on well with her, but he realised that this would never happen while they lived together. The Queen demanded too exclusive a devotion. By the year's end she had tried to build fresh barriers between Leopold and her elder children, ordering Collins to put him in his place where family matters were concerned; he was to stand up for her point of view, she said, 'in the presence of his sisters and brothers sh^d they at any time try to lead him astray', and he was 'never to tolerate any grumbling or finding fault with his mother'.[56] Clearly she guessed something about the summer's letter, and the thought rankled.

But events were about to draw everyone together. On 21 November telegrams went out from Sandringham to say that the Prince of Wales was ill, and as the news became more alarming, family and Household converged on the house. Leopold lived through a nightmare in the days that followed, terrified for his brother, and lost in admiration of his sister-in-law Alexandra, who 'looked like an angel from Heaven'. On 14 December, the tenth anniversary of the Prince Consort's death, the crisis passed, but writing to Stirling some weeks later, Leopold captured the atmosphere at the darkest time. Early on the morning of 11 December, the entire house was roused. Clutching a lit candle, Leopold made his way to his brother's dressing-room, passing crowds of servants, ladies and gentlemen, all in their night-clothes, who thronged the passages and staircases waiting for the end. 'It was too dreadful to see the poor Queen sitting in the bedroom behind a screen listening to his ravings', he wrote. 'I can't tell you what a deep impression the scene made on me.'[57] It was his most unguardedly tender comment about his mother since his return from Cannes.

SEVEN

OXFORD

At eighteen, Leopold was tall and slim, with wavy brown hair and the large, pale eyes of his mother's family. Called ugly as a child, he showed every sign of becoming an attractive man, perhaps the most attractive of the Queen's sons. He liked people, and approached them with the openness and vulnerability of those who are unsure of their reception, but want desperately to be liked; years of seclusion and frequent criticism had undermined any social confidence he might have had. This would always be true of Leopold: 'At the height of his popularity', his friend Frederic Myers remembered, 'his manner kept a certain wistfulness, as if he were asking for an affection on which he had no right to rely.'1 At times he was far too emotional, sharing his mother's tendency to the dramatic. He over-reacted: the least setback could throw him into a panic or make him say things he would later regret, but he was young, and very inexperienced. 'Wilful' is the word most often applied to him, but that was the Queen's word, and means no more than that Leopold, on the verge of adulthood, had a mind and will of his own.

His most striking quality was intelligence. With few outside distractions, he had reached a standard in many subjects that was way beyond his years. He spoke English, German and French from the nursery, and studied Italian with Professor Volpe, a master from Eton. He learnt Latin and Greek, reading and enjoying poetry in all these languages, and developing an early attachment to Shakespeare: in 1867 a special edition, *The Prince's Shakspere*, was dedicated to him. He shared his father's love of painting and the visual arts, and played the flute, piano and harmonium, but was equally fascinated by science. Politics and current events intrigued him and he read widely, and the only fault in his education was its patchiness.

Later, it was said that Leopold's education had been disrupted by illness, and this was true, but another equally serious disruption was never noticed. From the age of eight, Prince Arthur was raised by one governor and one principal tutor. Leopold had passed from Elphinstone to Sir John Cowell, to Stirling, to Duckworth, with Drs Legg and Poore as medical attendants, and, as tutors, Jolley, Buff, Shuldham, Prothero, Duckworth, Collins and others. Lacking consistent direction, he progressed in subjects that interested him, and in those for which a teacher was available; he felt the inadequacy of this acutely, and was embarrassed when people praised him.

From the summer of 1870, when Duckworth left, Collins had sole charge of Leopold's education, but he was not given the title 'governor', and was not permanently resident at Court. He faced a more difficult task than the others: Leopold was older and had his own ideas, and when he lashed out against the Queen's restrictions, Collins was often on the receiving end, as it was up to him to enforce her will. He and Leopold quarrelled at the start of 1872, and the next day Leopold wrote, 'I was very unhappy at leaving you yesterday, particularly after what had occurred the night before; but I couldn't help saying what I did, you know that in these cases I say things without knowing what I am saying.'[2] Collins forgave him, as he always did. He knew the strain the Prince was under, and was fond of him; he maintained a respectful distance, but in many ways he and Leopold were more like friends, or brothers. It had taken Leopold three years to use Stirling's Christian name, and he always wrote to 'My dear George Stirling'; Collins was 'Dearest Bob' from the start.

Only three months older than the Prince of Wales, Collins had been a schoolboy in his last years at Marlborough when Duckworth joined the school as assistant master. He went on to study at Oxford, adding to the ranks of Oxford men around the Prince, and was a barrister at Lincoln's Inn when he became Leopold's tutor. He thought he was too outspoken to make a good courtier; years passed before the Queen really trusted him, but he served Leopold well. His own stress and frustration he confided to Frederic Myers; Myers visited Windsor in 1868 and met Leopold, finding him 'a most engaging boy': 'from the very first', he wrote, 'it was observable how quickly the young prince learnt from men, how retentive was his memory for names, for faces, for anything which had been said in his presence.'[3] Myers knew about Leopold's situation, and at the end of 1870 wrote to Collins: 'I think there are very few men whom I know who would not in such a position do a boy as much harm as good, – but I don't think that of you; and in fact I can only say that if I had a son myself, of the same sensitive and affectionate nature, the very first person to whom I would be willing to entrust him would be you.'[4]

In the ten years since the Prince Consort's death, all the royal family had travelled a difficult emotional road, but none of the children was more deeply affected than Leopold. The older ones followed the courses their father planned for them; Leopold left a happy home in November 1861, and returned to find that home gone for ever, and the life he might have led gone with it. Only Beatrice had lost as much, and she was too young to remember for long. Leopold often thought of his father and missed him, certain that his unhappiness began with the Prince's death. He tried to live up to his memory: not to the 'Papa' who could be relied on to ratify any decision the Queen made, but to his own receding picture of a tall, solemn man with a German accent, who waved goodbye to him from the steps of Windsor Castle and was never there again. It is easy to idolise a dead parent, particularly when there are problems with the one who remains. Prince Albert was not perfect. He was too severe with his elder sons, and there is no telling how he would have handled Leopold. But he had a special feeling for his youngest son, and would have appreciated his desire to learn. He would almost certainly have approved the step Leopold was about to take.

When Leopold quarrelled with Collins in January 1872, he had a lot on his mind. For years he had dreamed of Oxford. His brothers, brothers-in-law and sisters, the Duke of Cambridge, his tutors and Dr Jenner all knew and encouraged the idea, but if it were ever to become reality it was time to raise the subject with his mother. Facing her in person was too dangerous; Leopold guessed how she would react and could not trust his own temper, so he decided to approach her by letter.

Through January and February, in the aftermath of the Prince of Wales's illness, the Queen kept him busy, writing letters on her behalf and sending out tickets for the Thanksgiving Service to celebrate his brother's recovery. She was preparing to take him to Baden in late March, to see her sister: 'Mamma considers this a mighty secret, so don't mention it to her when you write', Leopold told Louise.[5] He played piano duets with the Princess of Wales, and discussed his plans, and was almost ready to make a move when an incident took place which shocked them all. On 29 February he was in a carriage with his mother, Arthur and Lady Churchill, driving into the forecourt of Buckingham Palace, and as they came to a halt a young man pointed a pistol at the Queen's head. John Brown grabbed him, Arthur went for the pistol, for a moment all was mayhem, but the would-be assassin turned out to be a disturbed seventeen-year-old with a romantic attachment to the Fenian cause. His gun was not loaded. The bombshell Leopold had in mind would be a far more lasting shock to the Queen.

Leopold's letter was delivered on 6 March. It was long and carefully worded; he poured his heart into it, but he also used his head, and it was the most important letter he would ever write:

Dearest Mamma,
I have long wanted to speak to you about a subject, which I have very much at heart, & which I have thought much about for some time past. I have always expected & for years cherished the hope of being of use to you as far as would possibly be in my power, – and for the affectionate care bestowed on my education up to this time to more or less fit me for such a position I must ever feel most grateful. But beyond a certain point it is impossible that one's intellectual, moral, or social powers should be properly developed by a continual residence at home . . . I would most earnestly & with all the emphasis in my power strongly urge, that the time has arrived when (both for your own sake & for mine) residence for a period at a University would be an inestimable benefit & boon.

Oxford is close to Windsor, so that I should never be removed in reality more than a short distance from you; the terms too are short. . . . To Modern Literature & to History, to German, French & Italian, to art & to science I would chiefly desire (following dear Papa's footsteps as much as possible) to direct my attention. Socially besides it cannot but be evident to you, dearest Mamma, what an advantage such a life would be to me. To meet with such companions of my own age as would be carefully selected would tend to take away that shyness of manner, & general dullness of spirit in conversation & at all times indeed, of which you now so naturally & so much complain, & which must of necessity belong to one who has for so long led such a comparatively solitary life. . . . With all a child's duty and respect I put these, my very dearest wishes, before you & entreat you, dearest Mamma, to consider them as such . . .[6]

The reply was swift and predictable. Assuring Leopold that she was not angry, the Queen seized on an insignificant comment towards the end of his letter, where he mentioned that he had 'often talked to others' about Oxford. 'I own I have felt pained that you should have spoken to any one else but Mr Collins or Sir W. Jenner about such a thing', she wrote. 'I cannot speak to you as yet about it, for it would upset me far too much.' Ignoring everything he had said about his need to spend time away from home, she suggested that his object might be achieved without going into residence, and set out her own objection to Oxford and Cambridge – 'that tendency to High Church & extreme Episcopalianism, which I think so dangerous for any of the Royal Family'. She assured him that 'Dear Papa' would not have approved, even though Prince Albert, as Chancellor of Cambridge, had put enormous effort into reforming the curriculum of British universities, and was a university man himself. The final comment must have hurt most: 'I never doubt your affection, dearest Child. But you fancy you are stronger than you really are.'[7]

The same evening, returning a copy of the Queen's letter as she directed, Leopold defended his religious views, and appealed to her to speak to Collins, but his full reply took some days to consider. The sense that he was holding himself in check with some difficulty comes through the wording of his letter: 'It is not at all the case that any of my Brothers & Sisters ever thought of attempting to make any "schemes" or "plans" with me about my future, but I suppose it is only natural that they should take an interest in me, & ask me about my possible future, & that I should speak to them of my hopes and wishes with regard to Oxford. . . . It would make me most unhappy to think that you imagined I had tried to "<u>force</u>" this deeply cherished wish of mine upon you. I only waited to bring it before you, until it seemed to me that the improvement in my health warranted my safely doing so without causing you alarm.' But he thanked her for promising to think about Oxford, and pleaded for her agreement.[8]

It came, slowly. Leopold was forbidden to mention the matter to anyone and he obeyed, knowing that this could make all the difference. In the last week of March he left for Baden with the Queen, and if they discussed Oxford at all, it was not mentioned in any of their letters home. Leopold's reputation had gone before him, and his aunt was amazed to see how strong and fit he looked, and alarmed that he walked so fast; it was some years since she had seen him, and the Queen's letters had led her to expect an invalid.[9] He visited Strasbourg with Collins, and an English school with Ponsonby, and had lunch with his thirteen-year-old nephew, Prince Wilhelm of Prussia, but when a birthday present arrived from Alice and he asked permission to go and see her, the answer was no. He had to content himself with buying toys to send to her children. '"Heaven's will is inscrutable",' he commented to Alice, 'or rather "<u>Man's</u> will".'[10]

The visit to Baden was a short one. On 9 April Leopold had to appear at the Old Bailey as a witness in the trial of Arthur O'Connor, the Irish boy who had threatened the Queen. He had already given evidence in Bow Street Magistrates' Court, and the sight of a member of the royal family taking the oath caused great excitement. Leopold only spoke briefly, confirming his position in the carriage and his view of the incident, and identifying O'Connor, but the papers praised his loud, clear voice, and a few loyal souls in the courtroom even tried to applaud.

Afterwards, he enjoyed a few days of freedom. The Queen allowed him to take the train from Windsor to Paddington to meet

Arthur at Buckingham Palace, and the brothers rode to Chiswick in an open carriage. They met Stirling and the Marquess of Stafford, an old playmate of Leopold's; together the four young men went out on the Thames in a 'watervelocipede', and spent the rest of the day chatting to friends in the park. 'I had a nice talk with Patti who looked wonderfully pretty', Leopold told Collins. He was back at Windsor 'rather later than Eliza had desired, however there wasn't much of a row about it'. ('Eliza' was a nickname the Household used for the Queen, and Leopold had caught the habit).

A few days later he was out on the river again, rowing with Herr Sahl and Dr Marshall in a leaky boat, which had to be baled out with a flower pot. They stopped for strawberries and cream, and then rowed on, in defiance of a lock-keeper who told them they were certain to sink, arriving back at Windsor in high spirits, with damp boots and socks.[11] It was a 'rare lark', Leopold said, and he was right: adventures like this had been all too rare in his life. Perhaps something in his appeal for Oxford had touched the Queen: after all, she had once been an over-protected teenager longing for company and fun. On 14 April she gave him permission to stay with Arthur in camp, though this time the tight hand of parental control was much more apparent. Leopold was accompanied by Collins, who was told that there were to be no dinners or parties, and Leopold was certainly not to mix with the officers.[12]

Meanwhile, the Queen was thinking about Oxford and had drafted a list of conditions for her agreement. She sent it to the Dean of Windsor for comment, with copies of Leopold's letters and her own, and the Dean, with gentleness and immense tact, defended Leopold and praised the Queen for letting him go. He tried to put her mind at rest on the religious question, advising her to speak to Arthur Stanley, the Dean of Westminster, who could steer the Prince towards right-minded teachers. Dean Stanley, one of the most loved of Victorian clergymen, was well known to the royal family.[13] In 1864 he married Lady Augusta Bruce, Leopold's childhood favourite, and although the Queen disapproved of the marriage at first, the Stanleys continued to give her their support and friendship. They arranged informal gatherings where the royal children could meet interesting people; Max Müller described one luncheon party at the Westminster Deanery in February 1870 when the only guests were himself, Leopold, and a young Indian religious and social reformer, Keshub Chunder Sen.[14] Stanley was another link in the chain which drew Leopold towards Oxford: he had been Regius Professor of History, and was a good friend of Dean Liddell.

The Dean of Windsor asked permission to discuss Oxford with Collins, but the Queen wanted to speak to Collins herself first, and said Leopold was to know nothing until her mind was made up. Her conditions were severe: he was not to belong to any of the Colleges, and not to attend daily prayers in Chapel. He was not to go to large dinners or parties, but could invite a few selected people to his own house, which must be outside the city. If the Queen was at Windsor on Sunday, he was to join her, and he was to return home on demand, and 'always go with the Queen to Scotland, & not return earlier in the Autumn than the Queen; & also as a rule go with her to Osborne'.[15] The Dean suggested a slight modification, enabling Leopold not to miss lectures when his mother was travelling to Osborne; she ignored this, but was persuaded to allow nominal membership of Christ Church.

But still she felt aggrieved. For ten years she had believed that Leopold's loneliness was the result of his condition; now, he had come as close as he could to saying that it was the exclusive company of his mother and younger sister which made him unhappy. The implication was in his letter, and she was too intelligent not to see it and be hurt by it. Knowing that everyone else was in favour of his request made her feel worse. She refused to mention Oxford to Leopold at all for seven months: 'I cannot forget the way in which it was discussed behind my back, & I may say <u>forced</u> upon me', she explained, in a letter setting out her final conditions.[16]

Through the spring and summer the atmosphere between them was distinctly cold, and plans to give Leopold another outside interest by allowing him to join the Volunteers came to nothing, though both the Prince of Wales and Lord Lorne were working on schemes of this kind. Leopold had an accident in May which put him in a wheelchair for several weeks, but his mother gave him little sympathy. 'This accident is annoying', she commented to

Collins, 'but <u>yet</u> she thinks it useful too. The good Boy is so heedless & foolish that he needs reminders.'[17] She made similar remarks to the Crown Princess, complaining of the ingratitude of adult children, and her daughter tried, tentatively, to speak up for her brother. While agreeing the ever-present danger to his health, she warned, 'is not the lonely and secluded life he leads – also a danger? When he is once his own master will he not be tempted to rush into the very extreme of excitement and amusement, and will it not be doubly hurtful to him then? . . . a young man pining for liberty (justly or unjustly) is not likely to make the best use of it once he gets it within his reach.' Her simplest plea was the most telling: 'I wish with all my heart he were happier.'[18]

This was the one thing the Queen refused to admit, insisting that Leopold was perfectly happy alone with her and Beatrice; only other people unsettled him. He, meantime, was thoroughly miserable. At Balmoral his mother insisted that he should go out in his chair in all weathers – twice he was caught in the rain. 'Mamma has been as unkind & disagreeable as she <u>possibly can be</u> since she has been here;' he told Louise, '. . . & is in & out of my room all day, without giving me warning.'[19] He wrote to his Wales nephews, and passed the time reading Pepys's *Diary*. Some amusement was provided by a musical bottle Dr Poore sent him – 'such a jolly thing' – and it must have made him smile when the Queen recognised his advancing age (he was now nineteen), by ordering that in future he should say goodnight to her at 8.30, rather than 8 p.m!20

The summer brought new reasons to fret against the confines of home. In July, François, duc de Guise, a grandson of Louis Philippe of France, died at his father's house in Paris. He was a year younger than Leopold, and they had known one another all their lives; his death was a reminder of the fragility of life. Leopold wrote to his father, the duc d'Aumale, and received a touching letter in reply: 'he had real affection for you. He became . . . a perfect son in every way; I am certain that he is happier now than we are.'[21] A few weeks later Philipp of Coburg, one of the 'two fat boys' whose appearance amused the Queen on Leopold's sixth birthday, passed through England on his way round the world. He was to tour America, going on to New Zealand, Australia, Singapore, China, Japan, Java and India – and how could Leopold, whose mother put up such fierce resistance to his going a few miles down the road to university, not have felt envious? Philipp sailed from Liverpool on 10 August on the Cunard steamer *Java*, leaving his cousin eager for a detailed account of his travels.

On the day the ship landed in New York, Leopold suffered a loss. His dog Waldi, a constant companion for nine years, ran under the wheels of a dogcart he was driving at Balmoral and was killed. He was heartbroken and the Queen sympathised – she adored animals – but it would have been more tactful not to point out how often she had warned that it would happen. It would have been kinder, too, not to have repeated John Brown's remark that if Leopold had not run the dog over himself, he would have accused whoever had done it of carelessness.[22] Sadly, Leopold turned to Louise: 'he was more than a dog to me, he was a faithful companion and friend . . . you remember how he was content to lie all day on my sofa with me . . . I miss him at every turn, & am most unhappy.'[23]

In a final stroke of bad luck, he was crossing a stream in September when the footbridge gave way beneath his feet. As he lay in bed, unable to walk again, and far away in England the Oxford term began, the Queen made a last attempt to change his plans. She let Collins know, in confidence, that she was considering sending him to St Andrew's University instead of Oxford. Knowing Leopold's aversion to all things Scottish, Collins persuaded her to drop the idea, for the time being at least.

Behind the scenes, Collins and the Dean of Windsor had worked hard all summer to make sure that Leopold would get to Oxford. The Dean approached Dean Liddell about suitable lodgings, and on 19 July he warned Collins, privately, that the Queen was likely to delay the move if she could, advising him to take Leopold to Oxford as soon he returned from Balmoral in November.[24] A house was found in Oxford, but the agent discovered who it was for and wanted to raise the price; then, last-minute alterations were needed to the drainage and ventilation, '& there is no saying in what way such a state of things may influence the Queen, who will not be slow to prevent the Prince's going to Oxford at all this term . . .', Collins told Sir Thomas Biddulph. 'Excuse this ebullition of feeling . . . it is a relief to have a growl.'[25]

They had reached the decisive month. Sheer determination would probably have made Leopold walk again, however he felt. On 6 November he told Louise, 'I expect to go to Oxford on the 25th, & I trust by that time to be <u>all right</u> on my pins.'[26] At last the silence about Oxford was broken. Collins was instructed to notify the Prince of Wales, who sent his heartfelt approval, and Leopold was allowed to write to the Crown Princess. On 21 November, as they prepared to leave Balmoral, the Queen set out her final thoughts: 'Before we leave this beloved, beautiful, & graceful Place I wish to allude to your departure for Oxford. . . . The inconvenience that it will entail on me in not having a grown up Child in the House in case of Visitors will be considerable. However I have consented to give your wish a trial on the conditions which you are aware of, & on your clearly understanding that it is <u>merely</u> for <u>study</u> & <u>not</u> for <u>amusement</u> that you go there, & that you must conform in all to <u>what Mr Collins knows</u> are my wishes.' She composed a full sheet of regulations governing Leopold's life and activities.

It was a comprehensive list. He was to live quietly and simply with no luxuries, only meeting a few undergraduates 'marked out either by their birth or by their quiet & steady qualities as fit acquaintances'. Friendships were discouraged. He was not to attend Chapel, not to walk much in the town, and not to accept invitations. He was to write home frequently, and to receive regular visits from Herr Sahl, Dr Marshall and a doctor named Fox, and if he was ill in between, Dr Acland, head of the Oxford Medical Faculty, was to attend him.[27]

Henry Acland was a remarkable man, who would come to have great influence on Leopold. Like Dean Liddell and John Ruskin, both of whom were his friends, he was not only accomplished in his own field, running a busy medical practice and teaching medicine at the university, but was also a talented artist, a sailor, traveller, botanist and historian; the men whom Leopold was about to meet never thought that being a specialist in one field precluded other skills. They expected to do well in everything, and usually, they did.

Acland was no stranger to the royal family. With Dean Liddell, he was invited to dine and sleep at Osborne in the summer of 1858, to discuss the education of the Prince of Wales. Prince Albert thought well of him, and considered offering him the post of personal physician to the royal family, but was advised by the President of the Medical Council that Acland's work in Oxford was too important to curtail. When the Prince of Wales went to the university in 1859, his father entrusted him to Dean Liddell at Christ Church, with Acland as his medical adviser; so Leopold was following a path his father had already approved. It was Acland who found the house for Leopold, in a new development to the north of the city. Wykeham House in St Giles was the first home Leopold could call his own, and he would always regard it with affection.

The house was built in 1865–6 in the Gothic style, and took its name from a life-size statue of the medieval cleric and educational reformer William of Wykeham, set high on the front of the building to the left of the door. Acland inspected the house, and he was the one who insisted on the last-minute alterations which caused headaches for Collins. The house belonged to a local businessman, who owned a drapery and clothing store, and it was small, for a prince, but Leopold was enchanted. 'It is a dear little house', he told Louise, '(not exactly <u>little</u> as it is very <u>high</u> but it is very <u>narrow</u>, & hence little), it is a good ½ mile from Christ Church, & would be almost in the country were it not for the immense number of villas which have sprung up all round it, where most of the professors & "coaches" live. I showed you at Balmoral all the plans of the house, so I need not say anything about the inside of it, except that the three rooms on the ground floor, the Drawing-room, Dining-room, & Study (or rather <u>smoking</u>-room) . . . are very comfortable, as are also the bedrooms . . . & I have hung my own best pictures & engravings on the walls, & filled the rooms with my choicest ornaments, so that (in my eyes at least) the rooms look very pretty.'[28]

On the morning of Wednesday 27 November 1872, as the bells of Christ Church and the churches of Oxford rang in celebration, the Prince went through the ceremony of matriculation in the Deanery, becoming a member of the University and of Christ Church, and he adopted the nobleman's gown and velvet cap which he would wear while in residence. That evening, Dean Liddell and Dr Acland dined with him at Wykeham House. He had not entered a degree course, so was free to select his own subjects, and the days that followed were full and exciting:

On Thursday I went to my first lecture, which was one delivered by Professor Ruskin on the art of engraving, it was <u>most</u> interesting. . . . On Saturday I went to three lectures, one by Prof. Montagu Burrows on History, one by Professor Clifton on the human eye, & one by Professor Ruskin again on Art. . . . On Monday I attended a lecture given by old Professor Phillips on Geology, & in the evening a lecture on the last eruption of Mt Vesuvius by Mr Wyndham of Merton, which was very interesting. Yesterday morning I worked at Chemistry in the Ch. Ch. Laboratory with a Mr Harcourt & in the afternoon I went to a most interesting lecture delivered by Mr Chandler on 'the transmission of Genius &c, from father to son' which consisted mainly in proving that most great men had stupid parents & stupid children.[29]

The rest of his time was spent finding his way around and meeting people, mostly senior academics. Among his guests at Wykeham House were the Master of University College, who had been Collins's headmaster at Marlborough, Max Müller, whom he had known from childhood – in 1864 Müller gave a lecture at Osborne on 'The Origins of Language' which was attended by all the royal children – and John Ruskin, who was invited to dine alone with Leopold and Collins as they were told that he avoided large parties. An undergraduate named Lloyd was invited to play the piano with Leopold, and he met a few other young men from families known to the Queen. But the company of undergraduates was a sore point: twice the Queen wrote to Collins about men who might be suitable, 'sprinkled about amongst the older people'. She was certain that young men had been a bad influence on her elder sons, and wanted to keep Leopold from their clutches.[30]

Not content to rely on Collins, she sent Dr Fox to Wykeham House on Friday 29 November, and he stayed overnight. He visited twice the following week, and during the weekend in between, Dr Jenner arrived, and Herr Sahl. Jenner raised the possibility of a resident doctor being appointed, but left on Sunday morning before the Prince had a chance to speak to him privately. Alarmed, Leopold wrote to him that same evening: 'You know how very much I dislike having a Doctor continually with me when I am well; to be saddled with anyone one does not know is unpleasant; but to have somebody forced (very unnecessarily too!) down one's throat, as a kind of medical spy is a most unpleasant notion.'[31] He knew that the presence of a full-time medical attendant would mark him out as abnormal, and he was already far more closely supervised than any other undergraduate.

But even in these early weeks, Leopold's involvement in Oxford life had gone beyond anything his mother envisaged. On the first Saturday afternoon he was invited to the Deanery. He would have heard of Dean Liddell's family from Duckworth, but the elder daughters, Lorina, Alice and Edith, were no longer the bewitching children around whom Charles Dodgson had woven his stories. Lorina was twenty-three, Alice twenty, Edith eighteen, and their younger sisters, Rhoda and Violet, were thirteen and eight. Leopold grew fond of them all, and was drawn into the life of the family. The first meeting made its mark. 'I went to the Deanery & heard the charming Miss Liddells play & sing', he told his sister, 'they are very pretty indeed, & very nice.' The next day he heard Dr Pusey preach in the University church of St Mary's, 'for <u>an hour & twenty minutes</u>, I assure you, not a minute less, I never was so tired in my life; it was all about the Athanasian Creed'.[32] If the Queen had known this, she really would have been alarmed: Dr Pusey was the founder of the High Church 'Oxford Movement' which she thought so dangerous.

Leopold gained more insight into the ferment of religious ideas in Oxford in his second week, when an attempt was made to exclude Dean Stanley from the university pulpit for the liberality of his views; his speeches in the Lords and his decision to administer communion to a Unitarian had alarmed members of the Oxford Movement. The Prince attended the 'Stanley debates' eagerly, and was delighted to see his friend vindicated. 'I was present in the Sheldonian Theatre when the voting took place,' he told Princess Alice, 'about 700 people voted, it was a most <u>interesting</u> & memorable sight to behold.'[33]

He was entranced with Oxford, and nothing escaped his attention. Even the cook at Wykeham House earned unstinting praise. 'My housekeeper & cook, Mrs Scott, is a very nice, good-looking, rather fat woman of about thirty two or thereabouts,' he told Louise, '. . . she is also a very good tempered woman, & makes no difficulties, which in my eyes makes up for a multitude of defects, (if she had any) now haven't I described a model? & not exaggerated a bit, I assure you.'[34] But all too soon it was over. He had to be home by Saturday 14 December, for the anniversary of his father's death, which coincided with the end of term. He was sorry to leave, but went home full of excitement, and ready to be on good terms with everybody. Oxford had exceeded his expectations, and he looked back on it as 'the first time when I was really happy, & knew what it was to be happy'.[35]

Two weeks had worked quite a transformation. Sir Henry Ponsonby noticed that Leopold's conversation had improved, and that he was beginning to grow a beard.[36] The Queen was pleased to find him '<u>not</u> changed in the wrong direction, but in the right – not playing the fine young gentleman, which I have so painfully observed in your Brothers, but on the contrary more amiable, more friendly to others & much less irritable & touchy'. She was so pleased, in fact, that she decided to entrust him with a very sensitive mission. It pained her to see that Arthur had become less friendly to the servants since he had been out in society. 'Could you not give him a hint on this point?' she asked Leopold. She started by referring to servants in general, but really had one in mind: 'This applies especially to my excellent Brown, who <u>ought</u> to be treated by <u>all</u> of <u>you</u>, as he is by others, <u>differently</u> to the more ordinary servants (tho they should be treated with great friendliness).'[37]

For Leopold to be the blue-eyed boy, and Arthur the problem, was a real reversal. Leopold would no more have tried to persuade his brother to be nice to John Brown than he would have tried to fly, or run away with the circus, but he would have seen the funny side of it. He was disposed to enjoy everything that Christmas, and his only worry was that he would be kept for too long at Osborne in the New Year. Term began on 24 January 1873, but the Queen intended to stay on the Isle of Wight for two months, and she had already said that he must stay with her.

He would have been a great deal more worried if he had known what else she had in mind. On New Year's Eve he wrote to Collins anticipating the freedom they would have when he reached his twenty-first birthday in 1874, and was granted an allowance by

Parliament. He had no idea that his mother had already contacted the Prime Minister and offered to waive the allowance. Alfred and Arthur would need increased annuities on marriage, and the Queen foresaw opposition if she were to request an allowance for another son at the same time, so Leopold's income was to be sacrificed to ensure his brothers' future. After all, as the Queen pointed out, 'it is Her Majesty's earnest wish that Prince Leopold should live principally with her', and she felt that he would only need an independent income on her death or his marriage.[38] Leopold had achieved his dream, but new battle lines were already being drawn.

EIGHT

LOVE, AND A GATHERING STORM

By the end of January 1873, Leopold was itching to return to Oxford, where the new term had started, but he had to wait two more weeks and when he left, a fresh list of instructions went with him. He was to join the Queen at weekends if she was at Windsor, to accompany her to Osborne for Easter, and to leave for Balmoral with her in May, though this meant missing the best part of the summer term. He was disappointed, but determined to make the best of the time he had, and to deepen the acquaintances formed in his first two weeks. Already his 'inner circle' was taking shape.

If he had been asked at this early stage to pick out the Oxford figures who would be important to him, he would certainly have named John Ruskin. Publication of *Modern Painters*, *The Seven Lamps of Architecture*, and *The Stones of Venice* had established Ruskin as a leading critic of art and culture, whose views had a profound impact, but his social criticism was more controversial. Ruskin was a crusader, who longed to transform the lives of ordinary people through art, through his teaching, and through various practical schemes. In 1869, with the support of Acland and Liddell, he was elected Slade Professor of Art at Oxford. It was a new professorship, which he intended to use creatively to further his wider aims. Leopold attended his lecture on 'Sandro Botticelli and the Florentine Schools of Engraving' in November, and invited him to dinner the following week; the rapport between them was immediate.

It was an odd combination, the established art critic in his early fifties, and an undergraduate of nineteen with everything to prove, carefully shielded from the real world, but Ruskin knew what it meant to be almost suffocated by parental watchfulness and concern. He treated Leopold more as a friend than a pupil, and listened as much as he talked. During their first meeting, Leopold lent him a favourite book of poetry by Myers, and once he had read it Ruskin wrote, 'I am very heartily glad to know that your Royal Highness likes it – but it seems strange to me – you are very happy – in being enough sad to enter into the feeling of these poems – already . . . this note must read to you as if I only wanted to say what would please you. That is indeed true – but I should neither hope, nor attempt, to do so by praising what I did not like.'[1] It was the start of a lasting friendship, in which the imbalances of age, rank and achievement did not matter at all.

Ruskin lived alone, his loves always ending in torment and disappointment, but Oxford would also provide Leopold with a model of contented family life, on a much more human scale than he had previously known. His own family was surrounded by courtiers and servants, and their homes were palaces; their happiest days belonged to a time he could hardly remember. Men like Dr Acland, Dean Liddell and Professor Müller were happily married, living with their wives and children in ordinary homes, whose doors were always open to him.

Max Müller's wife Georgina had almost died in the 1850s when her father forbade the wedding. Once his objections were overcome, the Müllers sustained an intense and deepening love through forty-one years of married life, and their Oxford house was simple and comfortable, dominated by the dog Winnie, who claimed exclusive rights to the best armchair. There were four children, three daughters and a son; in 1877 the eldest, Ada, died of meningitis, and her father sent Leopold her photograph. 'I am so grateful to you for the photograph of your dear daughter', Leopold told him, '& I shall ever value it as a recollection of my visits to your house in Oxford in those happy bygone days.'[2]

The Aclands' home in Broad Street was a rambling house which Mrs Acland likened to a rabbit warren, made from three smaller buildings. A narrow, panelled entrance hall led first to the doctor's waiting and consulting rooms, then to his library and sitting room, but the heart of the home was on the upper floor. In the narrow, beamed drawing room, full of books, with so many pictures that the wallpaper could hardly be seen, the Aclands held open house, where visiting undergraduates and dons could mingle with their eight children in cheerful informality. Over the door was a notice, 'Pour out not words where there is a Musician', and music often filled the house, with the doctor playing the harmonium, and his wife accompanying him in her fine contralto voice. Sometimes, Mrs Acland would read aloud, and always the evenings ended with prayers at ten, and refreshments. By eleven the house was quiet.[3]

Sarah Acland was a gentle, reserved woman, who mothered everyone who came under her roof; Ruskin called her 'Mama', and her husband would often bring home overworked undergraduates for her care. She was intelligent and well-read, able to converse in several languages, and for Leopold, her home had an irresistible appeal, both for its intellectual and artistic atmosphere – the paintings on the walls were by artists like Rossetti, Millais and the Richmonds, all personal friends of Dr Acland – and even more for its openness and warmth. The Aclands taught him that illness need not be a bar to normal life, and he became especially friendly with their only daughter, never forgetting to mention her in letters to her parents.

But the centre of Oxford social life, and, for a time, of Leopold's life, was the Deanery at Christ Church. Mrs Liddell was not a gentle, self-effacing woman like Sarah Acland and Georgina Müller. Imposing and ambitious, the Dean's wife wanted to be seen and respected, if not loved, in her husband's world. Parties, balls and musical evenings at the Deanery were much grander affairs than the Aclands' evenings, but behind the grandeur was the same intensely loving family life, into which Leopold was drawn and welcomed. Dean Liddell kept a Letts' diary hanging by the fireplace in his study with his engagements for the day, and if his children wanted to spend time with him, they found a space and wrote in their names. The Dean and his wife were proud of their children and expected them to be seen and heard, and the young Liddells were involved in the social life of the Deanery from an early age. As Leopold discovered in his first week, the three elder daughters, Lorina, Alice and Edith, sang and played exceptionally well: the composer Hubert Parry wrote settings especially for them.

The Queen worried endlessly about the immorality of upper-class young men, whose wealth and idleness made them easy prey to temptation. This was as strong a motive as haemophilia for her determination to keep Leopold at home: she wanted to preserve in him the innocence of childhood. It never seemed to occur to her that there were positive as well as negative forces to be encountered in the outside world. Leopold had not yet had a chance to meet the temptations which so preoccupied his mother; in time he would, and he would succumb, but the image of family life and of deepening love in marriage learned in the homes of his Oxford friends proved a more lasting influence.

From mid-February until April 1873, the only interruptions to his residence at Oxford were weekend visits home. Returning to Windsor after a week, he had 'a <u>screaming</u> row' with his mother, which was soon smoothed over; 'Mamma will now see that I am not going to submit to all her little bullyings', was his optimistic comment. At the end of the month he was called on to accompany his younger sister to the theatre in London. He did not mind this; in fact, he was amused, because the play seemed such an unlikely choice. 'We are going to Covent Garden Theatre to see a play called "Babel & Bijou", which is very pretty but somewhat indecent, (so saith report at least)', he told Princess Louise. 'I believe the dresses of some of the fair females are not very extensive and somewhat transparent; I can't understand how they let Baby go to such a thing, however it is not <u>my</u> business.'[4]

The Queen had probably not thought of the content of the play, but she was keen to strengthen his relationship with Beatrice; she also insisted that he should spend the Easter vacation with his sister. Term ended at the start of April, and before Leopold set off for Osborne he snatched an opportunity to go to London and visit Dr Poore. Poore had recently set up home in Wimpole Street with his friend Marcus Beck, another doctor, and Leopold found them spring-cleaning, with the curtains down and the carpets up. He didn't mind, and spent an hour talking to Poore. Then he went to Osborne for three weeks, but Oxford was never far from his mind; Dr Acland sent him a paper on 'Faith and Knowledge', with greetings for his birthday, and he replied, 'I am looking forward with <u>greatest pleasure</u> to my return to Oxford this day week; I wish there were no vacations, for myself at least.' He must have been giving a lot of thought to religious questions, and greeted Acland's paper with interest, 'as it puts everything so clearly before one'.[5]

The Prince's interests were becoming known to a widening circle of people. He was fascinated by fine china – an enthusiasm which may have begun with the miniature tea service his mother gave him during his 1861 illness, or perhaps even earlier. Prime Minister Gladstone heard of it, and in April he wrote to Leopold in characteristically ponderous style, enclosing a paper on Wedgwood, whom he recommended as 'one of the most remarkable men . . . in the combined history of art and commerce'.[6] Leopold accepted it gladly: 'I am very fond of Wedgewood china, & I have a great veneration for Wedgewood himself.'[7] Gladstone had devoted the best part of two years to a fruitless attempt to make the Queen perform more public duties; now he was turning to her sons, and he was not the only man of influence and intelligence to recognise that Leopold, who could never live the conventional life of a prince, could use his talents and his position to play an important part in national life.

Leopold returned to Oxford on 21 April and threw himself back energetically into work and play, to make up for the fact that, for him, the term would be unusually short. Three weeks; then, like it or not, he must go to Scotland with the Queen, losing the best part of the summer, and the start of his second year. He did not like it. 'I always hate, as you know, going to that <u>vile</u> place', he told Stirling, 'but this year my dislike of it & my misery at being dragged down there is encreased a hundredfold; <u>this</u> is the time of the year to be at Oxford; the boat races begin the <u>very day</u> I leave, isn't it annoying. I must, however, submit & put a good face on it as far as I can; <u>but next year</u> (if I live) things shall be different.'[8] He still had no idea of his mother's plans and was eagerly anticipating his majority, and the greater freedom he thought it would bring.

The social life of Oxford, which the Queen had done so much to keep from him, was as important to him now as the chance for further study. As he told Princess Alice, 'one meets so many clever & distinguished men & at the same time one makes the acquaintance of a number of young men whom one is pretty certain of meeting later on in life'.[9] This was a good thing, whatever his mother thought; when Ponsonby discussed Wykeham

House dinner parties with Collins a few weeks later his first reaction was to hope 'that Leopold also saw some young men'.[10] Among the Prince's undergraduate friends were Aubrey Harcourt, the Earl of Sheffield's grandson, and Lord Brooke, son and heir of the Earl of Warwick, whose early life had been as blighted by ill-health as his own. Friendship with Brooke must have helped him put his problems in perspective and feel more normal, and they remained friends for life.

Leopold would have been less than human if he had not wanted to have some fun at Oxford, but this was not easy with the Queen watching his every move. In May he told Stirling, 'even here Collins & I receive bullying <u>letters</u> & <u>telegrams</u> from "Home, <u>sweet</u> home"; I may never <u>drive</u> out here; though we manage to go out sometimes after dinner, & I give three or four dinners a week in my house; I can hardly ever invite more than <u>four</u> to dinner, & I may never invite any of the softer sex, which is a great pity, as there are such <u>awfully</u> pretty girls here unmarried as well as married; & you know I am always a great admirer, & more than that, of fair females.'[11]

The adolescent bravado and mischief in this last remark – so far he had had no chance to be 'more than an admirer' to anybody – mask a serious intent. In the spring of 1873, Leopold was in love, and it ran deeper than his passing fancy for Miss Fitzroy. This lay behind his visit to Dr Poore in April: he wanted to talk about his feelings, and perhaps to ask advice. A few days after the meeting Poore sent him a picture frame for his birthday, and Leopold told him it would be used for 'the two loveliest females I know, or rather the <u>one</u> most lovely person I know, I daresay you can guess whom I mean'. In August Poore wrote again, having heard rumours that Arthur was engaged. Leopold denied it, but said it was sure to happen soon, adding, 'Then it will be my turn . . . I have most decidedly fixed on the fair one, <u>if</u> she will have me.'[12] He must even have been determined enough to mention his hopes to the Queen. The following January, when relations between him and his mother reached a new low, and he was certain that she had a wife in mind for him whom he did not want, he complained to Collins, 'I half think that she broke off the other match on account of this wench.'[13]

He was in love. There was talk of a marriage, which the Queen put a stop to. The question remains: who was the girl? The Queen's correspondence relating to Leopold in the Royal Archives contains not the slightest clue. The only references are in Poore's papers, and Collins', and no name is given, presumably because both men shared the secret. It was almost inevitable that a lonely, affectionate twenty-year-old, away from his family, would fall in love with somebody. More experienced heads may have foreseen that it was too early to talk of marriage, or that, for some other reason, a marriage could never be. But who was the girl? She must have come from Oxford; if she had been at Court, Leopold would not have complained so vehemently about being hauled off to Balmoral. The written record is silent, but tradition offers one name, and only one: Alice Liddell.

Hints of this go back a long way: back, in fact, to the spring of 1873, when Mrs Liddell's enemies in Oxford began to say that she would not be content simply to have a prince in the house. In March Charles Dodgson, whose own relationship with the Liddells had turned sour some years before, wrote a satirical drama, *The Vision of the Three T's*, attacking Dean Liddell's alterations to the buildings of Christ Church. He included a vicious swipe at Mrs Liddell, satirising her as the 'King-fisher': an allusion to Leopold's frequent presence with the family, which implied that the Dean's wife was angling for a royal son-in-law.

Dodgson was not the only person who watched Leopold's visits to the Deanery, and wondered. Lorina Liddell was married in February 1874, and shortly afterwards another satire was written, more vicious and more sharply aimed than Dodgson's. *Cakeless* was a verse drama in three acts, depicting the triple wedding of the daughters of 'Apollo and Diana', following the disappointing marriage of their eldest daughter. The three bridegrooms are 'Yerbua' (Aubrey Harcourt), 'Rivulus' (Lord Brooke), and 'Regius', 'a Pr*nce, the youngest of his race' – obviously Leopold. Identifying the brides is less easy. 'Ecilia', who marries 'Yerbua', is surely Alice, but 'Rosa', the next in age, usually equated with Edith Liddell, sounds more like Rhoda. The third bride in *Cakeless*, 'Psyche', who traps the Prince, would therefore have to be Violet, who was still a child. In that case, Edith is missing.[14]

It may be a mistake to identify the daughters too closely. The undergraduate author of *Cakeless*, John Howe Jenkins, may not even have known the Liddell girls as individuals: his targets were the Dean and Mrs Liddell, and all that mattered for his purpose was that they had a large number of unmarried daughters, for whom they were thought to want rich and influential husbands. But it is interesting to note that he singles out Leopold and his two friends as the objects of the Liddells' ambitions, and, therefore, as frequent visitors to the Deanery.

Cakeless was published anonymously, but the University authorities took steps to uncover the author's name. Jenkins was sent down, and his work suppressed; it might have been forgotten altogether, if the attention paid in recent years to anything connected with Dodgson and *Alice in Wonderland* had not ensured its survival. In *Cakeless* 'Kraftsohn', a thinly veiled Dodgson, tries to stop the wedding. And so, through Jenkins, and through *The Vision of the Three T's*, the disappointed romance between Alice Liddell and Leopold has become an accepted part of the *Alice* mythology. It is said that Alice and Leopold were in love, and hoped to secure the Queen's permission to marry, but that Mrs Liddell, seeing the impossibility of the thing, put a stop to it for her daughter's sake. The Queen, it is said, would not allow her children to marry anyone who was not royal.

This last is certainly untrue. Louise had already married Lord Lorne, and the Queen did consider non-royal brides for her younger sons. But the Liddells, for all their beauty and accomplishment, were not on a level with Lorne, the son and heir of the Duke of Argyll; Dean Liddell's father was the younger son of a baron, so his own children were three generations removed from the title, and though he was a wealthy man in the context of Oxford, his daughters could not expect the kind of settlement which would tempt the Queen – there were too many of them. More important, and more subtle, was their social position. Dean Liddell had been a royal chaplain, and several of his cousins were at Court. Court families could be allowed unusual intimacy with the royal family because they knew their place. Like the steps of a complicated dance, the rules that governed their world were unwritten, but powerful: any unplanned move would throw the whole dance out of step. Trusted to play host to the Prince of Wales in the 1850s, and then to Leopold, Mrs Liddell would have known the rules and, whatever Oxford gossip said, she would have known better than to encourage hopes of marriage.

The object of Leopold's love could have been Alice. She was beautiful, well-educated, artistic and musical; they had a great deal in common, and he would not have been the only undergraduate to fall under the spell of the Dean's daughter. In a very male world which offered few opportunities for love, there were many young men who longed for the next musical evening, and the next chance to dance at the Deanery. But modern attention focuses exclusively on Alice because of her association with the book. Had it not been for *Alice in Wonderland*, the Liddells would be lost now in the same respectful obscurity which cloaks the Aclands and the Stanleys, equally well-known names in their day. In the 1870s no-one would have singled Alice out from her sisters; they were all attractive, all desirable. Both Jenkins and Dodgson hinted at a link between the Prince and one of the Liddell girls, but they did not say which one. Leopold certainly loved someone, but could it have been a different Liddell?

It could very easily have been Edith. Two years younger than Alice, Edith was tall, with a mass of red curls and a wistful, Pre-Raphaelite expression. She was nineteen to Leopold's twenty, and she was lovely, and a great favourite. In the early 1870s John Ruskin took over the place in the Liddell family's life which Dodgson had once filled, and he described a visit to the Deanery one stormy night. 'I think Edith had got the tea made, and Alice was just bringing the muffins to perfection', he wrote. 'I don't recollect that Rhoda was there; (I never did, that anybody else was there, if Edith was . . .).'[15] That was Edith. Shortly after her tragically early death, Max Müller commented that her father would never get over the loss; she was 'a most charming, lovable creature, so natural, so beautiful, and he so fond, so proud of her!'[16]

Leopold mentioned Edith in a letter to Collins from Balmoral in the autumn of 1874, a year after his hope of marriage had ended. He had heard that Aubrey Harcourt had been sent to America to prevent him from proposing to Edith, 'who (poor girl!), I hear, returns his affection. Were she of higher rank I would myself take her to my — house, she is such a pretty bit of flesh.'[17] Behind the awful language, which was a mannerism Leopold affected at this time when he wanted to sound hard and experienced, there may be a hint of his real feelings. Princes were conditioned to accept that there were very few women they could actually marry, but if he had loved Edith, it would not have been easy to think of her marrying his friend.

Talk of marriage ended sometime in the autumn of 1873 without bitterness, and the friendship and affection between Leopold and the Liddell family continued to grow – as it might, if they knew that he loved one of their own, and had been forced to set that love aside. And the end must have come by letter. In mid-May Leopold left for Balmoral with the Queen, and did not see the Liddells again until December.[18]

The pleasures of Oxford had never quite taken his mind from one nagging anxiety. In the autumn of 1872, his beloved little Hesse godson 'Fritzie' had been ill, and by January it was obvious that the child had haemophilia. The news was especially painful for Leopold because he knew what it meant. On 11 May he wrote to his sister, 'I hope my godson is keeping well, & not having any more bruises, & in every way unlike his Godfather, except in being very fond of you & Louis.'[19] But they were only days away from tragedy. Alice was in her bedroom one morning a little over a fortnight later, with her two small sons. It was an L-shaped room, with two windows facing one another across the right-angle. The Princess saw her elder son lean out of the nearest window and ran to grab him; she did not see 'Fritzie' until it was too late. Climbing on to a chair to wave to his brother from the other window, the little boy toppled and fell out on to the pavement a few feet below. He was dead before the day's end.

'How can I express my deep sorrow for you', Leopold wrote in horror, the next day. '. . . I know how deeply you loved dear little Fritzie, & how he deserved it; he was always my especial pet, & I was very fond of him, poor child.'[20] He grieved for his sister, but was also angry and afraid, identifying with the death because it could so easily have been his own. When he heard people say that it was 'all for the best', he said nothing, but the thought never left his mind, 'if anything happens to me, that is what everyone will say', and he hated them for it.[21] The Princess sent him a photograph of the dead child, surrounded with flowers, and a lock of fine, fair hair, a 'last souvenir of his precious godchild'. He kept them for the rest of his life.[22]

It was cold, even snowy at Balmoral that May, and the Queen kept Leopold busy writing letters on her behalf. She was pleased to find him 'amiable and cheerful', and was feeling very protective after her grandson's death. She told Collins that she worried about Leopold slipping and falling if no-one was nearby, and expressed the rather fruitless hope 'that as Leop^d gets older & _more_ reasonable he will see that it is _merely_ out of useful precaution that he abstains from these sorts of things w^h are really full of _risks_ & not because he is an invalid'.[23] But at twenty, Leopold was old enough to decide what he felt able to do, and the apparent closeness between mother and son was only the calm before the storm.

At the start of the year, he had glumly anticipated spending six months at Balmoral, but the summer was more varied than he expected. Gladstone persuaded the Queen to return to Windsor in June to entertain the Shah of Persia, and Leopold was included in the welcoming party. Towards the end of the visit he was charged with taking his mother's exotic guest to see the kennels, dairy and gardens, and the mausoleum at Frogmore, which must have been a novel experience, though he would have been less than enraptured by having to wear full Highland dress – in England! When the Shah left they went to Osborne, but by August Balmoral was looming back into view.

At first, though, even that offered an exciting prospect, as he was allowed to visit Louise and her husband's family at Inveraray. He was delighted to hear that his brother-in-law was intending to invite Aubrey Harcourt to keep him company: 'he's a great friend of mine', he told Louise, '& I think you'll like him.'[24] Leopold spent a happy, uncomplicated week, talking ornithology with the Duke of Argyll and smoking cheroots with Lord Lorne's younger brother ('I would be very much obliged if you would ask him for me _where_ he gets his _cheroots_ as I took a fancy to them, please don't forget this!', he asked his sister. A few months later a box of cheroots arrived at Wykeham House.[25]) It was hard having to leave, but a week was all the Queen would allow, and he returned to Balmoral on 16 September with a cold in the head, a terrible cough, and no voice.

The storm broke almost immediately. For some years, the Queen had been looking for ways to promote the cause of Protestantism, to stem the revival of High Church practices within the Church of England. This movement, which began in Oxford in the early years of the century, seemed dangerous to her because some of its leading figures had been drawn back to the Church of Rome. In 1870 Papal Infallibility was declared, and Bismarck embarked on his 'Kulturkampf' to purge Germany of Catholic power and influence; the Queen looked on with admiration and a trace of envy – useless, then, for her eldest daughter to remind her of her own preaching of tolerance in former years. In the early 1870s she was militant, and determined. She wanted the low churches to show a united front, and in the autumn of 1873 she made it known at Balmoral that she intended to take communion in the Scottish church, at Crathie, and hoped that her family, Household and servants would join her.

At heart, the Queen responded most deeply to simple forms of worship, but it was unfortunate that other issues were drawn into the argument. The Scottish church was much 'lower' than the Church of England, and this gave her another Scottish stick to beat down objections; for Leopold especially, this made the question harder to disentangle. His own ideas on religion were still very open. He had tasted High Church Anglicanism at Oxford, and the aesthetic side of the worship appealed to him, but he was still close to liberal churchmen like Stanley. Stanley had expressed initial unease about the Queen's decision, as had the Dean of Windsor, and even the Archbishop of Canterbury. The Queen sent Leopold some papers written by the Minister of Crathie in October, setting out her intention and the theology behind it, and her wish for a united front to be shown, and he replied, rather cautiously, 'As you say towards the end of it that "<u>no-one need take it unless he wishes to do so</u>", I hope you will not mind my saying that I would sooner not do so <u>myself</u>.'[26]

If he had launched an armed rebellion against the throne, the Queen could hardly have been more angry. The leeway she had allowed for liberty of conscience had never been meant to apply to Leopold. 'Let me now more strongly and emphatically point out to you, that it is your sacred <u>duty</u> to take the sacrament with me on this occasion,' she thundered. 'Your <u>not</u> doing so, would be a great mistake and a want of respect towards me. . . . If even you have no wish for it, it is nothing which can affect your faith. . . . Indeed I have <u>never</u> known <u>any one refuse</u> to take the <u>Sacrament</u> with a Parent – and especially the Head of the Country – if asked to do so.' The Minister of Crathie would be sent to answer his questions, and, in an attempt to soften the blow, she added in PS, 'You are very affectionate and I hope very dutiful; indeed I have no reason to complain of that at all.'[27]

Then she turned to Collins, but he said that although he would speak to the Prince, he doubted that he could move him on so sensitive an issue. The pressure mounted as 3 November, the date of the communion service, drew nearer, and suddenly Leopold began bleeding from the kidney. A letter from the Queen to his sister implied that this was the result of a hunting expedition.[28] It was not a severe attack, but it confined him to the sofa for longer than usual, and the Queen commended Collins for showing him a letter from Princess Alice which stressed the need for him to take care: 'we must all take the line of frightening him now', she said.[29] Early in November he had a fit, the first for some time, which the Queen blamed on a change of medication and lack of exercise. She was beside herself with worry, thinking of the death of her grandson, but became rather annoyed that all the sympathy was directed at Leopold. 'You only speak of him', she complained to her eldest daughter, 'and not of my constant anxiety and the terrible difficulties I have to contend with from foolish, ill-judged people suggesting things which bring on illnesses. No-one knows the constant fear I am in about him.'[30]

Fritzie was on Leopold's mind too, and as he lay on the sofa, his thoughts often went back to his games with the Hesse children at Balmoral two years before, when no-one thought that the child was even ill. But he was also preoccupied with the future. The end of the year was drawing near, but the Queen had not mentioned the change in his status and income which would follow his twenty-first birthday. By the third week in November he was walking again; soon he would be well enough to go back to Oxford, and his mother was determined to settle the sacrament question before he left, but he was working himself up into quite a state, and it was not the moment to push him.

Faced with demands to move Leopold on the religious issue, Collins suggested that it was time for the Queen's whole plan for the future to be brought into the open. She ignored him. The sacrament was what mattered, and she was beginning to suspect that someone was influencing Leopold, probably Louise; Collins was to find out the truth. By the beginning of December he and Leopold were back at Wykeham House, and his efforts to follow the Queen's orders were meeting a blank wall of misery, and increasing resistance. As far as Leopold was concerned, his beliefs were a private matter, and he was deeply unhappy about the whole business. He did not want to be at odds with his mother, but would not be forced into supporting her when men whose opinion he valued were not in favour of what she had done. He had spent some time with Gladstone at Balmoral, and they may have discussed the issue; Leopold certainly asked the Prime Minister's advice on a matter they both regarded as 'delicate', and Gladstone offered to discuss it with the Dean of Windsor.[31] Gladstone was so strongly opposed to the Queen's decision that she had begun to see him as a closet Catholic.

They were at an impasse. Leopold wanted to discuss the future; the Queen refused to mention it until he took the sacrament with her. Poor Collins was caught in the middle, between two formidable tempers. His relationship with Leopold was compromised by the fact that he knew the Queen's plans, and was sworn to secrecy, and once again he tried to reason with her: 'It is evident that the Prince is still very strongly opposed to a different treatment being applied to him, on his attaining the age of 21, to that which was applied to his brothers, nor does he realise yet, that Your Majesty's mind is made up on this point. . . . The Prince, though still boyish in many respects, is certainly already very determined & independent, & can be, when he considers himself aggrieved, the very reverse of a pleasant or agreable companion.' The Queen had let him know that she wanted him to stay on with Leopold, and Collins warned that if the Prince, as a man, was forced to be 'an unwilling party to the arrangements made for him', that position would become impossible, for him or for anyone.[32]

It was hopeless. Beginning to feel that Collins might not have her interests at heart, the Queen sent Dr Jenner to Wykeham House, and produced a letter from the Dean of Windsor supporting her arguments. She suggested that Collins should threaten to leave unless Leopold gave way on the sacrament question – which may have been a threat to Collins himself, as well as to the Prince – but Collins, who must by now have felt that he had very little to lose, refused. As he pointed out, Leopold might take him up on it, and would certainly never trust him again. He then produced a trump card of his own, warning that the Prince would soon turn to other members of the family to break the deadlock: 'The Princess of Wales . . . & others visited Mrs Liddell & the Dean of Christ Church today, & Prince Leopold met them at the Deanery at lunch. The Princess also called here . . .'.[33]

Meanwhile Leopold, angered beyond measure by Jenner's appearance, defied a telegram instructing him not to write to his mother, and explained his position in writing once again, in as conciliatory terms as he could manage. 'If I <u>had</u> followed your wishes in this matter of taking the Holy Communion in Crathie Kirk, I would not have been able to take it in a true Christian spirit, in charity with all men, as I should have felt . . . that I was only taking it under constraint & not of my own free will. . . . I am <u>convinced</u> that, when you have read this, you will understand all my feelings, which could never be rightly expressed through other persons.' He said he was very unhappy not to have been able to speak to her directly.[34] With Christmas approaching, the Queen replied in an equally conciliatory tone, promising to talk to him, but reminding him that she, as his mother and sovereign, must have the last word: 'state therefore then <u>openly your wishes</u> and <u>ideas</u> & listen in a right <u>spirit</u> to what <u>I</u> shall have to say, & to what can & <u>cannot</u> be done'.[35] It was the 'cannot' she emphasised. The arguments between them were far from over.

NINE

THE GREAT STRUGGLE

With so much bad feeling in the air, 1874 did not look promising. Every issue had become a trial of strength between Leopold and his mother, and he expected the next round to begin with the start of the Oxford term, which he did not want to miss. On New Year's Eve he told Stirling, 'in a fortnight's time the great struggle between myself & H.M. will commence. I am looking forward to it with the greatest horror, but with determination, & a firm resolution to gain my point. . . . I have submitted for long years, but <u>now</u> I <u>must</u> & <u>shall</u> be free & independent.'[1] All the Queen's children feared rousing her anger; they loved her, no matter how difficult the day-to-day relationship could be. For Leopold that relationship was under intense strain.

Somehow he had discovered that the Queen did not intend to ask Parliament for his allowance, but the reasons he had heard made no sense, and still she had not spoken to him herself. He had resigned his hope of marriage without complaint, but in recent months the Queen kept hinting that 'someone in the family might marry an English lady with a great deal of money', and this was driving him into a frenzy. He worked himself up into believing that his mother might use his dependence to push him into marriage; if he married, Parliament would certainly vote him an income, and the bride herself would have money. But having given up the girl he loved, he was not about to accept another for so cynical a reason. 'I've no wish to be tied to a cat as yet for some time,' he told Collins, in a state of high excitement. 'I know well enough by experience how infernal it is to have anything to do with women.'[2]

It was all nonsense, but the strong language shows his state of mind. Opposition in Parliament to grants of money for the royal family *had* made the Queen think about royal finances. The girl in question was Frances Maynard, a fatherless twelve-year-old whose grandfather died in 1865 leaving her a considerable fortune – the rest of the family were so outraged that they threw butter pats at his portrait when the will was read. The Queen may have been giving vague thought to Miss Maynard as a bride for one of her younger sons, when the child was older. There would be a political advantage: Lord Lorne was a Liberal MP, the son of a Liberal peer, and some had seen unacceptable bias in Princess Louise's marriage. Miss Maynard was the step-daughter of Lord Rosslyn, a Conservative peer. But the possibility was far off, and the Queen was probably thinking as much of Arthur as she was of Leopold; marriage had never been one of her favoured options for him.

That New Year at Osborne was unusually quiet, with no family party. Leopold complained to his sister that there was 'no Xmas tree for the School children to-morrow, on account of the bad behaviour of all the people here last spring' – goodness knows what they had done.[3] Collins went on leave just after Christmas, and the Prince was left to stew in his problems alone, immersing himself in George Eliot's new novel *Middlemarch* to take his mind off things – 'I'm in the middle of [the] 4th volume, there are 8 of them.'[4]

For Christmas, Princess Alice sent him a bust of little Fritzie, and his heart went out to her: 'you could not have given me anything which I should have liked better, or more prized & valued. It is such a dear, sweet & innocent little countenance, that I cannot help saying to myself that it is perhaps well that the dear child has been spared all the trials & possibly miseries of a life of ill health like mine. . . . Oh dear Alice, I know too well what it is to suffer as he would have suffered, & the great trial of not being able to enjoy life, or to know what happiness is, like others.'[5] His anger had passed, leaving only deep depression.

Leopold was fortunate in his friends. Ruskin visited him several times in December and listened patiently. In January Acland went to Osborne; he was in regular contact with Ruskin so he may have had some idea of what was happening, and he had already been in touch with the Prince of Wales about a plan for Leopold's future which would keep him at Oxford after his studies ended, or enable him to make regular visits.[6] But Collins was the best friend of all. Loyally, he kept urging the Queen to clear up the uncertainty about her son's future, even though this put his own position at risk. He coped with Leopold's anger and unhappiness, and tried to offer good advice. Sometimes he touched a nerve. A guest at Wykeham House the previous term had told him there had been gambling. Collins suggested that this was not a good idea, and Leopold nearly exploded. Denying the story, he took refuge in pointed sarcasm: 'if you wish me to give up playing cards at Oxford, I shall as a matter of course submit; I fear we could not manage to get a billiard table into Wykeham House, but we might have readings in the evenings out of some nice books, say the Bible.'[7] The phrase 'you sound just like my mother' does not appear in the letter, but the sentiment is there.

When Collins came close to giving up, it was Ruskin who offered encouragement. An undated note which appears to relate to this time assures Collins 'that the office of a prince's tutor is quite one of the most honourable in the world – by whatever formalities discomforted or hindered. I quite truly and simply have always considered you are in a higher duty than mine; – more difficult, and requiring more various skill and power.'[8] At this stage it was an uphill struggle, because for all Collins' urging, the only issue the Queen would discuss was the sacrament, and she had lost faith in him and decided to hand the entire correspondence on the subject to Duckworth. She intended to tell him that she was sure Louise was behind the trouble.

One Sunday morning in early January, Duckworth took the service in Osborne House, and afterwards walked in the grounds with Leopold. Later the Queen sent for him to tell him about their differences, and gave him the correspondence. Evidently Leopold had said nothing; Duckworth was surprised, and promised to speak to him, but he assured the Queen that Leopold would not be acting out of a desire to hurt. He also spoke up for Louise, and faced the Queen with a stronger warning than anyone had yet dared to issue: 'desirable though it is that he should give the utmost weight to Your Majesty's earnest wishes and strong convictions, Your Majesty is far too wise and tolerant, and too well aware of the worthlessness – nay, the <u>immorality</u> of a religious act which is not <u>done from the heart</u> and from a <u>sense of duty towards GOD</u>, to put strong pressure upon anybody, however near and dear, whose feelings on a matter of such sacred moment differ from Your Majesty's own.' He suggested that the Queen should leave well alone, only assuring her son 'that he has still Your Majesty's undiminished love and confidence'.[9]

The argument niggled on for weeks. The Queen accused Leopold of an '<u>inclination to obstinacy</u>', but it was a quality they shared in full measure, as all those around them could attest.[10] By the time he returned to Oxford, at or near the beginning of term, they had reached a kind of truce, and in his luggage Leopold carried various commissions from his mother.

He arrived in time to share an important event in the life of the Liddell family. On Saturday 7 February, Lorina married William Baillie Skene, a Fellow of All Souls, at Christ Church. On a fine morning, bright with frost, she left the Deanery on her father's arm to walk to the Cathedral, passing through a line of small girls with flowers. The short route was marked with a red carpet, and the bride was followed by her sisters, her brothers, and other relatives, with Leopold, who walked in the family procession supporting her great-aunt on his arm. His gift to the couple was a silver enamel wall mirror with four matching candlesticks.

He was in his element again, and did not want to waste a moment. In a speech he made at the Birkbeck Institution five years later, he described the importance of knowledge gained at some cost, and there was more personal experience behind his remarks than his audience could possibly have guessed: 'many have known what it is', he said, 'to labour against the grain – to begin a lesson when they would rather have gone to a theatre; to finish it when they would rather have gone to bed; and such efforts of self-denial and conscientiousness form at least one-half of the benefit of education. It is a great benefit to fight for knowledge, to suffer for her, and to make her our own.'[11] He had fought, and suffered, to be at Oxford, and not only against his mother's opposition. In the spring of 1874 he had almost continual pain in his joints, particularly his knee, but was determined not to let it hold him back.

His studies centred now on political economy, history and languages, but he attended many special lectures, followed courses on geology and physiology, and had private music lessons at Wykeham House. Sometimes Dr Acland took parties of undergraduates into the villages to look for ways of improving the methods of sanitation used in the countryside, and Leopold went with them, following an interest which had been important to his father.

He loved Oxford, and Oxford was coming to love him, for the gentleness and consideration, the eagerness to learn and to be involved, which he showed everywhere he went. He didn't expect to be treated as a prince. A deep gulf was opening between Leopold as the Queen saw him – since their first clash over the sacrament she had called him spoilt, irritable and selfish – and the Leopold Oxford knew. Apart from his work, which he took very seriously – he was thinking of trying for a scholarship – he belonged to many of the university's clubs and societies. Christ Church's prestigious Loder's Club elected him a member almost immediately on the strength of his title, but that was only the beginning. In February 1874 he was elected to membership of the University Chess Club, because he was often seen playing chess in the coffee room at the Union. He attended debates, belonged to the Bullingdon Cricket Club (in a supportive role, as the game itself was far too dangerous), and was a founder member of the University Musical Club.

Leopold wrote to Louise from the Musical Club one evening in February, passing on a letter from the Queen: 'at this moment', he told her, 'there is a delightful trio being played by some friends of mine, on two violins & a violin-cello; we are of course <u>all</u> amateurs, & <u>nearly</u> all of us are undergraduates. We only allow strict & good music. It is like any ordinary club, only that once-a-week we meet for musical performance, & to-night is one of them. I write from here as I have so very little time in the day for correspondence, as I am <u>really</u> working <u>hard</u> this term.'12

Ruskin did not give any lectures in the spring of 1874, but he did attend a dinner party at Wykeham House, when Leopold and Collins introduced him to Frederic Myers, who was staying with them. Max Müller was there too, and there was another guest at the table, the painter William Blake Richmond. It was an awkward occasion for Leopold because the Queen had told him to return the artist's new portrait of the Princess of Wales and ask for a number of changes, but he liked the painting, and was terrified of giving offence. 'I pointed out to him <u>some</u> of the things wh Mamma w^d like to have altered', he told Louise, '& he was very nice about it, & said that he would do what he c^d; I c^d <u>not</u> say <u>all</u> that Mamma wished changed, as if I had done so I w^d have made a fool of myself, as she wanted to ruin it altogether.'[13] But Ruskin, sitting in apparently respectful silence, was really holding his tongue in horror. 'I didn't like the portrait', he later told Collins, 'and would have told the Prince exactly what I thought, by ourselves – but didn't like, among all those strangers.'[14]

He became more talkative later, when he and Müller, Myers, Leopold and Collins were left, discussing the deep questions which seem more real late at night. At the turn of the year, Myers remembered the evening and wrote to Collins. 'That long conversation with him & Ruskin on the next world was the only occasion in my life when I have found thorough sympathy in my own intense interest in the existence which awaits us, and which must in reality so utterly overbalance this mere fragment of life wch we have here – and the sight of the Prince's look of brave patience & Ruskin's look of yearning melancholy made me feel as if they two typified to me all that the world contains of dignity, delicacy and sadness.'[15] It was one of many similar conversations which Collins would remember even longer. Early in 1900 he wrote to Müller, 'Dear Old Ruskin has passed away. I remember so well you & he being together once at Prince Leopold's bedside, & I think F. Myers was also there, & some very interesting converse took place. Alas! For the days that can never return. They have a charm & an attractiveness to me that the present days sadly lack.'[16]

Good conversation was one of Oxford's delights, and Leopold and Collins found themselves increasingly drawn to the Rectory at Lincoln College; the attraction was not the Rector, Mark Pattison, a dry and profoundly glum intellectual who gave little outward sign of personality, but his wife Emilia. Almost thirty years younger than her husband, she was an acknowledged expert on French painting, fluent in four languages, who contributed articles to several journals; an attractive woman whose glamorous fashions, smoking, and support for women's suffrage, cut a striking figure. With Leopold she discussed poetry and art, played piano duets, and argued endlessly about politics; his bugbear, Sir Charles Dilke, was a close friend of hers, and after her husband's death she married him. George Eliot was another friend, and it is curious to wonder if Leopold knew, as he ploughed through the eight volumes of *Middlemarch*, that the characters of Dorothea Brooke and Mr Casaubon were supposed to have been based on Emilia and Mark Pattison.

Friendship with Emilia probably sparked his interest in the suffragist Josephine Butler, who visited Oxford in the spring of 1874; he told Louise that he was hoping to meet her: 'she is by many people considered the most beautiful woman in the world, & she is very clever & a great speaker', he wrote, apparently unaware that his sister was in touch with her already.[17] In the spring of 1868, the Crown Princess wrote to her on Louise's behalf, to offer her sister's support; since then, Louise had written herself, and watched Mrs Butler's work with growing interest.[18] Leopold approved generally of Mrs Butler's campaign for female suffrage and education, but her more recent cause, the welfare of prostitutes and the repeal of the Contagious Diseases Act, which condemned women in the ports and military towns to compulsory medical examination, was viewed by him with prim disapproval. He said it was 'a subject which had better be left alone, by ladies at any rate'.[19]

From a distance, the Queen kept him supplied with letters to write, which he accepted willingly. Her orders and complaints were another matter, and at the beginning of March it seems likely that he was finally told of her intentions regarding his allowance. Nothing else could have made him quite so despondent as he was when he wrote to Stirling: 'The shell which I told you was going to burst, has now done so, & I am on the <u>very worst</u> of terms at head-quarters. . . . I shall in a month be of age; but what then? I shall be still a miserable slave without a farthing! Don't think that I am always like this, but I have of late been goaded by savage letters & messages, & to-day I have been driven almost to extremities.' It was a very long letter, in which he complained bitterly of his mother's unkindness, and of the ill-treatment he received in a 'home' he was longing to leave.[20]

Fortunately the mood, if not the cause of it, passed; Arthur spent a weekend at Wykeham House, and together the brothers went around Oxford, attended Sunday services, visited the races, and were entertained at the Deanery. Leopold was much calmer when he returned to Windsor on 7 March, to meet his new sister-in-law, Alfred's wife Marie Alexandrovna, daughter of Tsar Alexander II of Russia. He was looking forward to the reunion with Louise too, and if he felt some trepidation about seeing his mother, he could at least be sure there would be other people in the room. Marie he took to instantly: 'all that you told me about her last winter is so true', he told Princess Alice. 'She gets on remarkably well with Mamma; I wish I could say the same of her husband!'[21] In time, Marie would become very fond of him too. His visit home was painless, and he was soon back in Oxford planning to receive Stirling at Wykeham House, and hoping to go to London to see his brother and sister-in-law's grand entry to the city, and perhaps fit in a play.

On 7 April 1874, Leopold came of age, and he celebrated his birthday at Osborne. It was a beautiful, sunny day; the band of the 102nd Regiment played during lunch, and there was a concert in the evening. His one regret was that so few of the family were present, with only Beatrice and the Queen and three friends to help him celebrate. The Queen was uneasy, because she believed that at twenty-one all young men become foolish and unmanageable, but she did appear to be relenting on the question of his allowance: 'As yet he has no allowance from Parliament', she told Louise, 'and I don't know if that will be proposed soon. We must see.'[22] For his birthday she gave him a pair of hand-coloured photographs of little Fritzie of Hesse in a double frame, and he wrote to Princess Alice to tell her how much pleasure they gave him. 'My money affairs are still very unsettled', he told her, 'but I look forward at present with more hope to their being settled to my satisfaction.'[23]

Collins now became Leopold's private secretary, and the Prince gained an equerry, the Hon. Alexander 'Alick' Yorke. 'I believe he does nothing manly which was his chief recommendation with the Queen', Ponsonby told his wife. '. . . He detests shooting hunting games and smoking – but is devoted to music.'[24] And at last, after nine years, the hated Archie Brown was moved to another position. Leopold had made his feelings known, and the Queen, who would always say that he had been unkind to Archie, found a new man. Leopold's reaction was hilarious: 'Eliza has found a servant for me, a <u>good one</u>! An <u>Englishman</u>!!! Oh Ye Gods! What a marvel!'[25] He visited Covent Garden before returning to Oxford, and had just arrived at Wykeham House when he unwittingly stepped into a minefield.

It all seemed so innocent. The Oxford Lodge of Freemasons invited him to join and he accepted cheerfully, because his elder brothers already belonged. There was no deliberate defiance in this; he continued to refer other invitations to the Queen through Collins, but placed this on a par with the Chess Club or the Musical Club. Writing to arrange his next weekend home, when he was to go to a reception at Buckingham Palace and perhaps visit the opera, he made a casual mention of the Freemasons, and the letter brought an instant rebuke from the Queen to Collins with a frenzy of underlining. It was Collins' job, she said, to advise Leopold: 'the Prince Consort <u>never</u> took <u>any</u> step <u>without consulting the Queen</u> – (who naturally <u>looked on him</u> as Her <u>Superior in everything</u>) – or his P.Sec^y & Treasurer, even when he was double P^{ce} Leopold's age.' She wrote to Leopold in the same vein, adding pointedly that she would be out when he came home.[26]

But this was not all. Sir Thomas Biddulph was told to write to Leopold, and to inform the Prince of Wales, instructing the Prince to supervise the London visit and prevent Leopold from going out in public. Colonel Elphinstone was sent to talk to Leopold; he did, and assured the Queen that, at worst, her son had been thoughtless. Leopold apologised, and Collins tried to defend himself: 'the Prince does to a great extent consult him, & of course, if it came to Mr Collins knowledge, that the Prince contemplated any positively wrong or harmful action, he would take extraordinary measures to save him from any such step.' Once again, he reminded her that Leopold was more determined to assert his independence because the question of his income was still unresolved.[27]

Next, Elphinstone was sent to Wykeham House to observe Leopold and Collins. Since the days when he had been Leopold's governor, Elphinstone had never liked the Prince particularly, agreeing with the Queen's assessment that he was spoilt and demanding. Now he spent several days at Wykeham House, and although he still said that Leopold's illness had made him too used to having his own way, he praised the 'quiet steady life' at Wykeham House, and spoke up for Collins.[28]

At the centre of yet another storm, Leopold probably felt he had nothing to lose, and he wrote to his mother appealing for permission to stay at Oxford until the end of term: 'I hope you will not think me unreasonable when I say that I am <u>most anxious</u> not to have my studies here entirely interrupted by going with you to Balmoral for the rest of the Term . . . my lectures this term are very interesting, & if they are cut off in the middle, they will lose more than half of their good.'[29] Twice in one day, the Queen turned to the Dean of Windsor, first with the business about the Freemasons, then with this new request, and the Dean suggested that it would be best to put the whole thing behind her and allow Leopold to stay on at Oxford, asking Dean Liddell for a report on his studies. She took the advice, after first referring everything, including her reply to Leopold, to Dr Jenner.

But only days later, at Wykeham House, Leopold was taken ill, with agonising pains in the back and legs which the newspapers reported as sciatica. Dr Acland attended him and Jenner visited; Arthur visited too, and Dr Legg was asked to stay at Wykeham House and support Collins. Acland's daughter sent Leopold her own special chair, but he was concerned because he knew she used it herself in the mornings, so he returned it, through Collins, asking permission to borrow it in the afternoons only.

Far away at Balmoral, the Queen believed that she had noticed something important about Leopold's attacks. 'It is very strange', she told Collins, 'that each time the poor Boy gets so obstinate & unamiable he is struck down by illness! She thinks that it <u>is</u> his bad health wch causes this & we must therefore make <u>every</u> allowance for it.' This was meant in kindness, but it became one of the hardest arguments to counter. If there was a connection between Leopold's state of mind and his attacks, it was the reverse of the Queen's theory. The tension of family arguments could have increased the severity of his bleeding attacks. They could have taken his mind off what he was doing, and so caused accidents. They could have been cause, they were not effect, but in future he would often face a brick wall of sympathy when he had a legitimate grievance, and his frustration was increased tenfold.

But the Queen really did mean to help, and she wanted Collins to keep her in touch with all the details. 'What does he read? The Queen hopes not merely exciting novels wch is <u>very very</u> bad for him. She sent 2 <u>most</u> amusing & delightfully written books wch she strongly recommends.'[30] Quietly, she made another, more generous gesture. On 16 June she sent a confidential note about Leopold to Disraeli, the new Prime Minister, and in mid-July her son's annuity was finally passed. She was still anxious, wanting to see the terms of the proposal before it was put to Parliament, and she asked Disraeli to write expressing his hope that Leopold would save some of his income, but the step was taken, and she did not withdraw it.[31]

Leopold still could not walk, but it was Commemoration Week in Oxford, when the University celebrates the end of the academic year. He had never seen Commemoration before and did not want to miss it, and he invited Dr Poore to stay. The doctor arrived shortly after the degree ceremony, but in time for 'a Fête in the grounds of Worcester College which was most enjoyable. P Leopold . . . went in a Bath Chair', Poore told his friend Beck, '& then sat in some rooms overlooking the festivities.' They returned to Wykeham House for dinner and music, and then Leopold was carried to bed while his guests went to the University Ball.[32]

Before the month was over, he was taken to Windsor, from where he wrote to Dr Acland to thank him for his care: 'It was most kind of you to think of so many little comforts, which you lent me, & which do so much towards alleviating the sufferings of an invalid.'[33] He was happy: Princess Alice had written with a very special request, and on 29 June he replied: 'Of course I <u>shall</u> be delighted to stand Godfather to the infant [her fifth daughter], & to feel again that I have a share in one of your Children. I <u>thought</u> of you a great deal, dear Alice, during all those sad anniversaries.' He told her that he could stand again, but not walk, and was feeling very well.[34]

But his problems were only just beginning. On 14 July he was taken to Osborne with the Queen, and shortly after arriving he tried to stand and slipped, hitting his knee. The joint began to swell. Two days later the swelling had spread to the thigh, with intense pain, and Dr Marshall telegraphed Dr Jenner to ask if he should give morphine. By 21 July Leopold was on regular doses of morphine, and delirious. His temperature was over 103°, and the doctors were worried by a red flush appearing on the affected thigh. Their anxiety continued for days, and in London it was even reported that Leopold was dead. Not until 11 August was Marshall able to declare that his temperature was normal, and the doses of morphine reduced, though not withdrawn altogether.

Mentally, Leopold sank into the profound depression which always came on when he was bedridden; he had hated dependence and lived in dread of its becoming permanent. On 19 August the Queen set off for Balmoral with him, and she was so worried by his mental state that she gave orders that stations where the royal train would stop should be cleared of people. Ponsonby was told to insert a brief paragraph about this into the newspapers, and to explain to the Prince of Wales 'that it w^d have been impossible & most unpleasant & painful for P^ce Leop^d to be lifted out of the railway Carriage into his <u>own</u> – <u>before the public</u>'.[35]

The recovery would be slow. Towards the end of August Emilia Pattison asked after Leopold, and Collins told her that it would be some time before he could use his legs, 'so deplorably weak & wasted are they'. There was little he could do for entertainment: 'the only music he can do at present is an attempt at a concertina,' Collins wrote. 'I also join in making horrid sounds on that instrument.' They both looked back fondly to Oxford, where their life was less restricted.[36]

Another week or so would pass before Leopold found movement returning to his injured knee, though it still hurt; his old, mischievous humour was returning too, alternating with fits of anger – a sure sign that he was feeling better. He had a new puppy which he wickedly named 'Vic', and she was busily tearing up everything in sight. But he had to bottle his anger, he said, because Collins had left, and Alick Yorke was just learning his job: 'I might swear & curse to my heart's content if old B was here.'[37] Dr Jenner never left his side, on the Queen's orders, and he found the attention oppressive; he was sure Yorke would feel that he was not trusted. 'Yorky & Jenner don't get on very well', he told Collins, 'the latter keeps such an eye on Yorke that everybody at the table remarks it.'[38] He was annoyed to hear from Sir Thomas Biddulph that the Queen had approved a salary for Collins which was far lower than he thought right – £200 a year from her, and £500 from himself, but this, at least, he could remedy: 'I will give you <u>apparently</u> £500 only; so that you will <u>apparently</u> only get £700-a-year; but I shall give you <u>besides</u> £300-a-year so as to make up the £1000, which I swore you sh^d have.'[39]

His impatience to be up and in control of his own affairs was growing. Early in September he heard from Mrs Liddell and Rhoda – it was at this time that news reached him of Aubrey Harcourt's feelings for Edith – and his longing for Oxford grew. He never liked Balmoral much, but in the autumn of 1874 it showed its most unfriendly face, with constant rain, wind and cold, which he felt all the more intensely because he was immobile. At the end of September Jenner encouraged him to try to walk, supported on both sides, but the experiment was a disaster. His right leg, which was still slightly bent, began to swell, and he was forced back to the sofa.[40] He began to feel that he might be there for ever.

Weeks passed, and by 23 October Leopold was finally thought well enough to leave for Oxford, though he still could not walk, and would not be able to attend lectures. The Queen told Dr Acland by letter that she wanted him to be very firm, and to make sure that Leopold did not try to stand again. She asked for regular reports, and was concerned to hear, a week later, that her son had a headache; still, there seemed no real reason to worry, and she let Collins know that she hoped Leopold would attend the christening of Alfred's baby son in Buckingham Palace. It was a grand occasion, in the presence of the baby's other grandmother, the Tsaritsa of Russia, but Leopold could not face it. He was bleeding internally, and by mid-November the newspapers were again discussing his illness. He invited Dr Poore for a weekend, and when Poore arrived to find Leopold ill, and Dr Acland also bedridden, he moved into Wykeham House and took charge himself.

There was no anxiety; the Queen was offended that Leopold had not attended the christening, and told Collins that people asked after him; she felt ashamed to say that he did not want to be at home. She had heard of a woman who died after falling into the fire during a fit and was careful to pass on the details as a salutary reminder.[41] This appeared to wash over Leopold; his mind was on the news that Stirling hoped to be engaged: 'You can fancy my delight at the contents of your letter of yesterday', he wrote. 'Do be quick and let me know who is the lucky fair one, whom you are going to make happy.'[42] There were lots of visitors to Wykeham House; regulars like Ruskin and Müller, and some new faces. 'One night Gladstone's youngest son came to dinner', Poore told his mother, '& this afternoon we have been visited by Bishop Colenso . . . Professor Jowett the author of one of the Essays & Reviews & Professor Martineau. It is very delightful to see all these men.'[43]

But Leopold's illness was more serious than anyone realised. Surrounded by friends, he was smiling and chatting to conceal an overwhelming sense of exhaustion. On 8 December, he confided in Lady Caroline, 'I feel no elasticity or wish to exert my self in any way; I should be quite content to remain here alone over Christmas, as I feel as if all capacity for enjoyment had left me.' Drained of his usual energy, his mind slipped back towards the affections of childhood: 'Whenever I live under the Queen's roof now, I miss dear Louise so very much, much more so than formerly, & home (if there is such a place) is so dreadfully changed.'[44] He had typhoid. The year that began with 'the great struggle' for independence would end with a struggle for life itself.

Term ended in mid-December and Leopold returned home, then accompanied his mother to Osborne. He was still in a wheelchair but seemed lively, and Ponsonby remarked on his antics one evening 'wheeling about in a most profligate manner after the maids of honour Old Car delighting in his larks and pretending they were amorous advances'.[45] But then it was said that he had a cold, and soon the seriousness of his illness became apparent; the Queen watched over him anxiously, and Arthur left Osborne, as it was thought necessary to keep the house quiet. The Prince of Wales was told, and on 28 December the Queen sent the news to Louise: 'You shall hear daily, after you get this letter, as I know how anxious you will be and how much you will feel for ME.'[46] But Louise already knew, from Collins, who was keeping in touch quietly with all the people who mattered to Leopold. He knew how much the Prince wanted to see his sister, and had told the Queen this; he was dismayed that Louise was not summoned. In the first week of January, the Queen wrote to Louise to say that the doctors thought the danger had passed.

One of the earliest photographs of Leopold, taken at Buckingham Palace on 1 April 1857, a few days before his fourth birthday (The Royal Archives © Her Majesty The Queen)

Queen Victoria and Prince Albert on the terrace at Osborne, 26 July 1859 (Private Collection)

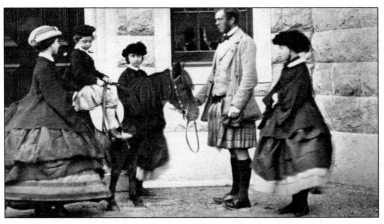

Leopold riding Topsy the pony on his first visit to Balmoral in August 1860, with John Brown holding the bridle. Princess Alice is standing beside Leopold, Princess Louise in the centre, and Princess Helena on the right (The Royal Archives © Her Majesty The Queen)

The reunion at Coburg – Queen Victoria's nine children at the Rosenau, August 1865: l to r, Leopold, Louise, Beatrice, Alice, the Prince of Wales, Arthur (sitting on the ground), the Crown Princess, Alfred, Helena (Private Collection)

Leopold with the Queen at Osborne shortly after his return from Cannes, on 15 April 1862 – the photograph was taken by Prince Alfred (The Royal Archives © Her Majesty The Queen)

Leopold and Louise, in about 1866 (Private Collection)

Leopold at Balmoral with (l to r) the Reverend Robinson Duckworth, unknown gentleman, probably Herr Sahl, Robert Hawthorn Collins, and Waldmann the dog, c. 1867 (The Royal Archives © Her Majesty The Queen)

Prince Leopold, 27 March 1871 (Private Collection)

Edith (left), Alice (standing) and Lorina Liddell, 1872–3 (The Governing Body, Christ Church/Mrs M.J. St Clair)

Leopold at Oxford, photographed by the Reverend C.L. Dodgson (Lewis Carroll), 2 June 1875 (Private Collection)

Leopold's first real love, Lady Breadalbane (Private Collection)

Princess Frederica of Hanover, whom Leopold wanted to marry in 1878; she remained one of his closest friends (Private Collection)

Princess Alice, Grand Duchess of Hesse (Private Collection)

The Hesse children, c. 1876:
l to r, Irene; Ernst Ludwig ('Ernie');
Leopold's godchild Marie sitting on
the knee of her sister Victoria; Alix;
Elisabeth ('Ella') (Private
Collection)

'Fritzie', Prince Frederick Wilhelm of
Hesse, Leopold's haemophilic godson,
taken in England in November 1871
(Private Collection)

The Prince's mentor and friend, John Ruskin (Private Collection)

Princess Alice's husband, Leopold's closest confidant, Grand Duke Louis IV of Hesse (Private Collection)

Leopold at Claremont, 1881 (The Royal Archives © Her Majesty The Queen)

Leopold with Princess Helen of Waldeck; one of the engagement photographs taken in Arolsen (Private Collection)

Leopold and Helen with baby Alice, 30 July 1883 (Private Collection)

The newly married Duke and Duchess of Albany on their visit to Boyton Manor in July 1882, with Mrs Fenwick (on the right) (Mr Robert Golden)

The son he would never see. Helen in 1885 with her children, Alice and baby Charles Edward, 2nd Duke of Albany (Private Collection)

They were wrong. Soon after the letter was written, Leopold began to bleed. Collins wrote to Stirling on 20 January: 'The Prince is most dangerously ill – Heaven grant he may recover, but Jenner thinks very badly of him indeed – When the fever had apparently left him, he was attacked by haemorrhage from the bowels – a concomitant of the fever that it was hoped he had escaped. It is very sad.'[47] He told Myers that when Leopold saw the blood he expected to die, and made him promise to send for Louise; still, the Queen delayed until 18 January, when she sent a telegram. This was followed by a letter from Beatrice, warning that the Queen did not want Lord Lorne to stay in the house for more than one night; if he did, the Princes would want to come, and their mother could not cope with them.

Anxiety made the Queen possessive. For years she had longed to be close to Leopold. Now, as she sat by what might be his deathbed, she did not want to share him with anyone. Louise was only supposed to sit with her brother for an hour, twice a day, but it was a rule Collins and the doctor had no thought of enforcing: the difference she made was obvious. She was critical of the way her brother's case had been handled, as she had been before, but on 23 January she wrote to her brother-in-law in Scotland, 'I am a good deal with my poor brother, he still looks very ill, but is gaining strength daily, and can now eat more. He takes interest in all that goes on and likes being read to.'[48] She sent news of his recovery to Dr Acland too, adding, 'He is wonderfully good & patient, it goes to ones heart to see him, & he is on the whole very cheerful, he asked me to show him how to make some comforters, which has been a little occupation to him.'[49] But a few days after this letter was written, Louise had to leave. 'The Queen was I think waxing jealous', Collins told Myers, 'at any rate she wouldn't let her tarry longer.'[50]

TEN

LEAVING WONDERLAND

The news that Leopold was near death produced an extraordinary reaction. As Collins nursed him, he was almost overwhelmed by letters of encouragement. Some came from colleagues in the Household, like the Reverend Dalton, tutor to the young Wales Princes, who was well placed to understand what he was going through. 'I cannot refrain from writing one or two lines', Dalton said, '. . . though the silent pressure of a friend's hand in real distress is almost all one can give, & often in truth preferable to many words. . . . One goes to bed thinking of him & of you, & one rises again with the same thought of you both first on one's mind.'[1] But above all, the letters came from the dons of Oxford, and they spoke of the tenderness, even love, they had come to feel for Leopold during his time in residence.

Today, it is a difficult body of evidence to evaluate. Much of it sounds overstated. Popular books and journals of the nineteenth century heaped glowing praise on the most mediocre of princes, particularly if they died young, but these letters were not written for public consumption. They were not produced by loyal subjects trying to please the Queen. They were private letters to Collins from men he knew well, many of whom would have scorned the idea of being adoring to royalty, sharing Myers's first reaction: 'it is not the flunkeys that appal me, many & scarlet tho' they be – but one has such an intense horror of appearing to thrust oneself in amongst exalted beings.'[2] Some sounded almost embarrassed by what they were trying to put into words, yet impelled to try, before it was too late.

So, for example, Bonamy Price, Professor of Political Economy: 'Love, if it be not presumptuous to say so is the real honest feeling. . . . Never have I seen, in my experience, so much simplicity and kindness, so much grace and refinement, so much tenderness of feeling and gentleness . . . [combined] with such a large amount of intelligence.' Or Sydney Owen, Historical Lecturer at Christ Church: 'Never have I seen one impatient movement, or heard one hasty or harsh word, though he often was evidently in much pain. While his kindness, considerateness of the most delicate and comprehensive kind, his sprightliness – amid all his weakness and illness – and the ready interest with which he followed up any suggestion I threw out, made the hours we spent together most enjoyable and – in spite of the difference of station – made me deeply attached to him as a man – or rather a <u>boy</u>. For there is, in spite of the maturity of manner and taste, a . . . boyish freshness about him that is <u>most</u> attractive.'[3]

This was the best of Leopold. There were other sides to him, of course, but people were usually attracted to him. Contained within these loving testimonials there is also a glimpse of the man he might have been – certainly of the man Oxford hoped he would be, for these are the voices of the men Collins called the 'inner circle', who were encouraging the Prince to look for positive ways of using his rank, and would continue to watch his career and cheer him on. Several wrote of his potential for the future: Owen was one. So was the Reverend Mandell Creighton, Fellow of Merton: 'There was work for him yet in life: it is not easy to be reconciled even to the prospect of loss.'[4]

But by some miracle, they had not lost him. Perhaps it was the quality none of them noticed, the intense strength of will inherited from his mother, which carried Leopold through. By 20 February he was well enough to write himself to Dr Acland, quite cheerfully, thanking him for an amusing letter, and sending 'kindest remembrances to Mrs & Miss Acland, as well as to the Liddells, & trusting that you will excuse my shaky handwriting'.[5] He anticipated returning to Windsor during the next week.

The next day he had a fit. It was not a bad one, but he was holding a pair of scissors which cut the fingers of his right hand before Alick Yorke could prise them away. At first, it seemed that pressure had stopped the bleeding and the Queen, still shaken, wrote to Louise, 'It is awful to think of what he might not do! I hope and think this will be a lesson to him.'[6] But within hours the bleeding began again, and the wounds had to be cauterised by burning, an agonising solution inflicting terrible pain and weeks of incapacity while the hand healed. Undaunted, Leopold still insisted on his right to return to Oxford. Pain was a fact of life which he accepted, but against dependence and control he would fight as long as he lived.

The Queen may have tried to make Dr Jenner forbid his return: on 18 March Sir Henry Ponsonby told his wife, 'Jenner is in a blue rage and came to see Bids [Sir Thomas Biddulph] frantic at a letter he had got directing him what opinion to give about Leo – and he says he wont.'[7] A few days after this she gave her consent, most unwillingly, stressing that Leopold must go to Balmoral for her birthday in May, and must now resign himself to being an invalid: 'you <u>owe it</u> to me & <u>to all</u> those about you, for the constant anxiety we are under, about you. It is not <u>yourself alone</u>, it is <u>every</u> one else – you owe it to.' He was told to dictate a reply to Beatrice or her governess, but he ignored this, writing himself and politely but firmly refusing Balmoral to make up for lost time.[8] He returned to Oxford as he had wished in mid-April, walking well but unable to climb stairs.

Oxford restored Leopold's spirits. 'I never saw him looking so well as when he gave me that kind smile across the choir of Christ Church', Ruskin told Collins.[9] Wykeham House had been redecorated in his absence, and he was delighted with it and threw himself back enthusiastically into university life. Knowing that, at best, he had only two terms left, he wanted to share Oxford with the people who mattered most to him. The Hesses were staying with the Queen, and he arranged for his three little nieces, Victoria, Elisabeth and Irene, to be sent to him by train for a day. At the end of the month their parents joined him for the ceremonies which marked the gift of Ruskin's art collection to the University. Leopold was to be chairman of the collection's trustees, who included Dean Liddell and Dr Acland, and Alice and Louis witnessed the signatures on the Deed of Gift.

Anticipating the pleasures of Commemoration in June, Leopold invited Louise and Lord Lorne for the week, to stay with the Liddells; Arthur would be staying at Wykeham House. Louisa, Lady Knightley, and her husband visited the Deanery at Whitsun, and on their first evening Leopold and Lord Brooke were among the dinner guests. 'It is charming to see him so well, able to walk about easily, and so much come out in every way', Louisa remarked.[10] She and her husband took Alice Liddell, 'a most fascinating girl, the original of *Alice in Wonderland*', to dinner at Wykeham House, and it was probably this summer that a boating trip to Iffley took place which Alice remembered years later; she accidentally gave Leopold a black eye with her oar, and he wondered how he would explain it to the Queen.[11]

Mentions of Alice Liddell raise again the idea of romance between her and Leopold. He loved her, as he loved all her family: his letters to Dr Acland often contained messages for 'the dear Liddells'. But talk of marriage with any of the sisters had ended in the autumn of 1873, and the mere fact that Alice was allowed to visit Wykeham House, chaperoned by the Knightleys, suggests that she was not Leopold's original choice. If she had been, her mother would surely not have allowed anything which could revive the attachment, knowing that it was hopeless. The river trip was probably a family outing, and it certainly would have been chaperoned.

May brought Leopold a first meeting with the man who had helped to inspire him with the dream of Oxford – and the world with the dream of *Alice*. After the Reverend Dodgson's contribution to his autograph album it may seem strange that the Prince had not sought him out sooner, but Dodgson was a shy man, and Leopold's identification with the Deanery at a time when he and the Liddells were not on good terms probably made the first approach difficult. At last, on 24 May, Dodgson sent a note to Collins asking if he might take the Prince's photograph, and he was rewarded with an invitation to lunch at Wykeham House. He was an honoured guest, seated next to Leopold at the table, and found the Prince 'particularly unassuming and genial in manner; I do not wonder at his being so universal a favourite'.[12]

Dodgson had some of his photographs with him and the Prince examined them after lunch, in a tent in the garden where the party had settled for coffee and cigars. The following week, Leopold visited Dodgson's rooms at Christ Church and spent an hour and a half there, having his photograph taken and looking through examples of Dodgson's photography, some of which he chose for himself. The tent in the garden of Wykeham House was a feature of the summer of 1875, remembered by a fellow undergraduate who described Leopold as 'always affable and unassuming and thoughtful for others; ready to show his photographs or pictures, or sing, or play the round game of cards which usually ended his dinner parties'.[13]

It meant a lot to Leopold to have his own house, but he knew he would have to leave in December 1875, when the Queen had said his Oxford career must end. He wanted a base in London but Collins, realising the arguments there would be if this was mentioned, suggested another idea, a country house which they might rent jointly. For some years Leopold had kept an amused eye on the progress of Collins' relationship with a Miss Wightwick. Now they were about to marry and could live in the house during Collins' leaves, when Leopold was with the Queen. By the end of May they had even found somewhere they liked: Boyton Manor, a Jacobean house under the Wiltshire downs. Leopold proposed the scheme to his mother, writing at the same time to Jenner and asking him to find a doctor prepared to travel with him when required. He wanted to be independent, but was sensible enough to recognise his need for medical help.

The Queen was horrified by the idea of Boyton. She agreed to let the scheme be tried, though she was frightened for Leopold and hurt that he wanted to leave her, and to Dr Jenner she confessed bitter disappointment in her son. She felt that she had done everything possible to make him comfortable at home, and could not see that he needed more: 'young men (who are odious) she thinks) seem not to be able to occupy themselves <u>at home</u>, by reading & writing, music (which he is so fond of) & as they ought to do, & ought to be so happy. If Prince Leopold has talked about this plan to Princess Alice or Prince Arthur or The Prince of Wales, The Queen will <u>never</u> forgive it.'[14]

Helplessly, Jenner, Collins, Ponsonby, and others in the Household watched the emotional temperature rise. They understood Leopold's need for freedom, but nothing they could do or say made any difference. 'Prince Leopold is wonderfully well', Jenner told Lady Ely, 'and cannot be regarded otherwise than as a man. He will not be driven.'[15] After the Oxford Commemoration, Leopold went to London to visit his sister Louise at Kensington Palace, intending to stay for a week to attend a State Ball and Concert. 'I don't see why he shouldn't', Ponsonby commented, but the Queen had not been asked and she was furious, lashing out not only at Leopold, but also at his sister for taking him in.[16]

At the same time, the outside world was starting to take an interest in the Queen's youngest son, and expecting him to be involved in its affairs. He was offered the Freedom of the City of London, and looked forward to a ceremony in the city. The Queen wanted it done privately at Windsor. Leopold tried to make his own arrangements with the authorities, but that was doomed to failure, as Ponsonby told his wife: 'the Queen telegraphed to the Ld Mayor to request that everything should go thro' her – of course the Ld Mayor – partly flattered partly frightened obeys implicitly. So Leopold is check mated. I have heard poor fellow that he has again got a bad knee. This really is most disheartening.'[17]

Leopold was allowed to go to London to be made a Younger Brother of Trinity House, but the Queen agreed to this unwillingly, reminding him that he was not to stand too long at the ceremony, and not to wear the Trinity House uniform instead of his Highland dress, or for important occasions; he was, in fact, to consult his mother on whatever he wore while he was under her roof.[18] This was an intolerable demand, and it set the tone for a very bad-tempered summer. At Osborne in August the Queen began to complain that Leopold was spending too much time with the Household when he ought to be with his younger sister. She sent Duckworth to speak to him, and composed a letter on the subject herself, warning that while there was no harm in the odd game of whist – one of Leopold's few amusements at home – he 'must not become the <u>ordinary daily intimate</u> at the <u>Hshld table</u> with the <u>Maids of Honour</u> & Equerries – nor spend the whole day with your gentlemen. . . . Beatrice is clever, & most amiable & I am sure in every family a Brother w^d like to be with his sister.'[19]

Leopold's trip to London in June had given her the chance to question his devotion to study, and she seized on this, suggesting to

Duckworth and others that the boy who had seemed so promising was turning into an idler, bent only on pleasure. After coming so close to death at the turn of the year, Leopold did want some fun, but the charge was patently unfair. All through the summer of 1875 he was writing privately to Ruskin, discussing future lectures, and taking an interest in Ruskin's Oxford School. He was as serious as he had ever been, but the knot of criticism tightening around him was beginning to tell on his nerves.

Crossing the Solent from Osborne in August, the royal yacht *Alberta* collided with a schooner and three people were drowned. When Leopold mentioned at dinner that he had been watching the schooner before the accident, the Queen pounced on him immediately, saying that he should have warned someone. But he had not foreseen the collision, and Ponsonby told his wife how disturbed Leopold was by the suggestion that he could have prevented the accident.[20] At Balmoral in September, he was kept busy writing letters, yet found himself continually under fire: he was too silent and unsociable, he was not polite, he didn't visit the tenants, he showed no respect for his mother, he quarrelled with Beatrice, he was wasting his time. Collins was not there to keep him calm, and his temper probably did give way, but when he left Balmoral to visit his sister at Inveraray under a cloud of family disapproval, Ponsonby commented: 'I did not perceive that he was ill tempered but suppose he must have got soured.'[21]

The complaints followed him. Duckworth had sent a rather stiff letter from Westminster on the Queen's instruction; this involvement of a friend whom he loved and trusted depressed Leopold, and he told Duckworth so, angrily denying the charges against him. He wrote to his mother from Inveraray in a very low spirit to say that he was sorry, but didn't understand why she was so angry: 'I have endeavoured to do my best to please you . . . & I really <u>cannot</u> find out what has happened to make you so annoyed with me. But as my company seems to be so distasteful & detestable to you, I beg to propose that instead of returning to Balmoral after my visit to Blythswood I should return South straight.'[22] The response was a long catalogue of his faults, and a demand that he should return to Balmoral by the end of the month to make amends.[23]

At least Collins was back. He joined Leopold at Inveraray and accompanied him to visit friends, the Campbells at Blythswood, near Paisley. Lord Brooke was there and several others, and when the Queen reacted to newspaper reports suggesting public welcomes and lavish entertainment, Collins was on hand to deflect her anger and assure her that the party was quiet.[24] They were still at Blythswood when the news reached Leopold that Stirling was engaged to Lady Clifden, one of his favourites among the Queen's ladies. He was delighted, but the Queen disapproved: she never liked her people to marry, and had never forgiven Stirling. When Leopold returned to Balmoral as ordered, her disparaging remarks about the wedding provoked him to retaliate, souring the atmosphere even further. He would have loved to accept Stirling's invitation to be best man, but felt he could not: 'I would have to <u>ask permission</u> to be "best man", to which I sh[d] receive a point blank refusal, which would only cause more bitterness.' It was a miserable letter to have to write, and he appealed to Stirling not to ask Arthur in his place, 'as it will make me so <u>horribly jealous</u>'.[25]

This was a tense and unhappy time. As Leopold went south in early October, accompanied by his new doctor, Arnold Royle, the Queen took measures to bring him into line. His every move was to be observed and discussed, and even Royle, whom he liked, was drawn into the web, reporting his activities to the Queen. The Dean of Windsor was told of Leopold's behaviour at Balmoral, and asked to contact Dean Liddell, to warn him and tell him to keep the Prince in order during the next term. Liddell was surprised. He knew of no problem, and the dons who taught Leopold had no complaints. He would watch the Prince, he said, 'But you will perceive that I cannot speak strongly unless I find some good ground to go upon, to which I can refer – I <u>cannot</u> take the report of the idleness at Balmoral as the foundation of my remarks.'[26]

So Leopold returned to Oxford, with a full programme of lectures prepared, and all eyes upon him. He worked hard, but his heart was not in it; all he could think of was the future. Life at home with his mother and sister, dogged by continual criticism, would be unbearable. The Prince of Wales had discussed his future with Collins, and invited his brother to serve on a literary committee, while Collins tried to introduce Leopold to people who gave their time to particular causes. He was taken to a temperance meeting, and became involved with the work of an Oxford vicar who ran a Sunday School for the city's most deprived boys; Leopold assured the boys that however poor they were, all were equal before God, and even the poor had a right to learn. He was being guided towards the public role which he would make his own. 'The Prince is sadly in want of some definite aims & serious views of life', Collins told the Queen, trying, with as much subtlety as he could muster, to bring her round to the idea that Leopold must have an existence outside the home.[27]

It was difficult, because when Leopold was not in favour, all his gentlemen came under suspicion. Alick Yorke was now thought too young and frivolous to attend Leopold alone, and Major Pickard, who normally attended Arthur, was brought in to add moral fibre to the small establishment. Collins knew that direct confrontation in these circumstances would be pointless; his only hope of success lay in telling the Queen what she expected to hear, angled in such a way as to guide her response. He told her that Leopold appeared to have no natural aptitude for study, but needed to be in a studious environment, with others to spur him on. He suggested that idleness or boredom would be disastrous. He sounded as if he agreed with the chorus of Leopold's critics; even so, his letters were being referred silently to the Dean of Windsor for comment, not only on Leopold, but on Collins himself.

But while others discussed him, Leopold was making his first steps towards a constructive public role. On 25 October he accepted the Freedom of the City of London, making a speech before 700 people at the Guildhall – not quite what the Queen had envisaged when she gave permission for a quiet and private ceremony in London. Ponsonby attended and was impressed with Leopold's performance, and a second speech, on the work of English designers, at the Oxford School of Science and Art, was praised in the press. Leopold was so intent on doing this well that he took elocution lessons beforehand.[28] He presented prizes at the Kensington Art School, but when a request came for him to open an infirmary the Queen refused, 'for he will also be asked to do every sort of thing, – people being now most indiscreet in expecting the Royal family to lay stones & open buildings &c &c on all occasions' – activity which she felt was particularly unsuitable for Leopold.[29] Collins' careful arguments had had little effect.

Term ended, and with it, Leopold's Oxford career. He took at least one exam, in modern languages, and passed creditably. He bought gifts for his teachers, and their response showed again how fond they were of him and how highly they regarded his abilities. Max Müller's thank-you letter was a six-page exploration of the importance of Sanskrit and Indian literature to European culture: 'I feel convinced that the true solution of many of our theological difficulties – difficulties which will become far more terrible than they are at present – is to be found in the study of the history of all religions . . .'. He would not have written in this way if he had not known that Leopold would understand and be interested, and his letter included the words 'Life is precious, and we must try to make the best use of it we can', which might have been a motto for the Prince's future.[30]

Leopold's first wish, now Oxford was behind him, was to travel – in particular to see Italy, which had been his dream ever since 1862, when he stood above the gorge at Napoule and glimpsed the country on the skyline. Collins prepared the ground in November by warning the Queen that the request was coming. On her orders, he tried to put Leopold off, and failed. Then he attempted to bring the Queen round by playing the health card: 'if one dissuaded him from going & he did happen to fall ill again this winter, the responsibility would be an unpleasant one.'[31] So the Queen did agree, but she made sure that Leopold knew how selfish she thought him, and imposed stringent conditions for the journey. He was to be accompanied by Dr Royle, and as Collins could not be available for the whole time, Major Pickard would go. Leopold was to take his hated wheelchair in case of need.[32]

Relations between mother and son could hardly have been worse. In February 1876 Leopold was installed as Provincial Grand Master of the Oxford Masonic Lodge in a ceremony in the Sheldonian Theatre, and, by a disastrous oversight, the Queen's first inkling of this was a newspaper report. She was furious about it; furious too to hear of alterations to Boyton, which suggested that her son was becoming more settled there than she intended. As the argument circled around him, Collins came close to losing his temper with his sovereign, and sent her a sixteen-sided letter in tiny, meticulous handwriting, defending the Prince, and himself, on every point. He was polite, but obviously angry, and it was left to Leopold to restore the peace, which for once he did with great success. Showing unusual self-control and perception, he abandoned argument and resorted to charm, delighting his mother with an unexpected gift.[33]

As the holiday drew near, he was in high spirits. He joined the Household one Tuesday evening after dinner, and persuaded the Duchess of Edinburgh's lady-in-waiting, Lady Mary Butler, to play the piano with him, and to sing all the Irish rebel songs she knew. 'I do like Prince Leopold', she confided to her diary afterwards, '. . . He is not goodlooking exactly, because he looks ill often, but he has a nice face, & is very intelligent, & at present he seems well enough. I do like his intense enjoyment of life & his pluck in face of his delicacy.'[34]

On 2 March, Leopold left England and made his way to Paris, to spend a few days with his godfather, the exiled King of Hanover. He was delighted with the welcome the Hanover family gave him, and very taken with the King's two daughters, particularly the younger, Princess Mary, who reminded him of his sister Louise. Passing through Cannes, he attempted to call on Queen Sophie of the Netherlands, whom he knew from her visits to England, but it was too early in the day: 'When a sick old woman is dressing she can neither hurry, nor keep a Royal Prince waiting: she therefore submitted to the real sorrow of missing your dear visit', she told him, inviting him to call again.[35]

By April the Prince was in Venice where an old friend of Ruskin, Rawdon Brown, acted as his guide. 'I cannot imagine anything more rapturous than the good old man's feelings', Ruskin told him, 'in being able to interest Your Royal Highness . . . or in having the pride of taking your Royal Highness first in to the Great Council Chamber of his beloved and reverenced State.'[36] In conversation with Brown, Leopold suggested that Ruskin should prepare a new edition of *The Stones of Venice*, and the suggestion was welcomed. Meanwhile, Ruskin called on the Prince's help in saving a collection of classical art for the nation. He had discovered that the authorities at the British Museum were packing various items to send to Philadelphia: 'quite priceless Greek marbles – quite marvellous Etruscan gold . . . just think of it, Sir; – here we spend half a million as if it were a handful of dust – to build an iron ship and sink her – and here is an entire history and substance of Greek art – offered us for forty thousand – and we send it to the Americans.'[37]

Collins joined Leopold in Venice, and in mid-May they went on to Milan. By June they were back in Paris, where the Prince heard that he was to receive the degree of DCL by diploma. He wrote gratefully to the Vice Chancellor, agreeing to be at Oxford for the ceremony on 21 June. Arrangements had been made for him to stay at the Deanery during Commemoration, and he arrived in Oxford on Friday 16 June, attending a Freemasons' meeting that evening, and a banquet at the Clarendon Hotel. In the next few days he heard concerts, watched a procession of boats on the Isis, promenaded in the Broadwalk and danced at the University Ball, and everywhere he went, Mrs Liddell and her daughters were with him.[38]

It should have been a very special week for the Liddells. Three days before Leopold's arrival, Edith finally became engaged to Aubrey Harcourt. There was to be an announcement during Commemoration week, but Edith was taken ill in church on Sunday and missed the festivities. Shortly after noon on the Wednesday, Leopold received his degree in the Sheldonian Theatre, wearing an academic gown over his Trinity House uniform and Garter ribbon. Everyone cheered and sang; it was a wonderful day for him, which ended with an evening ball at Christ Church; the next morning he left Oxford, with no idea of the tragedy to come. Edith had peritonitis. On the Sunday her condition worsened, and on Monday 26 June she died. 'It is horrible – happening at this very moment of their greatest joy', the Queen told Dean Stanley. 'Leopold, who had only just told me of the engagement which caused them so much happiness, is greatly distressed.'[39]

He was allowed to attend the funeral and played an unusually prominent part as one of the first pair of pallbearers, carrying the coffin from the Deanery to the west door of the Cathedral, then on, after the service, to the new family vault. With the other mourners, Leopold laid his own wreath of white roses and, as a last, fond gesture before leaving, he took the white flower from his button-hole and placed it on the coffin. 'Though the weather was as beautiful as in Commemoration week', he told the Reverend Creighton, 'an air of gloom pervaded the whole place; & as long as I live I shall never forget the sad ceremony at which I was present.'[40]

Was it any accident that only then, after Edith's engagement and death, did Leopold start thinking about marriage again, though he had no particular person in mind? He knew that only marriage would give him the independence he envied in his brothers. Sir Howard Elphinstone became engaged at the end of June and Leopold was curious: 'He wanted particularly to know what had especially attracted me towards you', Elphinstone told his fiancée.[41] Something Leopold said a few days later stung the Queen into issuing an emphatic reminder that he could do nothing without her consent: '<u>no nice</u> people or <u>any one whom I c^{ld} receive w^{ld} wish</u> their <u>daughter</u> or <u>Sister</u> to <u>become engaged to you, without my knowledge</u> or <u>permission</u> or <u>sanction</u>', she said, though this was one thing he was not likely to forget.[42]

The Queen had made it clear that her son's travels were over, and she expected his company; she was determined to keep him occupied at home. 'We must <u>try</u> to <u>find</u> something wch w^{ld} force him to work', she told Collins in May, when Leopold was offered the Presidency of the Royal Society of Literature.[43] It was a tragic indication of the lack of understanding between mother and son: both wanted the same thing for Leopold, even using the same words 'real work', but their meanings were poles apart. He was elected to the society's presidency in July, despite his mother's misgivings, and also became president of the new Royal Tapestry Manufactory in Old Windsor, a small-scale attempt to unite manufacture with the very best in art and design, which was close to the ideas Leopold had expressed in his Oxford speech. This was a cause to which he would devote endless effort, but still his mother saw outside appointments as an excuse to socialise: worthless and morally dangerous.

For five years, Leopold had cheerfully assisted her with her private correspondence. It was varied and interesting work, bringing him into contact with a wide range of people. He was involved from the start in liaising with Theodore Martin, for example, whose biography of the Prince Consort would eventually run to five volumes. Leopold was often first to receive new sections of the work for the Queen's approval, and he passed back her instructions and requests; he was fascinated by the book himself, and enjoyed discussing it with the author. But this could not keep him occupied full-time, and in July the Queen began to prepare him for closer involvement in her official workload.

A selection of letters and despatches from overseas was set aside which Leopold was to read; then, he must prepare written abstracts. Ponsonby was told to show him what to do, and make sure that he did it, for the Queen was convinced that Leopold lacked application. Once, the Prince Consort had shared her burden of paperwork, and in 1864, when Prince Alfred turned cold on his future as heir to Saxe-Coburg, she had looked forward to receiving the same help from one of her sons. She was determined now that Leopold would take up the charge his brother abandoned. In the summer of 1876 there was a crisis developing in the east, where Turkey's repression of her subject peoples in the Balkans looked likely to lead to war with Russia, and this would be the testing-ground. Ponsonby was instructed to discuss the crisis with Leopold and to keep him hard at work on the despatches.

Uneasily, Leopold was drawn in. He was fascinated by international affairs, but knew perfectly well that there was no need for him to duplicate work which was being done by the private secretary, whose experience was far greater than his own. He knew, too, that he could not cope with life at home. The Queen expected him to amuse her and Beatrice when they had no other company, but 'society' was an enemy from which he must be protected, and suddenly his lease on Boyton became a weapon in her armoury. He wanted to spend time at Boyton? What better time than Cowes week, when undesirable elements descended on the Isle of Wight, and Osborne was not safe from their influence. On 19 July the Queen told him, 'the society at Cowes during the Regatta is about as bad as any & I am extremely anxious that you should avoid it & not go there to lounge about or pay visits to fashionable ladies or indeed get familiar with people'.[44] So, at the very times when Leopold might have found home bearable, he was to be somewhere else.

It was the same with Balmoral. Leopold asked to leave at the end of September, but was refused. He was told that he might pay one or two short visits in September, perhaps another in October, but when the rest of the family and their guests travelled south, he must rejoin his mother and sister – and he must enjoy it: 'I have stated everything clearly', the Queen wrote, '& trust that you will find this a <u>pleasure</u> as well as a <u>duty</u>.'[45] In vain Collins tried to plead Leopold's cause: 'he has always felt, (& as he grows older he fears he will feel this still more) that a lengthened stay at Balmoral, where he has no pursuits whatever & where there is little society for him, & nothing practical for him to turn his mind to, has been so trying to him, that, struggle against it as much as he will, he is apt to become morose and discontented, & quite unfit for making a cheerful companion to anyone.' He tried to explain that the Queen need have no fear of her son's friends, and it was a fair point: left to himself, Leopold often sought the company of older people like Ruskin and the dons of Oxford, and it would have been safe to trust him. Instead, his mother was pushing him towards the excesses she dreaded.[46]

Once again, the Dean of Windsor and Duckworth were drawn in, and Duckworth promised to speak to Leopold and to present him with good resolutions for the future. But his reply to the Queen suggests his true feelings: 'It is impossible not to be touched by Prince Leopold's petition, and it must have cost Your Majesty no little pain to have to dismiss it.'[47] And although the Queen may not have realised it, one of the resolutions pointed Leopold back towards the public role he had begun so well: Duckworth advised him 'To master the <u>social questions</u> of the day, and to look out for all opportunities of making myself publicly useful'.[48] This was not what the Queen intended, but it may have spurred Leopold on. Shortly before leaving Osborne in August, he discussed his need for meaningful work with no less a figure than the Prime Minister.

ELEVEN

THE MERRY-GO-ROUND

The result of Leopold's conversation with Lord Beaconsfield in the summer of 1876 was disappointing. Beaconsfield listened, then went straight to the Queen, and his famous letter of 25 August, urging Leopold to become the Queen's confidential assistant for foreign affairs, was only another attempt to push the Prince towards work he was already being made to do. There was something almost insulting in the assumption that he could be bought with flattery, and the promise of inside knowledge and power: 'You would become acquainted with all the secret springs and motives of public action – with the characters and conduct of the principal agents – and, in time, acting for the Queen, you would find yourself in a position to influence events.'[1] Leopold knew how far this was from the reality that faced him, and he replied with a heavy heart, and complete candour:

Will you let me speak quite unreservedly in this letter? & destroy it when you have read it?

You speak of my 'undoubted ability & acquirements' – now I know that I have the <u>credit</u> of possessing what you say, but frankly speaking I don't think I have much ability, at any rate not as much as my two <u>eldest</u> Brothers have; though I feel that from the good & careful education which I have received I <u>ought</u> to possess much more ability, but the fact is I am & always have been most indolent, a fault which my frequent illnesses have not tended to improve or remove. . . . It is on account of the fault above mentioned, that I am so anxious for <u>settled work</u>.

Of course I am very glad (& it interests me exceedingly) to see all the despatches which the Queen receives & to make 'précis' or analyses of them for the Queen, as I have been doing lately. . . . But then all this is done, & much better done, by her Private Secretary, & I feel that the Queen only gives me these kind of things to do to keep me employed, & not because it is of any necessity to her; as whatever I do, has been done a day or two previously, by Genl Ponsonby for instance. . . . Were my relations with the Queen more cordial, or could I ever hope that they might become more cordial, I should not be so very anxious as I am; but, as I fear, you are only too well aware, we are not on such terms as we ought to be, & we are never on such good terms as when we are absent from one another.'2

The letter showed how deeply Leopold's confidence had been undermined by the criticism which surrounded him from childhood. Though far brighter academically than the Prince of Wales or Prince Alfred, he felt inferior, and had come to believe the legend of his own idleness because it was repeated so often. This was particularly sad in someone who had struggled so hard against illness and recurrent disability. Despite his disrupted education, Leopold had reached a standard respected by some of the country's foremost academics. He was a gifted pianist, yet Max Müller recalled how nerve-wracking it was to play duets with him, because playing made his fingers painful and sensitive to the slightest touch; few people would have persevered against odds like these, and the comfortable invalid's couch the Queen offered would have attracted many a weaker character.

Leopold's hope for the future, as he now told the Prime Minister, was for a peerage, which would enable him to attend the House of Lords and to serve on committees: real employment, which would take him away from home. The peerage was in the Queen's gift, but Beaconsfield was one of the few people who knew how to influence her, and as the elder Princes were honoured in their early twenties the idea was not unreasonable. Leopold knew that the Prince of Wales supported him, and with the Prime Minister on his side too, perhaps. . . . In the present circumstances he was whistling for the moon.

He should probably have guessed that Lord Beaconsfield's letter had been written with the Queen's sanction, since it followed her plan so closely, but he had discussed confidential matters with Gladstone before, and thought that this conversation and its outcome would be equally private; he was horrified and very angry when the Queen demanded to see his letter from Beaconsfield (which she had seen already, as the Prime Minister sent her a copy), and rebuked him for not telling her about it himself. It was a misjudgement which would cost him dearly in aggravation as the weeks dragged by; the Queen was indignant, and returned to the subject at regular intervals: 'How can <u>you</u> for <u>a moment think</u> that any of <u>my Ministers</u>, whoever they are, could keep <u>from me</u> your Mother & your & <u>their</u> Sovereign such a conversation? . . . I am grieved to see that you <u>still</u> think you can <u>act</u> behind my back.'[3] Time and again she urged him to write down his views on foreign affairs, but he tried not to hear her.

Instead he danced at Abergeldie, attended a very wet and windy Braemar Gathering, and picnicked by Loch Callater with Ponsonby, Dr Marshall and Alick Yorke, and if this was idleness, it was idleness he had done his best to avoid. Princess Alice was at Balmoral that autumn, and he spent as much time as possible with her. He may have suffered a slight recurrence of his haemophilia, probably joint trouble: on 24 September Ponsonby told his wife: 'Leopold is better but Alice prefers dining with him to dining with the Queen which I am not surprised at.'[4]

Slightly later than planned, he set off on his round of visits: first to Lorina Liddell, now Mrs Skene, and her husband at Pitlour, near St Andrews. From their house he made several visits to St Andrews University, something his mother had been urging for a long time, and explored the town and the cathedral. He visited other friends in the area, and was made Captain of the Royal & Ancient Golf Club for a year, attending a dinner, and striking the first golf ball of the new season. From St Andrews he went on to see the Butes, and the Duchess of Roxburghe at Floors Castle, before returning to Balmoral. By the end of October he was finally allowed to return south, pausing for a few days at Lamington, near Perth, with Collins and his friends the Baillie Cochranes. Then, on the train journey home, something happened which seemed so important to Leopold that he remembered it five years later, when making the same journey. He was travelling north on this later occasion; it was 22 May 1881, and he noted in his diary: 'Did not "turn in" till after Rugby – & woke up at <u>Carlisle</u>, & thought of her & of <u>Oct 27 '76</u> – then slept on.'[5]

The Court Circular notes that on 27 October, Leopold, Collins and Royle were travelling south, bound for London, and ultimately for Boyton. There is no clue to 'her' identity, no clue to what happened – indeed, very little is likely to have happened as Collins was there and also Royle, who was in the habit of reporting Leopold's activities to the Queen. But there must have been a meeting at least, and in the absence of evidence the most likely chance is that this was Leopold's first significant meeting with Lady Breadalbane, the ambitious and beautiful wife of Gavin Campbell, the 7th Earl, one of the Queen's lords-in-waiting. By 1877 Leopold was friendly enough with the Breadalbanes to attract gossip, and at the time the diary entry was written, Alma Breadalbane inspired some of his most rapturous comments. A few weeks after 22 May 1881, she and her husband joined Leopold on the train at Perth and played whist until they reached Carlisle, so it was not unknown for them to travel on the same train. Whatever happened on 27 October 1876, it left Leopold in a good mood as he went on to Boyton, and a small house party of his own.

The company of Louise and Lord Lorne, then of Louis of Hesse, provided distraction from his problems, and he attended a Grand Lodge of the Wiltshire Freemasons. He planned a visit to Oxford to fulfil an engagement and see friends before the Queen required him at Windsor. Repeated demands from Balmoral for his views on foreign affairs fell on deaf ears: after six years of clashes with his mother, Leopold appeared to be developing a thicker skin; his letters were stronger and less emotional, with a sarcastic edge that had not been there before. Submitting his plans for the rest of the year, he suggested that as he had not been needed at Osborne during Cowes week, perhaps he could leave before the New Year, because in winter the damp and windswept island always affected his joints. When refused – 'it is for <u>me</u>, Dear Child, to say where I shall wish you to stay <u>with me</u> or not' – he replied, 'I shall of course be very happy to spend New Year at Osborne as you so kindly ask.'[6]

Behind his back, attempts were still being made to bring him into line. He was invited to take the Chair of a charitable institution for elderly Freemasons; Collins asked the Queen, who told him she had strong objections to Leopold's attending 'Public meetings or anything wch causes gt excitement'. Conceding that at times this might be difficult to avoid, she added, 'what she <u>does</u> decidedly however object to (tho she will not absolutely forbid it) is his taking the <u>Chair</u>'.[7] If the duties of the post could not be kept to a minimum, she said, Leopold's knee should be used as an excuse for refusing the request.

Quietly, the word had gone out from Balmoral that the Prince was not to be invited to balls or social events, or to participate in sports, to protect him both from injury and idleness; a letter from Lord Hertford to Lady Ely in mid-November expressed regret that he was not even to attend quiet house parties with people who could be trusted.[8] The visit to Oxford annoyed the Queen, and once again poor Collins found himself in the firing line: 'Had Mr Collins known Your Majesty would have objected so strongly to his being the 4 days at Oxford he would have tried to prevent it, but he really finds himself so <u>constantly</u> in the position of having to advise the Prince to take some course that is contrary to the Prince's private inclinations, that he is unwilling for many & good reasons to be brought into conflict with the Prince, if it can be avoided.'[9] Once again, he urged Leopold's need for regular, meaningful work. Once again, the correspondence was passed to Jenner and the Dean of Windsor for their opinion.

Leopold and his mother, and all those associated with them, had become locked into a predictable cycle of arguments, like a merry-go-round spinning them helplessly through the year: arguments about Osborne and Balmoral, home and society, arguments about what did and did not constitute real work. The Queen was trying to force Leopold back to her side, to assist with what she saw as the true business of the sovereign – writing letters, reading reports, keeping a finger on the pulse of events at home and overseas: this was her sphere, and no-one handled it better. But he had grown up with his eyes on the world outside, acutely aware of the damage done to the monarchy by his mother's seclusion, and resentful of a situation he had no power to change. Now his friends, his education, and his own nature all inclined him to look for work away from home.

It was sad that the Queen placed so little value on the contribution he could make to the educational, artistic and charitable concerns which were beginning to seek his patronage. Intelligent and able, full of serious interest in social issues, the Prince also had a gift for organising and energising people. A founder member of the University Musical Club, he went on in later years to create the Bachelors' Club in London, and while this was just the sort of society venture his mother thought so dangerous, it showed skills which could have been useful elsewhere. A fellow member of the Bachelors' Club, William Gillett, recalled that Leopold brought the founder members together and made their discussions flow; he was 'wonderfully clever in helping us out of any difficulty & some of the more important rules were entirely drawn up by him'.[10] This was a talent wasted on the Queen's assistant.

But the Queen's assistant he must be, and when she told the Dean of Windsor about the latest round of arguments he wrote to Collins, and then let the Queen know that his letter had given a clear warning 'that the position to be held hereafter by Prince Leopold in this country would greatly depend upon his mainly residing with Your Majesty, and thus becoming useful to you'. The element of threat in this was softened a little by the suggestion that if Leopold was too shy to give his views on foreign affairs, Collins might help him work out what to say.[11]

As so often in the past, a rise in the emotional temperature was followed by an attack of bleeding. Shortly after the Dean's letter was sent, Leopold suffered a painful bleed in the calf muscle. He was at Boyton with a small group of friends, and had just enjoyed some amateur theatricals which were originally planned for Louise's visit. Acting had been on the forbidden list for Leopold ever since his brush with death at the start of 1868, though it was something he particularly enjoyed, and Alick Yorke was passionate about the stage. They put on two short plays, one a comedy, the other based on the story of Ulysses, and Leopold acted in both, with Yorke, Walter Campbell of Blythswood, who had a talent for comic singing and was one of the Prince's closest friends, Collins' sister and sister-in-law, and a Mr Nicolson. When the bleeding began, Dr Royle suggested that it was the result of exposure to cold when changing. Leopold mentioned to Dr Paget that he had climbed on to a low chair and stood down quickly, and this might have caused a strain. The Queen was furious, and all those present, except Collins, scrambled to cover their own backs, leaving Leopold to take the blame.

It was Royle who did the most damage by writing to Dr Marshall, for the Queen's eyes, to say that the acting was not his fault: 'I am happy to say that I had nothing to do with these theatricals and did nothing but protest against them from the beginning.'[12] This was not true: in February Duckworth spoke to the doctor at Osborne, and discovered that all he had done was to warn Leopold not to overdo things at rehearsals, so as to be fit for the actual performance.[13] By February, though, the harm was done, and the Queen had confidently accused her son of 'imprudence & total disregard of your kind doctor's advice'.[14]

This was not the only time Royle's words would be harmful to Leopold. The doctor was not an unpleasant man and, in fairness to him, he did not know the Prince's situation so well as Collins, Duckworth and Jenner, who had known Leopold since he was a boy, and understood the tensions which helped to shape his character. New to the Court, Royle was bound to be in awe of the Queen and to want to please her; the life of her son was a huge responsibility, and this was the first serious bleeding attack he had seen. Besides, it was in his nature to speak before he thought. In January Ponsonby told his wife, 'Royle – Leopold's doctor speaks out whatever first comes into his head and I should be afraid of his getting into difficulties if he remained here long – so is he.'[15]

Letters about the acting passed backwards and forwards for three months, with the Queen demanding details and names; it was a lot of fuss about a very harmless activity, which exposed one of the main reasons for Leopold's bouts of frustration and anger. Even Duckworth wrote now of the 'unwarrantable risk when he indulges in amusements fitted only for the strong & healthy', yet there was no inherent danger in acting: it was a pleasant recreation which made Leopold's life more bearable – and if he was never to act, Alick Yorke was quite the wrong person to have chosen as his equerry.[16] A year later Royle was still complaining about the number of theatrical entertainments staged in country house parties for the

Prince, but Ponsonby's reaction was more sympathetic: 'what else can he do – he cant shoot ride or do much walking.'[17] Leopold was right to suspect that his illness was being used as a means of control; after all, the accident with a pen at Reinhardsbrunn nearly cost his life, but no-one suggested that he should give up writing. The blunt truth was that any activity, or no activity at all, could produce a fatal bleeding attack. Death was a reality he had to live with, and only he could decide how best to come to terms with it. This was a freedom no-one was prepared to allow.

He was confined to his sofa at Boyton over Christmas, and contrary to the Queen's dark predictions it was a happy, peaceful time. He amused himself with reading and chess, and listened to his mechanical piano, and he invited Dr Poore to stay, joining Royle and the Collinses. Snow fell, and at 3 a.m. on Christmas morning the household at Boyton woke to the sound of carol singers. Single clergymen from the neighbouring villages came in to share the turkey and plum pudding, and even a rise in the temperature on Boxing Day, which turned the snow to grey sheets of rain, did not dampen the atmosphere. But Christmas could not last for ever, and the Queen was expecting her son at Osborne. Early in January Duckworth was sent to Boyton, to urge Leopold once again to be useful to his mother, but he returned complaining that he had no chance to speak to the Prince alone; Collins told the Queen he had not asked to, and the stand-off continued for another fortnight. On the afternoon of 24 January, Leopold arrived at Osborne. He had to be carried, and so had asked that no-one should be there to receive him.

In this state he had no escape, but he was restless and found it hard to concentrate. Illness affected Leopold emotionally as much as physically; he knew how short his time might be, and wanted to see, and do, and taste all the experiences other men enjoy in a lifetime. He dreaded the thought of dying in pain; still greater, at times like this, was his dread of permanent disability and helplessness. Ponsonby thought him 'looking older and more set', and told his wife that although Leopold's conversation was good, Royle complained that he would not settle to anything.[18] The Prince was depressed because the swelling in his leg refused to go down; at the end of February the knee was still bent, making it impossible for him to walk without a stick. But the pressure was on. Duckworth pushed him to embark on 'a course of regular study of history, political economy and social science', and letters and despatches relating to the crisis in the East, which was about to escalate into war between Russia and Turkey, were handed over for his attention.[19]

Leopold worked, and he worked hard, and as February gave way to March, and March to April, his relationship with the Queen improved. Shortly after his birthday, she spoke to Lord Beaconsfield about obtaining a Cabinet key for him, to give him access to official papers. This was a privilege none of his brothers enjoyed, not even the Prince of Wales, and to avoid questions or objections from the Foreign Office, Beaconsfield advised her to ask for a second key for her own convenience; on 18 April she told Leopold, 'Your getting the Official Gov^t Key is a gt privilege & I will let you see what Ld Beaconsfield wrote about it.'[20] She praised him for his helpfulness, and for the comfort he had given her at this difficult time, and Leopold seemed to enjoy his new standing; replying to a birthday letter from Dr Acland, he said, without a murmur of complaint, 'as you can imagine, in this very critical time I have a great deal to do for the Queen'.[21]

Between themselves, the Queen and the Prime Minister were beginning to see Leopold as an alternative private secretary. Lord Beaconsfield dealt with him directly, and he wrote and received important letters for the Queen, corresponding even with other sovereigns. But there were dangers in this sudden elevation which he had recognised from the start. He was not qualified for some of the things he was being asked to do, and his presence complicated the work of the real private secretary, Sir Henry Ponsonby, who found himself being by-passed. At heart Ponsonby was a Liberal, though he was careful not to allow his private opinions to influence his work. Still, it was tempting for the Conservative Prime Minister to communicate with the Queen through a younger and less experienced man, who might be open to influence.

Fortunately Ponsonby liked Leopold and understood his situation, but there was a difficult moment at the end of April when the private secretary heard that the Queen was unhappy with his anti-Turkish perspective on the eastern crisis; she thought him too close to the Opposition. It emerged that she had picked up this impression from Leopold, whose own instinctive preference for the Turks had been challenged in a series of discussions with Ponsonby – on the Queen's orders Ponsonby had been trying to educate Leopold in his new duties and to increase his enthusiasm for them since the previous summer. The storm blew over in a few days, but it confirmed some of the fears Leopold had voiced to the Prime Minister in August 1876, and its warnings were heeded by no-one but Ponsonby, who took care in future to guard his words.

Though the eastern crisis absorbed most of Leopold's time, he was called on to deal with other matters too: in March, for example, his cousin Count Gleichen wrote to him about new regulations governing naval dress. But beneath the surface, as the weeks passed, his resentment grew. In the outside world his brothers enjoyed busy social lives and travelled widely, while for him there seemed to be only work. He missed his friends, and the dullness of home began to grate on his nerves. The crunch came with May, and the compulsory journey to Balmoral.

Having worked steadily for four months, Leopold felt that he had earned a break, and some consideration of his own long-term plans. The Cabinet key was an honour, but it was granted only to enable him to share his mother's work; his heart was still set on the peerage. He wrote at first for permission to leave Balmoral the day after the Queen's birthday, perhaps returning later; he wanted to go to Oxford to open a new wing of the Radcliffe Infirmary, at Dr Acland's invitation, and he was to stay with the Liddells. The Queen turned to Collins: would he make Leopold stay longer at Balmoral? Back on the merry-go-round, Collins once again tried to explain that the days when he could *make* her son do anything were long over.

Then the Queen expressed her feelings to Leopold, and he was stung into replying immediately, with far more anger than wisdom. All the pent-up resentment of his brothers spilled out in his remarks: 'You speak of Affie's and Arthur's duties, I cannot quite see the severity of the latter's duties, as he was amusing himself all January & February, & during the two months he was on duty, he was continually visiting about, & now he has again been having leave.'[22] This was not a wise moment to mention the peerage, but he was obviously too agitated to stop and think, and he set out his dearest wish, and his arguments for it, even though the Prince of Wales had recently approached the Queen about the peerage on his behalf, and been firmly refused.

The letter resulted in a bitter row in which the Queen complained of Leopold's ingratitude and cruel jealousy of Arthur, 'who is a pattern to all young men & whom you always find fault with', and although mother and son went to Balmoral together, the feelings did not subside.[23] Leopold left as soon as he could, and went on to Oxford, then to Boyton. In another letter he attempted to explain his confused feelings about his brother and his wish for the peerage, and as there was no reply he assumed that what he said had touched a chord. This was unfortunate, because the Queen was so angry she had destroyed the letter without opening it, and it had also included Leopold's plan to stay with his sister at Kensington and spend some time in London.[24] When this piece of news broke, tempers flared all round.

This time, Louise was drawn into the argument. She had welcomed Leopold on condition that he told their mother about the visit, but was annoyed to find that he had plans of his own, which he preferred to the arrangements she made for him. She thought of calling Duckworth in, though this had been tried rather too often and, as always, it was left to Collins to restore peace. Tentatively he set out Leopold's proposed London activities to the Queen: a dinner at Trinity House with the Prince of Wales, laying the foundation stone of Duckworth's church, perhaps a State Ball and Concert. He was worried about Leopold's state of mind: 'Even now the knowledge that the letter was not read rankles very much in the Prince's mind, & Mr Collins cannot help feeling that the state of affairs is rather critical.'[25]

But Leopold's anger was giving way once again to depression and the fear that, for him, things would never change. His nephew Wilhelm of Prussia was due in England, and both the Crown Princess and the Queen looked to him to be responsible for Wilhelm and protect him from unsuitable company. The Queen also wanted Leopold to go to Boyton again to avoid Cowes week; she asked him to warn his nephew that 'objectionable' people gathered at Cowes. This was too much. Leopold knew that at eighteen Wilhelm had experienced far more of society than he had.

He would be happy to have his nephew's company, he told her, 'but I could not be responsible for his doings in any way; I should feel I was a "Killjoy", & that he would wish me away; & if he is to be <u>at all</u> with Bertie he will <u>very soon</u> find out how dull & dreary he would be in <u>my</u> company. . . . I hope, dear Mamma, you will not mind my saying this, it is only that I <u>know</u> the often unhappy results of locking young men up, so to speak, & keeping them from all harmless & innocent amusements; their eyes <u>must</u> be opened sooner or later, & the longer it is put off the worse it is pretty sure to be in the end.'[26]

Clear in this letter, though it could not be put into words, is the growing humiliation of a young man tied to his mother and under continual supervision. Most men of Leopold's class and generation would have had some sexual experience by the time they were twenty-four; they would at least have been free to discuss sex with friends in the regiment or the club, where they would pick up enough information to sound experienced. When Leopold was younger he had been able to laugh at his over-protected state; at nineteen he wrote to Collins, 'you ought to call me "Pamela" . . . on account of <u>my purity</u> of mind and body'.[27] By now he must have known that he himself would be a joke to many men and he felt shamed by his situation: the laughter had all left him.

Something in this letter touched the Queen. She seemed to notice for the first time that her son really was unhappy, and Collins, who had tried so often to explain this to her, pushed the point home, adding 'as Your Majesty is aware, the Prince is a little apt to look on the dark side of things, especially as regards himself, & to think that no one would care for his company'. He took advantage of the moment to repeat a request on Leopold's behalf which she had already refused, for permission to make a series of visits from Balmoral in the autumn.[28] This time the Queen agreed, and through the summer she and Leopold worked harmoniously together.

The most pressing issue was still the war in the East, which Russia showed every sign of winning eventually, though the struggle would be hard. Through July and August, Leopold submitted his ideas on British policy with growing confidence. On 24 July, he was told that the Germans were urging Britain to annex Egypt. 'Neither <u>Turkey</u> not <u>Egypt</u> have done anything to offend

<u>us</u>', he remarked, 'why should we make a wanton aggression? . . . How can we protest against Russia's doings, if we do the same <u>ourselves</u>?'[29] He advised on the text of the Queen's telegrams to Lord Beaconsfield, and commented on plans put forward by Ponsonby – fortunately, in view of the earlier spat, his comments were favourable. He was becoming very involved, and interested, and the work did have a lighter side: at the end of the month the Prime Minister sent him a Colorado beetle to show the Queen![30]

August brought a more social duty. Prince Bernhard of Saxe-Meiningen, the fiancé of his niece, Princess Charlotte of Prussia, came to Osborne to meet the Queen, and Leopold was asked to look after him. He was not impressed: four years later he told Louis of Hesse that Charlotte and her brother Wilhelm had both made 'stupid marriages'.[31] But at least it made a change from paperwork, and he must have been delighted at the same time to see the Liddells at Osborne. Whenever friends visited, Leopold enjoyed showing them places and things which had particular meaning for him. At Osborne it was always the Swiss Cottage, with its reminders of childhood, and his favourite corner of the beach, where once he built sand-castles and set light to his paper boats, watching them disappear between the flames and the water. The Dean and Mrs Liddell were accompanied by one of their daughters, presumably Alice; she dined with the Household, but joined the company after the meal, and Ponsonby remarked to his wife that 'Leopold [is] devoted to her'.[32]

By September the Court was at Balmoral, and Leopold and Alick Yorke were getting ready to set off on the promised round of visits, and scheming for a break from the disapproving presence of Dr Royle – for two days only, while they travelled to the Breadalbanes' house party at Taymouth. Royle was in London, so Leopold telegraphed him to meet them later at Taymouth, but this plan did not please Jenner and the Queen, who insisted that a doctor must be present at all times. When questioned, the two young men said Royle was in Perth, never suspecting that Jenner would contact Buckingham Palace to discover his real whereabouts and bring him racing to Balmoral. Ponsonby told his wife how delighted Jenner was by the thought of their anger when they saw they had been outwitted.[33]

Taymouth Castle, in a spectacular riverside setting, with high wooded hills on either side, was far more palatial than Balmoral, and the Breadalbane Campbells entertained royally. The Queen and Prince Albert visited in the summer of 1842, and were greeted by an honour guard of Breadalbane Highlanders; at night there was a lavish firework display and the Highlanders danced sword-dances and reels by the light of flaming torches. For Leopold, the Killin Rifle Volunteer Corps was called out, and triumphal arches erected in nearby Aberfeldy. There were banners, flags and cheering crowds; a prince was a coveted addition to any guest list, and the Breadalbanes celebrated his arrival in style.

He had been to house parties before, but still knew very little of society and its ways. Alma Breadalbane was young. She was beautiful. She was one of those women who like to be surrounded by a circle of adoring men; her attention to them was no more than a game. Montagu Corry, Lord Beaconsfield's private secretary, captured the flavour of her parties when he stayed at Taymouth in 1879: 'a . . . host of men and boys, all worshippers of our hostess, have raised our numbers to 30 or more at dinner. We have danced a little too much; and "tableaux" have caused some trouble. . .'.[34] There was no harm in the game while everyone knew its rules, but Leopold was an innocent. He had dined with the Breadalbanes before and may already have been nursing a slight infatuation for Alma, but he was not prepared for the impact which seeing her each day would have on his feelings.

At first he basked in her attention, but soon he was hopelessly in love; the other guests noticed and were amused, and wild stories began to spread. When Lady Breadalbane heard them, she backed off completely from him to show that there was no truth in what was being said. Unfortunately, this only offered more meat to the gossips, who assumed that something sensational had happened to upset her, while Leopold, without the faintest idea of what was happening around him, was hurt by her sudden coldness. He sulked. He argued with her about a picture. It was childish, but he was immature emotionally, and he knew it. He did not know, until it hit him, how quickly and completely infatuation can stifle judgement, and he left Taymouth feeling miserably silly and very annoyed with himself.[35]

His next stop was Aberdeen, to hand over the presidency of the golf club before visiting the Coutts Lindsays at Balcarres, but he was in no mood for another party. The literary gentlemen invited to Balcarres to meet him complained to Royle that Leopold had not made any literary conversation (they seemed to equate a prince with a performing monkey). They looked down their noses at the tableaux vivants Alick Yorke arranged, though Arthur Sullivan and the artist Richard Doyle were involved, so the music and scenery were in a class of their own. But Leopold was beyond cheering, and Royle, who hated house parties anyway, complained that allowing him into society did nothing for the image of the monarchy. Leopold's mood would not have been improved on the Sunday morning by a telegram from his mother ordering him to the Kirk, which arrived as he was about to set out for the Episcopalian church with the rest of the party.[36]

He still had no idea that anyone had noticed his embarrassment at Taymouth, but as the house party dispersed, the gossip was taking wing. Ponsonby heard of 'Leopolds larks at Taymouth', and appealed to his wife to find more details.[37] Royle was told the story by one of the Taymouth guests on a visit to Wemyss Castle, and it was not long before rumours reached the Queen. Her son was back at Balmoral by this time, so she sent for Royle who, even though he had been at Taymouth himself, repeated the gossip he heard later: that Leopold had had an affair with Lady Breadalbane, and had then upset her.

The explosion that followed can only be imagined. On 14 October Leopold wrote to the Queen, telling her that he had not answered her letters before because he did not know what she wanted him to say: 'I can only say now that your wishes shall be complied with, & that, if there was any harm in it, the blame was <u>mine</u> & <u>mine</u> alone – at any rate it shall not happen again.'[38] She must have imposed some form of sanction: two months later Helena tried to intercede for Leopold, assuring her 'that your poor sick boy does not deserve the severe judgement you have passed on him. – Of course knowing <u>only</u> what you did you had no other course.'[39] But suddenly an unnatural silence descended over the incident: on 21 October, Leopold began bleeding from the right kidney, and suffered considerable pain.

TWELVE

THE LOSS OF A SISTER

To be ill at Balmoral was one of Leopold's nightmares. The Queen visited him daily, and sometimes played the piano to him in his room. She meant to be kind, and promised not to say more about Taymouth until he was well, but the thought of this hung over him like a threatening cloud. Through October and into November the bleeding continued; the Princess of Wales visited each evening, and Lord Brooke and Walter Campbell were there. Early in November, Ponsonby called in, and found Leopold 'looking thin and worn but lighted up very much in talking'. Then, a few days later, Princess Beatrice came down with mumps: 'Poor Leopold is in terror of them very naturally in his sick bed', Ponsonby told his wife, 'and when he heard rumours yesterday about it refused to see the P^ss last night, which made the Q angry and she washed both Marshall's and Royle's heads for putting such ideas into his head.'[1]

Beatrice recovered much sooner than Leopold. The weeks dragged by, and the Court was stuck at Balmoral because the doctors would not risk moving him; only the Queen was glad of a reason to stay. Some days he seemed better, others not; Royle became increasingly worried, though Marshall and Jenner laughed off his fears. Then, three weeks into November, Leopold developed a cough at the base of both lungs. He was low and depressed, and his friends had all gone. In a desperate attempt to inject some life into him, Royle tried to persuade him to have an argument with Ponsonby about the Turks, but Leopold was too listless to care.

Even so, right through the illness he continued his work for the Queen. He was in pain, he was not allowed to stand, and he was sick with embarrassment about Taymouth, but still he dealt with papers relating to events in the East, and discussed the design for a new order for India and the ladies who should be listed to receive it. He was sent a book on the workings of the Long Parliament. Two Council meetings were held in the adjoining room with the door open, though Sir Thomas Biddulph remarked to Ponsonby that it was useless to make him work when he was still in bed. At the end of November Collins was sent for, and he brought a request for help that was much more to Leopold's taste, and more likely to divert him from his problems.

For nearly twenty years, Ruskin had tried to persuade the Trustees of the National Gallery to release drawings from the Turner bequest for use in education. He mentioned this to Leopold in 1876, a few days before Edith Liddell's death, but then the matter went no further. Now he had written to Collins: 'In an underground room of the National Gallery are some twelve or more tin boxes, containing sketchbooks of Turner's and perspective diagrams . . . I want to ask the Prince to get me – He will best know how – these perspective drawings for our Oxford schools; and a portion of the sketchbooks to be mounted leaf by leaf, and brought into use. They are <u>now absolutely waste paper</u>. No mortal can see them – nor can they be handled without destruction being in soft pencil, or chalk.'[2] Revived by this appeal from a world he still missed, Leopold wrote to the Trustees.

His confinement at Balmoral was almost at an end. On 5 December he was finally judged well enough to travel; he dreaded Windsor and longed to be allowed to go to Boyton, but it was not to be. A few days after making the journey, he began to bleed heavily again. The Queen blamed Royle for allowing him to walk, and Leopold clung to his room, doing the work that was asked of him and saying little about his plans. Collins warned the Queen that once he was better, he would probably want to travel. He still needed morphine for the pain, and when his mother set off for Osborne after Christmas she had no choice but to leave him. That day Helena visited her brother, and Leopold poured out the whole story of Taymouth, admitting his stupidity but denying that there had ever been an affair. 'What is really keeping him from getting well now', Helena told their mother, 'is the thought that <u>you</u>

believe him guilty of having behaved disgracefully and being unprincipled.'[3]

In a second, much longer letter (her first cautious note ran to thirteen sides), Helena related the whole story, adding that she had spoken to Royle, who agreed that the account he gave the Queen was only hearsay. She pleaded with her mother to forgive Leopold and say no more about Taymouth, to relieve the tension he had been under for months. And the Queen did forgive, though her conditions were hard: Leopold was to give up his friends in 'that fine fast heartless dangerous set', and to make no visits in the country, except 'to quiet sober people without large parties'. She was convinced now that his physical illness was combined with a dangerous weakness of character, and only one future was possible for him: 'He sh^d devote himself to be useful & to improve his mind, to read and help me in <u>every way</u> – wch is all he <u>can</u> do.'[4] Dr Jenner was asked to give this message to Leopold, but wisely, he declined.

In some ways the Queen was as innocent as her son, and she failed to see something which stood out in both Helena's letters: Leopold still worshipped Alma, and would not hear anything said against her. On 26 October, surely without his mother's knowledge, he had arranged for a dachshund which he wanted to give her to be delivered to the mews at Buckingham Palace; it was to be kept there until her husband collected it, and he asked an official from the Privy Purse Office to buy a good collar engraved 'Countess of Breadalbane'.[5] To his sister he said 'How can I ever meet Lady B. again knowing what has been said' – a sure sign of his real feelings.[6]

Help came from an unexpected quarter. As the year turned, Ruskin arrived to stay with Leopold at Windsor. He was not impressed with the castle, comparing the view from his room to 'a big modern county gaol', and it did not take him long to sense Leopold's mood.[7] Ruskin knew all too well the pain and confusion of loving the wrong person, and he listened, touched that the Prince chose to confide in him. There was nothing practical he could do, but his company helped. He brought news that Leopold's appeal for the Turner sketches had made a difference; the detailed negotiations would last several more months, but eventually 251 drawings and sketches by Turner and eight sketchbooks were released for the University of Oxford, an achievement which Leopold shared.

They talked of other things too. In 1871 Ruskin had tried to broaden the audience for his ideas of social justice and reform by issuing monthly letters 'To the Workmen and Labourers of Great Britain'. Leopold knew about these *Fors Clavigera* letters and had often discussed them with him in the past; now, much to Ruskin's delight, he asked to receive new letters as issued – '"You <u>promised</u> to do it long ago" said he – "and forgot me!"'8 Early in the *Fors* series, Ruskin undertook to set aside a percentage of his income towards a fund to support the reforms he advocated, and Leopold is said to have followed his example – certainly he approved of what Ruskin was trying to do.

By the second week in January, the Prince was well enough to go to Osborne. He had continued to work for the Queen from Windsor, and as soon as he arrived, she set him to sorting out her telegrams. But he was aching to get away, and speaking to Ruskin had fired his enthusiasm to see Italy again, this time to visit Rome, which was forbidden on his previous tour. His first request met a flat refusal, but later his mother relented a little, saying that, though she might allow him to go south, 'for quiet & rest & being in the open air', she was certain that 'cold churches & galleries, & visiting frivolous parties' would be bad for his health. She left the final decision to Jenner, and he must have agreed with Leopold, who set off at the end of February, travelling incognito as 'Lord Boyton', with Collins and Royle to keep him in order.

After Taymouth, Collins worried about the scrapes the Prince might fall into, given his inexperience, and his craving for freedom. Leopold was not dangerously weak as his mother believed, just a normal young man who had been kept on too tight a rein for too long, but he needed to learn, and sometime between the end of 1877 and the early months of 1879, somebody decided to show him what he had been missing. It would not have been Collins or Royle, or anyone whose livelihood depended on the Queen. It might have been a friend or a brother, but shortly before Leopold's departure for the continent a new person came into his life, who had all the experience he lacked.

Crown Prince Rudolf of Austria was one of the most promising figures of his generation. Five years younger than Leopold, he was attractive, politically astute and highly intelligent. Sent to Britain shortly after Christmas to study the country's government and economics, Rudolf stayed at Claridge's and travelled widely. He visited Osborne in January 1878 while Leopold was there, and was at Windsor in February: 'We liked the young Crown Prince of Austria very much', the Queen told her eldest daughter. 'He is so simple and unaffected and yet so well informed and with such charming manners.'9 Leopold's godmother, the Duchess of Teck, even joked to the Austrian ambassador that the Queen was in love with Rudolf, but would not be thinking of marriage!

Victoria might not have been so enchanted if she had known the other side of the Crown Prince. Like Leopold, he was possessed by the urge to live at a feverish pace, snatching every chance of happiness. The thirst for knowledge which had made a writer, scientist and political theorist of Rudolf before he was twenty-one, had also taken him into the night life of Vienna. He did no more than other young men of his time; sexual experience with 'actresses' and 'dancers', and with some aristocratic married women, was a normal part of their growing up, accepted, if rarely discussed, but in 1878 Rudolf was still young enough for it to be new and exciting. Leopold may have spent some time with him in London early in February, and accompanied him to the station when he left Windsor. Towards the end of the month he took his own leave of the Queen and was soon in Paris – and Rudolf was with him.

The two Princes were entertained at the Elysée by the French President. They spent two days together, though Leopold was careful to suggest to the Queen that it had only been a brief, chance meeting. But their time was not given only to pleasure. After a long, earnest conversation about events in the East, Leopold reported to the Queen that Rudolf was anxious for an alliance between Austria-Hungary and England, and had advised that the Hungarian Count Andrassy 'was England's best friend, & was <u>the</u> man who wanted us to work together'.10 Rudolf warned that the Austrian ambassador in England, Count Beust, could not be trusted because he was friendly with the Russian Count Shuvalov; he undertook to send proof of this, and to do all he could to have the ambassador recalled, though in reality he had as little influence on his father as Leopold had on his mother.

They parted firm friends, and Leopold went on to Nice, where he attended the carnival. 'It was very unfortunate that the Prince should have arrived at Nice just at the time when the town was gay', Collins wrote, uneasily, to the Queen.[11] She was particularly angry that a French squadron had fired a naval salute to 'Lord Boyton', whose identity they were not supposed to know. Leopold visited Corsica on board the Duke of St Albans' yacht, and made plans to buy a yacht of his own, the *Hildegarde*, from the Prince of Wales; when he mentioned this in a letter to the Queen she took immediate steps to prevent it. On 1 April he and his companions set out for Naples on board the *Moeris*, bound for Alexandria. There was an English clergyman, the Reverend James King, on board, and Leopold questioned him eagerly about Palestine and the Holy Land. Learning that King needed to go ashore quickly, Leopold took him to Naples as part of his own party.[12]

Rome was still forbidden, but the Prince climbed Vesuvius, explored Pompeii and saw Milan and Turin, visiting monasteries, churches and museums, with Collins in the background trying to fend off the Queen's complaints and help her to understand her son. 'It would be useless to deny that Your Majesty's chief complaint against Prince Leopold – viz – his love of pleasure & of the excitement of society – is founded upon fact. . . . At the same time Mr Collins is convinced that there exists beneath this love of excitement a taste for & an appreciation of higher & nobler things. . . . It would seem sometimes as though the Prince wished to make up for his long illnesses & sufferings by crowding a great deal of enjoyment into a small space!'[13]

The only surviving letter from Leopold to his mother in May 1878 was written from a hotel by Lake Como, and describes his surprise on learning of Arthur's engagement. He was happy: 'Here the whole place is one mass of roses, azaleas, lilies of the valley &c – all the summer flowers already out – & the nightingales singing so loudly day & night.'[14] He had certainly gained in self-possession and in confidence; four days later he wrote to his mother again, and this 'shameful heartless letter' was passed round the family – except to Alice and Louis, an interesting omission.

Copies were given to Ponsonby and Jenner, even to the Prime Minister; in it Leopold informed the Queen that he did not intend to return home for the spring visit to Balmoral. She was outraged: officials at the embassy in Paris were warned that he was on his way in defiance of his mother's wishes. If he tried to stay in London, the Queen wanted his brothers and sisters to make sure that he would not enjoy himself.[15] But many of those who were shown the letter sympathised with Leopold's stand. Ponsonby told his wife, 'He was firm against coming to Balmoral and protested against the Queen regulating his every movement – but he was respectful and dutiful in expression. Lady Ely says that Jenner was pitched into for not condemning Leopold sufficiently, that the Prince of Wales offered some mediation on his brothers behalf and that Beaconsfield declined to interfere.'[16]

Undaunted, Leopold spent two weeks in Paris, where his time was divided between the International Exhibition and the Hanover family. He told his mother that at their first meeting the King seemed cheerful, but later it became obvious that 'he was suffering a good deal of pain . . . though he strove to conceal the fact. Though I saw the Queen, Ernest, & the sisters, almost every day, I did not see the King again till the Thursday 6th, the day I came to take leave of him . . . in parting he gave me the Hanoverian Order of St George, & blessed me, asking me to bend my head so that he might make the sign of the Cross on my forehead – I was a whole hour with him, during which he talked most affectionately to me of you & of all the family.'[17] A few days later, the King died.

All summer, Leopold was involved with the tangled legal and political aftermath of the King's death, and the Hanovers trusted him to put their case to the Queen. The King had lost both country and fortune for taking up arms against Prussia in 1866; now there were questions about the standing and inheritance of his heir. Leopold had grown very close to the family, and was beginning to think of marrying one of the daughters: not his first favourite, Mary, but her older sister Frederica. She was thirty to his twenty-five: a tall woman, stately rather than beautiful, and quite shy. He would certainly have confided his feelings to Alice, who visited England with her children; he hurt his knee getting out of a train at Windsor in July, and the whole Hesse family could often be found in his room. When the Queen left for Osborne, Lord Brooke and a few other friends were invited to Windsor to keep him company, but on arrival they were forbidden to eat or sleep at the castle. Brooke was furious, and it was said in the Household that he wrote a letter of complaint, saying that he would have left immediately, but was unwilling to abandon Leopold.[18]

The tensions created by Taymouth and Leopold's refusal to go to Balmoral were still unresolved. He went to Osborne in August, but had to resort to subterfuge to join a party which other members of the family, including children, attended quite openly. Elliot Yorke, Alick's elder brother, was the host, and one of the guests was Lillie Langtry, who remembered Leopold as her first friend in the royal family. 'The Prince was a tall, transparent-skinned young man, of gentle manners and extreme simplicity', she wrote, 'artistic and of marked intellectuality; at our little London house he was a frequent visitor.'[19] To get to the party, Leopold asked permission to cruise on the royal yacht *Alberta* 'for his health', though his real intentions were an open secret. 'What I don't understand is Why shouldn't he', Ponsonby asked his wife. 'Why this mystery?'[20] The cruise took Leopold straight to Elliot Yorke's, and some of the guests, including Lillie, joined him on the yacht, hiding below decks until they were out of sight of Osborne. The game almost turned sour when Sir John Cowell included Leopold's attendance at the party in a draft for the Court Circular; fortunately he realised his mistake in time, and the Queen thought it was a huge joke. She even told Leopold. According to Ponsonby, 'he smiled a ghastly smile'.[21]

Tensions persisted into the autumn, but Leopold's wish to marry Princess Frederica did meet with a more sympathetic response. In October the Queen allowed him to visit the Hanovers at Gmunden, officially to see the widowed Queen on her behalf, but really to assess his chances. Unfortunately, this only deepened his feelings for another woman who was out of reach. Frederica was in love with her father's secretary, Baron Alfons von Pawel-Rammingen. The old King would not hear of marriage, nor would his son, and she would marry no-one else. Leopold did not propose because he sensed that it was hopeless; he sought comfort in Darmstadt with Alice and her family, and Louis broke the rules by taking him shooting, much to the Queen's annoyance. Then he returned home, and spent a few days at Buckingham Palace with his brother.

Arthur was disturbed by Leopold's depression. They spent an evening entertaining a homesick young cousin of Arthur's fiancée, Prince Alexander of Hesse-Cassel, who had just begun his studies at the College of Music for the Blind. While the boy played the piano, the brothers discussed Gmunden and the future. Afterwards Arthur approached the Queen about Leopold, and a few days later he confided his disappointment to his fiancée: 'Mama has written me a vy long letter which has made me vy unhappy: she does nothing but abuse Leo in it & nothing makes a man more annoyed than to hear his brother abused. . . . Mama is most kind to me & I am most grateful to her, but she is vy hard on Leo & constantly imagines him guilty of things of which he is really entirely innocent & this of course rubs the boy up the wrong way & makes him feel aggrieved – Why will dear Mama write these disagreeable letters which annoy one so much; she does the same to all of us but especially to & of Leo.'[22] He thought of trying to intercede, but it would not have helped: the Queen had already decided to send Leopold on a long voyage, probably to Australia, with a reliable older man to control him.[23]

But all this paled in the face of tragedy. Shortly before Arthur wrote his letter, fifteen-year-old Victoria of Hesse complained to her mother of a stiff neck. She had diphtheria, and in the days that followed the disease enveloped the family: only fourteen-year-old Elisabeth, 'Ella', escaped. Even Louis was ill, and Alice nursed them all, patiently, and in dread of the outcome. It was hard. Little Marie, Leopold's second Hesse godchild, died on 16 November. For him this was devastating: he had only just left Darmstadt, and the news revived the pain of Fritzie's death five years before. But worse would follow. Exhausted and pulled down by an indefinable sense of hopelessness, and by grief for her child, Alice succumbed to diphtheria herself, and on 14 December 1878, the seventeenth anniversary of her father's death, she died.

No loss would affect Leopold more deeply than this, and, sensing his feelings, his Oxford friends closed ranks around him. They had seen him with his sister, and knew how much she meant to him. Mrs

Liddell wrote. So did Dr Acland, who had lost his wife only six weeks before, while Leopold was still travelling – he wrote to the doctor as soon as the news reached him: 'To know dear Mrs Acland was to honour & reverence her – for her many acts of kindness, for the brightness she shed over her house, & for her constant sympathy with all those who suffered, mentally as well as physically.'[24] Now he responded sadly to Acland's condolences. To Max Müller he said that as soon as he heard his sister was ill, he guessed that she would die: 'It is a dreadful sorrow to me, she & I had so many thoughts, opinions, feelings in common – I was with her only a week before her eldest child fell ill, & she had told me all her wishes regarding her children's future – I do wish they did not live in Germany, as it will be almost impossible for me to do anything for them, being so far away . . . it is only by thinking of them that I can try to drive away the pain which is gnawing at my heart – I feel dreadfully knocked up, & both morally & physically unwell.'[25]

With the Prince of Wales, Leopold insisted on going to Darmstadt for the funeral, though the doctors advised against it for fear of infection. They went anyway, and in January Louis followed them back to England with his children; the brothers met them from the ship and took them to Osborne. Later, all moved on to Windsor where, in the weeks that followed, Leopold went out with the Hesses in the mornings, and spent most afternoons playing with the children in the Round Tower. After dinner in the evenings he sat up with Louis, smoking and looking at books, and talking late into the night, and a new friendship grew between the two men. For Leopold, taking an interest in the Hesse children helped to fill the aching gap left by his sister. He felt that he was doing something for her, and found himself able to confide in Louis without reserve. For Louis, stunned by the loss of a wife who had been the stronger partner in the marriage, the presence of a brother who also loved her, and who often thought and felt as she did, provided comfort. When the time came to go back to Darmstadt he told the Queen that he could not face it without Leopold and, reluctantly, she let him go.

They set off with the children on 28 February. Leopold strained his knee getting out of the railway carriage at Darmstadt, and though he tried to keep quiet about it, he was soon unable to walk.

179

The Queen was annoyed. She had been particularly keen for him to be a supporter at Arthur's wedding; now this was impossible, and Alfred had to take his place. But she could hardly ignore the warmth in her grandchildren's letters: 'It was such a pleasure Uncle Leo coming with us', Ella told her, ' & it made our parting not so sad as it would have been.' Eleven-year old Irene described their homecoming: 'It was so sad to see those dear rooms again looking so desolate & dreary! the birds were singing & that was the only bright thing there. It has been so nice having Uncle Leo with us on our arrival, & I hope his knee will soon be well again.'[26]

The children had to return to their lessons, and Louis to his duties, and during the day Leopold's only companion was six-year-old Alix. He was especially fond of the little girl, closest in age to his two lost godchildren, and he delighted in her company. 'Alix of course is with him the most', Ella told the Queen, '& they play little games of cards to-gether. She has learnt a trick which she does very knowingly.'[27] Sometimes Alix sat and painted in Leopold's room. On 10 March, she fell on a cucumber frame in the garden and cut her leg, and was proud to display her bandages beside her uncle's. 'I wish his were as trifling as hers', Ella said, though she could not help being amused.[28] With their father, the children spent most evenings playing cards in Leopold's room, but on the day of Arthur's wedding, Louis and his elder daughters celebrated with a small dinner party by the bedside.

Leopold was enjoying himself so much that it is almost tempting to wonder about his leg, which seemed to give way with impeccable timing. He was just walking again at the start of April, according to Victoria, who was about to celebrate her sixteenth birthday – 'it will be nice to have Mama's brother here', she told the Queen.[29] His own birthday fell two days later, and the whole family went out for a long drive and a picnic, but their time together was almost at an end. On 9 April the Crown Princess and her children came to collect Leopold for a short stay with them at the Palais Wiesbaden on his way home. 'We miss Uncle Leopold so very much', Ella told her grandmother a week later, '. . . poor Papa is so lonely without him.'[30]

Leopold was lonely too. From the Palais Wiesbaden, in rooms which his dead sister had often used, he wrote to Louis, 'I can't tell you how very, <u>very</u> unhappy I was yesterday as I parted from you and your dear children. I felt so happy and comfortable with you, and so much at home, if I can use the word. And I know that you miss me, and that you already feel yourself to be so very much alone. Oh! my dear brother, you know how much I share your feelings. I will <u>never</u> forget how good you and your dear children have been for me, and it hurt me so much to leave you.'[31] He did not look forward to returning home, with his future still unresolved, and he seized the chance to take a few days to himself in Paris on the way back.

But things at home had begun to change. Alice's death, and mounting pressure from her other children, were beginning to soften the Queen's attitude to her youngest son. Lord Beaconsfield may have had a hand in this too; after a difficult beginning, Leopold had come to see him as a friend, and to value his help. And Leopold was becoming more mature himself: the stand he made in the spring of 1878 had demonstrated that he could take independent action and come to no harm. From the start of 1879, he was gradually allowed more freedom, and was able to take on more of the public engagements which he handled so well.

In February 1879, he embarked on a series of speeches. In the Egyptian Hall of the Mansion House he spoke in support of the London Society for the Extension of University Teaching. Ruskin had fired his enthusiasm for educational reform, and the occasion gave him a chance to praise his old teacher and friend. It was a large meeting, and Gladstone was one of the other speakers. He wrote afterwards to the Dean of Windsor: 'As I passed Mr Collins in hastily leaving the meeting on Wednesday, I said to him "excellent" and the word will bear development. It applied to manner, voice, articulation, matter – keeping close to the subject, it was full of mind and it was difficult for anyone acquainted with the speeches of the Prince Consort not to recognise the father in the son. . . . The reception of it by the meeting . . . was not merely ceremonial and not merely loyal – it was thoroughly appreciative and was given to the performance on its merits.'[32]

At the Birkbeck Institute in London, Leopold praised the teaching of foreign languages: 'with every real increase of understanding of our fellow-men of different races', he said, 'some unkindly illusion disappears; we learn to realize their likeness to ourselves'.[33] Gladstone was not the only one to make comparisons with the Prince Consort. Princess Louise received a letter from her father-in-law, the Duke of Argyll, telling her that her brother's speeches 'have been remarkable indeed – a quality about them which unmistakably reminds one of your Father's thoughtfulness and power of expression. They have attracted great notice and deservedly. I always knew he was studious and reflective but I had no idea he had such powers as those speeches indicate.'[34]

In May, Leopold spoke at Grosvenor House at the annual meeting of the Royal Association in Aid of the Deaf and Dumb, showing considerable knowledge of the teaching methods used to unlock the silence of the deaf. Instinctive sympathy with the handicapped and disadvantaged would become one of his hallmarks, and, looking forward to a day when the state might take over responsibility for all such work, he reminded his audience that until that day came it was up to them; there should be 'no sorrowful list of sufferers whose intelligence might have been developed, and whose lives might have been brightened had our exertions been more timely and more sustained'.[35]

He went further afield in October, visiting Sheffield, where he opened the Firth College and spoke again on education, praising the town's schools for offering girls an education to degree standard. He went to Walkley, where Ruskin's Guild of St George was busy with plans for a new museum, intended as 'a working man's Bodleian Library'.[36] The tour opened his eyes to the hard and often thankless work people across the country gave to causes they believed in; in response to the Prime Minister's praise for his speech he wrote 'in praise of my host, whose generosity is only equalled by his modesty. He has given over £100,000 in charities to Sheffield, which is the more surprising as he has a family of 9 children.' Cautiously, he asked if official recognition could be given.[37]

This was real work at last, which suited his abilities and had no political or personal complication; the country noticed, and was impressed. But beyond a certain point, the Queen would not go. Leopold still wanted the peerage, as a confirmation of his adult status and a widening of his opportunities for work, but repeated appeals by him and on his behalf had got nowhere. He was not the only one to sense its importance. The press was beginning to comment on his exclusion from the Lords, and in February 1879 Arthur told his fiancée that he hoped to persuade the Queen to make the gesture on the occasion of their wedding: 'I hope she wont refuse me. Poor Leo is <u>so anxious</u> for it & I think that as Bertie, Affie and I all sit in the House of Lords, Leo <u>ought</u> too: I was quite sorry to see him sitting among the ladies upstairs while the three other brothers sat in the House.'[38]

But as far as the Queen was concerned, Leopold's first duty was to support her, and any gesture she made was designed to encourage this. She tried to recognise his need for independence by granting him the use of a suite of rooms at Claremont, one of her favourite houses, but as she retained suites for herself and Beatrice and their servants, and the right to occupy the rest of the house, except his private rooms, when she chose, his pleasure in the decision was limited, and the move to Claremont ended his life at Boyton, where he had been happy. Arthur and Louise, Alice and Louis and their children, and many of his closest friends, had been entertained at Boyton, and he had found a place in the local area, where he is still remembered. In 1877 he provided a new organ for the village church.

Dividing his time between Claremont and the Queen, Leopold continued his secretarial work, and the ending of Russia's war with Turkey opened a wider range of issues to him. These were interesting, and his working relationship with his mother improved, but this only made her more determined to hold on to him. She was no longer sure about the long voyage; Alice's death had made her nervous, and Lord Beaconsfield was all ready to send Leopold to Australia for the opening of an exhibition in 1879, when the Queen took up her pen: 'Since the loss of her beloved child . . . she cannot bring herself to consent to send her very delicate Son, who has been <u>4 or 5 times</u> at <u>death's door</u> . . . to a great <u>distance</u>, to a climate to which he is a Stranger and to expose him to dangers which he may not be able to avert. Even if he did <u>not</u> suffer, the <u>terrible anxiety</u> which the Queen would <u>undergo</u> . . . would unfit her for her duties at home and might undermine her health.'[39] Instead, Leopold was promised a trip to Canada in 1880 to see Louise, whose husband had just become

Governor-General, and in August he was allowed to sail from Osborne to Balmoral in the Admiralty yacht HMS *Lively*, cruising west to the Scilly Isles, then around the coast, via the Isle of Man and past Cape Wrath to Aberdeen.

That year, 1879, had brought many positive changes for him, but the central problem was unresolved. He was still tied to his mother, with rewards if he was good, and storms if he acted independently. As the first anniversary of Alice's death came round, the pain of her loss was sharp, and on a dark morning in December Leopold stood with the rest of the family in the mausoleum at Frogmore and cried for her and her children. He invited the clergyman to his room afterwards, and they talked about the clause in the Litany which appeals for deliverance from sudden death. Quietly, Leopold said: 'I think a sudden death would perhaps be happiest.' He paused for a second, then added, 'For oneself, I mean, but it must be such a shock to others, and it leaves so many things unfinished & incomplete.'[40] He still felt desperately alone, and craved acceptance and affection: without that, the emptiness would remain.

THIRTEEN

SEARCHING FOR A WIFE

Leopold needed to marry. On a practical level, this was the only way he could gain a home of his own, and the space to make his own decisions. For himself, he needed confirmation that he was normal and acceptable. He needed the affection which he felt he had known only as a visitor – with the Hesses, or the Hanovers, or his friends at Oxford. Whatever objective view may be taken of his situation – there is no doubt, for example, that the Queen loved him and thought she was acting in his best interests – his own analysis was painfully clear. He believed that he had been without love at home ever since his father's death. When he was nine Major Elphinstone had said that continual scolding and criticism were necessary to correct his tendency to selfishness; sadly, this unhappiness was the end result.

By 1879 he saw two possibilities: either he could meet someone and fall in love, with the same thrill of emotion he still felt for Lady Breadalbane – only this time the 'someone' would be suitable and available, and would return his feelings. Or, perhaps more realistically, he could find a pleasant young woman who would accept him, and their marriage would be a practical arrangement, giving them both a home, a family and a degree of freedom. Gratitude, and his own gentle nature, would have made a kind husband of him. His fear, as he launched on the search in earnest, was that no-one would accept him at all. He still doubted that people really wanted his company, and even if he had not, his health would always be a barrier.

No woman could be asked to marry him unless she had been

told the truth about his condition, and issues which had been unspoken for years now had to be put into words. The Queen had never really understood Leopold's haemophilia. She knew that he had problems with his joints, and she knew that he bled, but she was still waiting for him to grow out of it. Sometimes she thought he had. This was not so surprising because the doctors themselves did not fully understand what they were dealing with; by the 1870s the symptoms of haemophilia were recognised, but the cause was still open to guesswork – and the Queen would not accept that the bleeding was hereditary. She took Leopold's fits far more seriously, and so did his would-be brides.

Since 1866, when the fits began, they had hardly been mentioned, and the Queen seems to have regarded the subject as a secret to be kept within the family – understandably, at a time when epilepsy was regarded with suspicion and fear. Leopold was often reminded of the danger of fits when he wanted to travel, or to appear in public, though, in fact, he never had a fit in a public place. His seizures occurred rarely, at yearly, sometimes two-yearly intervals, and always during or at the end of serious episodes of bleeding. They may have been triggered by pain, or anxiety, and started at one of the most difficult periods of his boyhood, when he was subjected to the unwelcome presence of Archie Brown, and surrounded by arguments between Stirling and the Highlanders.

His fits appear to have been mild attacks, involving loss of consciousness, but not the convulsive movement of the limbs which occurs in a 'grand mal' seizure. Twice he was said to have fainted; during the prolonged illness of 1870 he said it himself: 'I fainted after dinner, & of course afterwards I had an awful headache.'[1] Once there was doubt about a particular episode being a fit, and unlike haemophilia, the problem seemed to be something Leopold would outgrow: 'During the last nine years', Jenner wrote in 1881, 'the Prince has had two attacks, and in the spring of this year may possibly have had a third – as to the occurrence of this last some doubts exist.'[2] For the Queen though, and for the girls he wished to marry, the word 'fit' was too ominous to ignore.

After his failure to propose to Princess Frederica, Leopold felt very dispirited. In January 1879, she arrived in London, and he was sent to meet her. He found it hard to shake off the longing that things could be different between them, and as the weeks passed, that longing grew. In February, two weeks before leaving for Darmstadt, he told his mother that he wanted to marry and she was sympathetic, though she advised caution. Frederica was not mentioned. The Queen suggested that Leopold should see several princesses, and then take time to think – perhaps Louis could make up a list, and Leopold could visit him and make a tour of inspection in the autumn. She warned that the search would be hard, and if he were ever to find happiness he would need to curb his selfishness and learn 'self control & amiability . . . anxiety to <u>sacrifice</u> your own wishes & your own <u>will</u> & to follow the advice of others – all which you never do <u>willingly</u> . . . if no <u>fit Princess</u> can be found, we must <u>try</u> & find a young Lady <u>here</u> – who would answer all your and our expectations'.[3]

The dream of Frederica was doomed to failure. Leopold still hankered after her when he returned from Darmstadt in April, and Alick Yorke appealed to friends to speak to her on his behalf, but soon Frederica took the matter in hand and confessed her feelings for Baron von Pawel-Rammingen. To his credit, Leopold's attitude changed as soon as the truth came out, and despite all that was said about his selfishness, he set his feelings aside and did his utmost to help her. As a member of the House of Hanover, Frederica was also a Princess of Great Britain and Ireland, and the Queen could give permission for her marriage. This she did, undertaking to pay for the ceremony and provide the couple with a home. 'Leopold has been her great help throughout', she told the Crown Princess.[4]

That November he set out for Darmstadt with two princesses in mind, Elisabeth of Hesse-Cassel and Viktoria of Baden. He was inclined to favour Elisabeth, having liked what he saw of her in the spring, but after this visit she slipped from the list, and when Arthur recommended her for him a year later no-one listened. Viktoria was the Queen's preference, but she was only seventeen; her mother wanted nothing to be said for another year, so the whole visit was inconclusive.

Once again, Leopold squeezed in an unannounced stay in Paris on the way home, much to his mother's annoyance. He dined with the ambassador, and tried to pack as much as he could into a limited time. 'It was horribly cold . . .', he told Louis, 'snow on the ground, & the streets like glass, on account of the tremendous frosts, & hardly a cab to be got – <u>most</u> inconvenient – I went to the "Assemblée" on the Monday, & saw Gambetta & Jules Ferry, Léon Say, Clémenceau (the future "Robespierre"), & other persons of interest – I went to two very good plays – a most improper one called "Jonathan" – & a very pretty little opera by Lecocq, called: "a jolie Persane" – very pretty scenery & costumes.'[5]

During the winter, his mind turned again to Viktoria of Baden. He had promised not to mention marriage, but surely it could do no harm to see her? The Queen was planning to go to Darmstadt the following Easter for the confirmation of the two elder Hesse girls and she asked him to make the arrangements; he assumed he would be going, and told Louis, 'I have told Mamma that before going to you for the confirmation, <u>I</u> should like to go a little to Carlsruhe to see a little more of V of B & to make myself a little more known to her. . . . You see there is no chance of the girl caring to marry me if she does not <u>know</u> me.'[6]

His mother had other ideas. On 16 March, with all the arrangements made, she let him know that he would not be going with her. He was stunned, and very bitter. 'After months of working hard for her, & doing everything I can to please her, & saving her trouble on every possible occasion, I am repaid by insults & most studied unkindness', he complained to Louis.[7] It might have surprised the Queen to know why he was so upset. It was not missing Viktoria of Baden that bothered him, nor yet being cheated of another holiday; he was afraid that this might be his last chance to see Louis and the children. Much as he wanted to go to Canada, he accepted that a long and probably stormy sea voyage might be an ordeal he would not survive.

The Queen gave his health as her reason for forbidding Darmstadt, but it is hard not to suspect that she had another reason. Six years earlier, Leopold had told Stirling that he feared she wanted to push him into marriage with the heiress Frances Maynard, who was then still a child. In 1880 'Daisy' Maynard was old enough to marry, and very pretty. In her autobiography, *Life's Ebb and Flow*, she described meetings with the Prime Minister and his secretary to assess her suitability, followed by an invitation to 'dine and sleep' at Windsor in December 1879, with her mother and her stepfather Lord Rosslyn. The Rosslyns were delighted by the prospect of a royal son-in-law, and Lord Rosslyn's equerry, who had been in love with Daisy for more than a year, had to promise complete silence to give the royal match a chance. That equerry was Lord Brooke, Leopold's closest friend.

Leopold never proposed, though he would have liked to. According to Daisy, he gave a house party at Claremont, with Brooke and herself among the guests. 'One afternoon', she remembered, 'the Prince opened his heart to me. He cared for someone else, whom he took great care not to name. . . . He knew all about Lord Brooke's feeling for me, and he said that if there was any understanding between Lord Brooke and myself, it would be easy to engage the Queen's sentiment in favour of my first love. Again and again the footman came in to pull down the blinds and light the lamps, but the Prince would say "Come back in ten minutes time" and the poor footman kept coming and going for at least an hour while we made our plans.' The next day, Brooke took Daisy for a walk in the rain-drenched park, proposed and was accepted, but the three conspirators kept this news to themselves.[8]

Leopold did give a large house party at Claremont in January, which may have been the occasion Daisy described. If so, their silence was kept for a long time, and he must have invented the 'someone else' as a gentle way of letting her down. Rumours of an engagement between him and Daisy began to spread, and on 21 March the Crown Princess told her mother, 'Another report is in the German newspapers – wch I suppose I may consider a mere invention, viz: that Leopold is engaged to a Miss Maynard, Ld Rosslyn's step-daughter.'[9] Louis saw the same newspapers, and made some comment to Leopold, who replied, 'What you said about Miss Maynard amused me very much – I wish it were true! But she is as good as engaged to my friend Lord Brooke, & I could not do anything so dishonourable as to try & cut him out.'

He went on to say he had abandoned the idea of Viktoria of Baden, because her mother was making difficulties. But engagements seemed to be in the air, and this must have made him all the more anxious to succeed; his nephew Wilhelm was engaged, and the news that Crown Prince Rudolf had just been accepted by his second cousin, Princess Stephanie of Belgium, really made him think. 'He wrote me a long letter', he told Louis, 'calling her an Angel – & saying he was going to lead such a virtuous life, & had quite done "with the old life". How long will that last, I wonder?' His own search was still intense: 'I have my eye on another young lady', he added, 'never mind what her name is. . . . She is English, well-born, pretty, very nice, & very rich. But of course it is still quite in the clouds. And I trust you will not <u>breathe</u> a word to Bertie or Alix or anyone, <u>save Mamma</u>. Lord Beaconsfield is helping in the matter.'[10]

A few days before this letter was written, Beaconsfield had indeed received 'a most extraordinary box . . . about the young Lady', and had sent for Montagu Corry for an urgent conference.[11] The young lady in question was Mary Baring, the only surviving child of the late Baron Ashburton, and as the Queen set off for Darmstadt, plans were afoot to arrange a meeting between her and Leopold, under the watchful eye of Lady Ely, one of the Queen's ladies, who arranged a dinner which all parties agreed to refer to as 'afternoon tea' for the Queen's benefit. It was a great success: Leopold was delighted, so were Mary and her mother, and they invited him to lunch; further meetings were being discussed when Beaconsfield inadvertently dropped the word 'dinner' into a letter, and the Queen exploded in fury. Telegrams and letters flew – 'I don't know what I'm to do', Leopold told Corry, 'I <u>wish</u> you could come here! And I was <u>so</u> happy yesterday. The lunch went off very well, and we visited several studios afterwards together – and we talked over the proposed visit to her place in Hampshire and I liked her more and more – and now I have this <u>exceedingly</u> unpleasant letter.'[12]

But the storm soon passed. The Queen was far too worried about the impending fall of the Conservative government to give much thought to the propriety of dinner parties, and quietly, Leopold's romance blossomed. Early in April he spent a weekend with Lady Ashburton and her daughter at Melchet Court, their Hampshire home, and his mind was made up. There was another meeting at Windsor, and he was ecstatic, telling Louis, 'You must not think she is a <u>beauty</u>. For she is not that. But she is very good-looking "très <u>Grande-dame</u>" a very good figure, tall, dark, & a very sweet & fascinating expression, decidedly clever. And I <u>believe</u> she loves me! I <u>have</u> proposed! & she asked time to think, she evidently does not jump at the <u>position</u> – on the contrary she rather dreads it.'[13] He was hoping for an answer when they met two days later, little knowing that Mary's response had already been given. On 27 April she wrote apologetically to Corry, telling him that at nineteen she felt too young to marry, and she hoped Leopold would 'forget all about Windsor – and then sometime (perhaps a year?) hence if he still thinks the same he can revive the subject – if not I shall quite understand'. Her true feelings only slipped out at the end of the letter: 'his health, between ourselves, is what I should dread.'[14]

It was over, but Corry and Beaconsfield said nothing and Leopold continued to hope. The Queen returned and took up the negotiations with Lady Ashburton, who made endless difficulties about her daughter's future position, though she too confessed to Corry, 'the <u>fits</u> are what terrify me'.[15] There were letters exchanged, hopes raised and lowered, but by the first week of May it was obvious that there would be no wedding. The Queen was furious, but profound misery was all Leopold felt. Two weeks earlier, when his hopes were high, he had seen Frederica married – now Mary was lost to him too. But he was soon lifted out of the gloom by a hand no-one could have expected, least of all himself. On 10 May, the day before Mary's final refusal arrived, he met Lady Breadalbane, and found that the cloud over their friendship had disappeared, giving way to deeper feeling on both sides. At that moment there was probably no other comfort that could have reached him. 'What happiness', he remembered in his diary a year later, 'but much, much too brief.'[16]

The moment of his departure for Canada had come. On the day of his meeting with Alma, he had left Windsor for London to make a round of visits to family and friends – with the unspoken fear that this might be his last chance to see them. Louis of Hesse came to England with his elder daughters, and on Thursday 13 May, he accompanied Leopold to Euston station for the midday train to Liverpool. Several officers of the Household were there to see Leopold off, and a friendly crowd; there were cheers, and shouts of 'God bless you, sir', and 'the train steamed out of the station, bearing one of our most popular Princes'.[17] The ship sailed from Liverpool that evening, carrying Leopold, Collins, Royle, Alick Yorke, and Leopold's fox terrier, Vic, and they were delayed by ice in the gulf of Canada before reaching land ten days later.

So Leopold was away from home in June, when Daisy Maynard's engagement to Lord Brooke was made public. In July Alice Liddell became engaged to Reginald Hargreaves, an Oxford contemporary of the Prince's who had waited patiently for four years. Leopold might have felt rather left out, but at least Canada provided a wealth of activities, new sights and sounds. Shortly after his arrival a grand review of Canadian troops was held in honour of the Queen's birthday, in sweltering heat. There was a dinner party in the evening, and the next day Louise and Lord Lorne took him around the hospitals and educational institutions of Toronto, before going on to Quebec and Montreal. Here, they attended a performance of *The Pirates of Penzance*. On 27 May they toured a gun factory: 'It was very interesting', one of Louise's ladies told the Queen, 'as one saw the whole process & the finished guns. . . . In the muzzle of one of the guns was a lovely bouquet for the Princess & a button hole bouquet for Prince Leopold in the touch hole.'[18]

Next, Leopold and Louise were due to tour the United States; they visited Niagara Falls, and then headed for Chicago, where Leopold had a meeting with General Sherman, and was intrigued and fascinated to attend part of the Republican Party Convention. He saw General Garfield chosen as presidential candidate, and when questioned about his impressions by a local reporter, he said, 'my sensations were conflicting, and I have thought much and will think long upon what I saw. This Republic is certainly a remarkable institution' – a diplomatic answer which gave absolutely nothing away. Before their departure, Collins had been warned to treat the press with civility, giving them as little information as possible: 'if they press you too hard you can always appeal to their feelings by asking them if they would like all the details of their own private life published.'[19]

American impressions of Leopold were curiously mixed. The reporter from *The World* felt that he resembled 'a young French-Canadian gentleman, having the . . . breezy, curly hair and the sallow complexion which distinguish the better class of that race', though according to the Toronto *Mail*, he was 'a fair skinned young man, who looks younger than he is'. One paper made fun of his way of walking. Most thought him well below average height: in fact he was a little less than 5 ft 10 in, but may not always have stood very straight. The *Milwaukee Sentinel*'s reporter, who was enterprising enough to secure an interview with Leopold and his sister, came closer: 'Prince Leopold is rather tall, well knit frame, fair[?] hair and complexion and in his manner entirely unaffected.' He was taken with the friendliness of brother and sister, commenting on the 'total absence of that chilling hauteur which persons of far less significance and worth so often assume'. Their mother would have been proud of them.

They toured Chicago, then took the two hour train journey to Milwaukee. Leopold told the reporter from the *Sentinel* that he was hoping to explore California, 'but late advices from Her Majesty, my mother, have led me to forego this extensive trip' – another part of the report that had the ring of truth.[20] After ten days Leopold and Louise rejoined Lord Lorne in Quebec, exhausted but happy, and set off for a restful salmon-fishing trip in the wilderness by the Cascapedia river. Unfortunately, Leopold fell over while trying to draw in a salmon, injuring both legs, and it was thought wise to return to Quebec. At the end of the month he and his sister set sail for England.

By August he was at Balmoral. There would be no more talk of marriage for the rest of the year, only reminders. On Wednesday 15 September, Alice Liddell was married in Westminster Abbey, wearing a handsome brooch in the shape of a horseshoe – Leopold's gift. He wrote to her from Scotland the night before, enclosing a photograph of himself, signed and inscribed with the date of the wedding, and told her, 'I shall think much of you and your family tomorrow; for you know how I have felt and sympathised with you and yours, in your joys and your sorrows, Your dear sister, Edith, will also be much in my thoughts tomorrow.'[21]

He resumed his work for the Queen, but in his absence it had become a political minefield. Leopold was steered into the job by Lord Beaconsfield, and in the four years they had worked together, he had come to rely on the Prime Minister's judgement and to see him and Corry as personal friends. Both men used him as a channel for communicating with the Queen; they used him for their own ends, at times, and the extent of their influence is obvious. The Prince was fascinated by politics from an early age, and his first sympathies were all Liberal. He got on well with Gladstone, whose son was one of his friends at Oxford, and when the Conservative government came to power in 1874, he complained to Stirling, 'I am very much grieved at the results of this election, I did not think that the English were such idiots as to be carried away by beer; but we are still very ignorant & have evidently much to learn.'[22]

The election result of April 1880 found him utterly changed, voicing sentiments which could have been his mother's. 'It shows what wretched, ignorant, misled, idiots most of the electors must be . . . . I really cannot conceive what has come over people', he told her. He perceived the new House of Commons as a hotbed of 'atheists, home rulers, republicans &c', hiding under the name of 'Liberal', and predicted doom.[23] Blinded by pity for Lord Beaconsfield, his first reactions were extreme, and even when the shock had passed he did not adapt to the new situation; the change of government caught him when his mind was on Mary Baring, and he did not consider its implications as carefully as he should have done. For four years he had discussed his work with Beaconsfield and Corry, and he did not see that with the change of government this had become inappropriate.

The first problem that faced all the Queen's advisers in April was the need to persuade her to send for one of the Liberal leaders to form the new government: either the Prince of Wales's friend, Lord Hartington, Liberal leader in the Commons, or Lord Granville, who led the party in the Lords. She liked neither, but had a positive horror of Gladstone, who renounced his leadership some years before, and was now making a triumphant and popular return to public life. Leopold spoke to Corry, who advised Granville. Beaconsfield advised the Queen to call Hartington, probably knowing full well that neither man would accept office over Gladstone, whose appointment was inevitable.

With a Liberal government in power, Leopold found himself in the position Ponsonby had occupied for six years, dealing with politicians whose ideas he did not support, but he lacked the political maturity of the private secretary. He was critical of government policy, and the Queen made things worse by using him as a buffer; ministers who wanted to speak to the sovereign found themselves conducted to Leopold instead, and he could only act as messenger, saying what he was told to say and denying them by his presence the opportunity to explain or argue their case. Many Liberals had an instinctive resistance even to legitimate royal authority; they were quick to resent this forced intrusion of a young man with no official position into the work of government. When they disliked the message, they blamed the messenger.

Worse still, the Queen was not prepared to give up her discussions with her former Prime Minister, or her reliance on his advice. She wanted to communicate with the Tories in secret, and when Ponsonby refused to handle the correspondence for her she turned to others, particularly Leopold, who was already in touch with Corry and Beaconsfield on his own behalf, and seems not to have seen that this new development had wider implications. In the 1920s and '30s, the publication of extracts from the Queen's letters and journal produced a flurry of interest in her political role, and it was then that constitutional historians noticed the part Leopold played. Picking up on the impropriety of his discussions with the defeated Conservative leader, and on the comments of his Liberal critics, the idea grew that he had exercised a mischievous influence on the Queen, encouraging her extreme Conservatism. A favourite authority, often quoted, was Sir Almeric Fitzroy, who was said to have spoken of 'the persistent and unremitting interference of Prince Leopold in State matters. Not content with influencing the Queen's action in its relation to individuals', Fitzroy went on, 'he appears to have aimed at being her political guide, and . . . his intervention was often the cause of acute difficulty.'[24]

In fact, Fitzroy was no authority at all, as he had nothing to do with Court or government until after Leopold's death; at best, his information was only stale gossip. His version of events was obviously wrong: if Leopold had been able to influence the Queen in any way, he would not even have been working as her assistant. But from comments like Fitzroy's the legend grew, and biographers developed it further, suggesting that the Prince of Wales, who was denied access to Cabinet papers and kept away from the centre of affairs, bitterly resented the favouritism shown to his younger brother. This too has no basis in fact. From the time Leopold reached his late teens, the Prince of Wales did his utmost to support him, and to help him find ways of breaking into the adult world. If the future King resented his exclusion from official business – he was not allowed a Cabinet key, or access to sensitive papers, because he was thought to be indiscreet, and to lack the application for serious work – he knew better than to blame Leopold.

The Queen and Beaconsfield had manoeuvred Leopold into a situation he never wanted and was not qualified to handle, and from 1880 onwards, the dangers of this became apparent. He may at times have acted unwisely or spoken out of turn; for the most part he simply spoke for the Queen, using her words or Beaconsfield's, but while some members of the new government resented him and muttered, the two men who had most cause for grievance, the Prince of Wales and Ponsonby, were close enough to the situation to understand. Ponsonby often disagreed with Leopold's opinions, but respected his ability; during a particularly sensitive argument about senior military appointments in 1881 he remarked that it was strange that the Queen should consult Leopold rather than Arthur, who was a career soldier. Then he thought again, adding, 'She is right – I don't think there is anything in the good amiable Prince Arthur.'[25]

By the autumn of 1880, Leopold was beginning to understand that his political views were best kept quiet. In an ironic reversal of their earlier relationship, he was careful now of what he said to Ponsonby. At Balmoral in October he spent some time with the secretary, who told his wife, 'I walked yesterday with him to and from Abergeldie Main. He was very talkative including politics though he did not dwell upon them and shifted his subject incessantly – in London gossip he was much more at home and rattled away.'[26] Leopold was in a good mood and perfect health that day, and about to leave Balmoral for the south: 'I'm leaving tomorrow at 12.30', he told Louis, 'and I am absolutely delighted about it. I miss you and the dear children very, very much.'[27]

Unfortunately, he was about to suffer another fall which would confine him to bed at Claremont for weeks. At first he suffered agonies with his knee, and the tight bandaging and splints applied by the doctors did not succeed in keeping the joint straight, so that even when the pain subsided his leg was bent, making the recovery long and hard. Inactivity confined and depressed him: in his own words he was 'tied by the legs', and haunted by the fear of permanent disability. There seemed to be so little for him to look forward to: he was still pushing for the peerage, with the support of his brothers and Lord Beaconsfield, but with no sign of success. After nearly two years his search for a bride had led nowhere, and now even Royle, in his mid-forties, was about to marry 'a most lovely young girl of 20!' – Leopold was openly envious.[28]

The beginning of December found him still at Claremont, restless and ill at ease, and barely able to walk. This had been a difficult time of year for the royal family since 1861; now it was even more so, and he wrote to Louis; 'As the sad 14th draws near, I write a few lines to tell you (what you know without any words of mine) how very much you & yours will be in my thoughts on Tuesday. It seems but yesterday that the fatal news came, & that Bertie & I took that sad journey. . . . When I feel lonely & unhappy (as I so often do) I often think with deep regret how I can no longer write to darling Alice, & confide in her, & receive her affectionate, but always sensible advice.'[29]

He was about to embark on another unsuccessful attempt at marriage, which would be doubly painful since it involved the opposition of members of his own family. In February, Princess Helena and Prince Christian had welcomed an extended visit from two of Christian's nieces, Princesses Auguste Viktoria and Caroline Mathilde of Schleswig-Holstein. The elder of the two, Auguste Viktoria, was engaged to Wilhelm of Prussia, but the younger, known as 'Calma', was prettier, and the Queen took to her straight away. Leopold had his heart set on Mary Baring at the time, but as the year turned he remembered Calma, and the Queen was prepared to encourage him. 'I (in my heart of hearts) dislike his marrying & dread it, for many reasons', she told the Crown Princess, 'but as he will do so, – we must prevent a bad mistake being made.'[30]

Calma's father had died at the beginning of 1880, and Christian was her guardian, so the way looked clear, but Leopold's first enquiries met with a baffling range of objections. He was told that

Calma was in line to marry Alfred's brother-in-law, Sergei Alexandrovich of Russia; to the Queen this seemed to be no obstacle, as she trusted Sergei's sister to put him off – Calma's younger sister, Luise, she suggested, would be far more suitable for Sergei. But at the same time, Helena hinted that Calma had 'nervous attacks'; the Queen wanted one of her own doctors to investigate this, and argued that if it were true, then Calma should not be marrying at all. She sensed that her daughter was making difficulties: 'What is annoying abt. all this', she wrote, 'is the want of truthfulness & openness in Lenchen who governs Christian entirely.'[31]

The water became muddier by the day. Alfred and his wife Marie were drawn in, and Marie also came away feeling that Helena and Christian were not being honest. Then the Queen decided to make a fight of it, indignant that she was prevented from speaking to Calma, who was a granddaughter of her own sister. It was not until February that another objection emerged, which the anti-marriage camp clung to as a drowning man to a lifebelt. They said that in 1879, Calma's father had written a letter positively forbidding a match between her and Leopold. Much as they wanted to support the engagement, they claimed, they could not possible ignore this command from beyond the grave.

The Queen had to accept that they had won, but she was not pleased. Wilhelm and his fiancée opposed the marriage, though she had counted on their support, and it was obvious that her daughter and son-in-law had been spreading stories about Leopold's fits, which were meant to be kept within the family; there was no telling what else they might have said. The really interesting question was the one nobody asked: why, in 1879, would it even have occurred to the Duke of Augustenburg that Leopold might want to marry his daughter? No hint remains of Leopold's feelings after this, but it must have been painful for him to find that his own sister and brother-in-law, and the nephew he was always kind to, had joined forces against him. It must have made the search seem more hopeless than ever.

FOURTEEN

THE TURNING POINT

In 1881, Leopold made use of a small green Letts' office diary to record his activities and impressions in a vivid, clipped style. There is no evidence that he kept a diary before, or would do so again, but if this was an experiment, it was an amazing chance. He could not possibly have known that 1881 would bring the two things he most wanted – the peerage and a promise of marriage – and the diary provides a valuable snapshot of his work and pleasures, his attitudes, character and friendships, at a turning point in his life.

The New Year found him at Osborne. It was bitterly cold, making his back and legs painful, but he expected this on the Isle of Wight in winter, and his mind was on politics. At the end of December he wrote to Louis of Hesse about the situation in Ireland, where bad harvests and repression were causing dangerous unrest. 'The "reign of terror" in Ireland still goes on', he said, '& the number of assassinations, & other atrocities of every kind is appalling – Still the Gov^t sit with folded hands. It will come to a terrible smash soon, & much (probably innocent) blood will be shed.'[1] He anticipated that the trouble could spread to England, so it was not with particularly friendly feeling that he saw four Cabinet ministers brought up from Cowes on 5 January, squashed together in a small carriage drawn by a single horse, to present his mother with the text of the Queen's Speech.

The day would go down in history, because the Queen refused to approve the Speech. She objected to a passage spelling out her government's intention to evacuate Kandahar in Afghanistan, because she thought it dangerous to announce the move in advance. The ministers were annoyed by her stand, and several hours passed before a compromise was reached. The whole incident was a government bungle; Lord Hartington had deliberately avoided the normal courtesy of sending the Speech in advance because he knew that the Queen would not like it. This was not the way to treat her, and a lot of unnecessary indignation was all he achieved. Sir William Harcourt, the Home Secretary, annoyed her further by his blunt assertion that the Speech was the speech of the ministers, which the sovereign was obliged to approve: 'Harcourt showed his <u>customary tact</u> (?)', was Leopold's only comment.[2]

Later, Leopold was criticised for his part in the day's events. It was said that he encouraged his mother to act unconstitutionally; in fact, he was just an intermediary, speaking the words others gave him. His only independent action was helpful: when the Queen set out her objections in a memorandum, which the ministers refused to take, he managed to modify her language, finding a form of words acceptable to both sides. With so much bad feeling in the air this was an achievement, but no-one gave him credit for it. The politicians resented him simply for being there.

A few days later he went to London with Alick Yorke, to hear Lord Lytton make his maiden speech in the Lords, and to call on Lord Beaconsfield on his mother's behalf to discuss Lord Harcourt's words. He only had two days, but made excellent use of them, attending debates in the Commons, and spending evenings in the club and the theatre. Lord Brooke joined him, and he saw as many other friends as he could. London had always drawn Leopold, because it offered company, stimulation and entertainment, away from the stifling atmosphere of home. He particularly loved the theatre at all levels: high opera, plays, concerts, music hall – every outing was a treat. He saw some plays several times, and knew the actors well. On a later visit in January his diary records: 'to Gaiety Theatre. "The forty thieves" burlesque – Nellie Farren (looking as wonderfully jolly as ever, & as amusing). Kate Vaughan (quite lovely but stupid) Connie Gilchrist – & dear little Phyllis Broughton whom I'd not seen since April . . . in the intervals of the acts Phyllis, Connie Gilchrist, Miss Hobson, & Lizzie Wilson came & sat with us in the smoking room at the box. Phyllis has much improved, grown stouter, her figure is now perfect.'[3]

The Gaiety was a favourite haunt, and occasionally he and his friends gave supper parties for the actresses, particularly Phyllis Broughton and her sisters, lasting into the early hours. He liked pretty women, and they liked him. Later in the year, in June, he saw Sarah Bernhardt at the Gaiety in *Froufrou*, 'an interesting and affecting play, beautifully acted – went in the 1st entr'acte to see Sarah in her room (had not seen her since '79) she was dressing. We had a very pleasant talk.'[4] She must have told him she was about to leave England; he saw her again a few days later in *La Dame aux Camélias*, and made a special visit to her dressing-room to say goodbye. Lillie Langtry appears in the diary too, in July: 'I spent a <u>delightful</u> hour with <u>Lillie Langtry</u> who was looking as lovely as ever', he wrote, 'though very sad at the death of her brother who has been torn to death by a tiger in India – She recounted the whole Shrewsbury & Battenberg affairs to me, & I gave her some advice.'[5]

On 12 January Leopold returned to Osborne, to be engulfed in a fierce snowstorm which isolated the house for days. A week later came 'a day such as not even the "oldest inhabitant" remembers – a terrific hurricane blowing with snow drifting every way. The snow had been blown into my room in the night right through the double windows – no possibility of going out . . . one side of the house was uninhabitable as the smoke was blown down all the chimney.'[6] On the roads the snow was ten, even sixteen feet deep, and horse-drawn snow-ploughs struggled in vain, but three times Leopold waded through the drifts to Osborne Cottage to see the Empress Eugénie; one afternoon he sat for two hours, fascinated by her account of her early days in France, and the problems that faced an empress who was not of royal birth. No-one prompted him to do this; once, the sound of his mother's arrival was enough to send him hurrying away through the snow – 'VR arrived & I fled.'[7] He liked the Empress as he liked most older people, whose stories were a constant source of interest.

The Queen's concerns about Leopold and 'society' had never eased, and she never seemed to see the breadth of his friendships. He did enjoy the company of actresses and dancers, and his 'society' friends, and sometimes did things with them which his mother would not have liked, but he was equally happy to spend an afternoon with an elderly aunt, and his frequent bouts of illness made him sensitive to suffering in others. He never went to London without spending time with his great-aunt, the Duchess of Cambridge. At one of his house parties at Claremont, his old nurse Mrs Thurston was a welcome guest; one evening he drove her to a dinner party with the Collinses. This attentiveness was one of his most attractive qualities.

But in the spring of 1881 one friendship was drawing to an end. For some months Lord Beaconsfield had been urging the Queen to give Leopold the peerage. In March the discussions reached a delicate stage, and Beaconsfield told him: 'With respect to the Queen's wish, that you should give an undertaking that you will not make your Peerage an excuse for constantly running up to London, I have advised Her Majesty not to press for any declaration of that kind, & have offered myself to receive your honourable engagement not to abuse Her Majesty's generous favour.'[8] The Queen's fears were not unique to Leopold: she had felt the same about Arthur's peerage, though she granted it when he asked. Only Leopold faced refusal, but now Beaconsfield drafted a letter for him to send his mother; he copied it, with a few alterations to make the authorship less obvious, and at long last, she gave way.

It might never have happened without Beaconsfield, but the triumph was muted for Leopold by the knowledge that his friend was dying. He kept in touch through Corry, now Lord Rowton, and on 16 April he called on the ex-Prime Minister at 19 Curzon Street; he was not able to see him, but the news was hopeful. Leopold was on his way to a house party at Sandringham, and it was there three days later, with an east wind tearing through the trees and hail falling, that the final telegram reached him. On 21 April he went to Curzon Street again: 'I was taken up to the bedroom & there was the open leaden coffin on trestles in the middle of the room, which was pretty well lit up with candles – the body up to the chest was covered with beautiful flowers. The face was really handsome, so calm and contented. . . . There was nothing painful about [it] – but <u>how</u> sad! He had been <u>such</u> a good & true friend to me, & we had been so intimate during the last 5 years.'[9]

Leopold came close to tears at the funeral, but gradually, the breaking of this tie did help him to get to know members of the new government, and his political understanding deepened. His working life also changed: the idea that he would be the Queen's confidential assistant for foreign affairs had been her own, but it was Beaconsfield who gave it life. Without him the role no longer existed, and although Leopold maintained a lively interest in world events, his only working involvement came in March and April, when he dealt with papers relating to the trial of an anarchist newspaper editor, who praised the assassination of Tsar Alexander II and advocated further murders. Leopold still assisted the Queen, but the issues he dealt with were more domestic, often concerning appointments in the universities and the church.

In the past, he had sometimes tried to use his position to help friends, and people occasionally appealed to him for favours. But by 1881 he was grown up enough to realise that personal friendship could not be his only criterion, and though he did try to bring forward people he liked, he did so with caution. In this field at least, the Queen began to take his advice. In the summer of 1881 there was a possibility that Dean Liddell would leave Christ Church, to take up the Deanery of Westminster. Leopold was in Germany, but she telegraphed him under cipher to ask his advice on a new man for Christ Church. He offered suggestions, then Liddell decided to stay put and Westminster became the vacancy; again the telegrams flew, and when Westminster was filled, the successful candidate was G.G. Bradley, an old friend of Leopold's Oxford days, whose financial problems had worried him for years.

But the diary shows how far he had been able to move to work outside the home. One afternoon in January, he took the chair at a large public meeting in Kensington Town Hall, sharing the platform with William Morris, Sir Frederic Leighton, and others; he spent the morning at Buckingham Palace, working on his speech. The meeting drew together the National Health Society, the Open Spaces Society, and the Kyrle Society, which had Leopold as its president, and they discussed ways of improving air quality in the city; the Kyrle Society was dedicated to raising the living standards of the poor by providing public gardens and open spaces, and by taking good music and art into the most run-down areas. Environmental concerns mattered to Leopold. He was as keenly aware of the natural world as he had been in childhood, and he wanted the things he enjoyed to be accessible to everyone. At a meeting of the Charity

Organisation Society in May, he spoke on the need to curb air and water pollution: 'Light and air and green fields and pure water are the first, the most essential of pleasures.'[10]

As his reputation grew, more and more causes looked to him for support. He sometimes felt overwhelmed by the scale of the need, and by a sense of his own inadequacy, but he did his best, and quietly devoted much of his Parliamentary grant to good causes.[11] In February 1881 he was elected president of the Consumption Hospital at Ventnor. In May he made a speech at a dinner at University College Hospital, with Drs Jenner, Poore and Günther in the audience. In the spring of 1882, he spoke for the National Hospital for the Paralysed and Epileptic, appealing for funds to save epilepsy sufferers from the asylums, which were often their fate. He was developing a unique voice, and the claim made years after his death – that his speeches were actually written by Dean Stanley – cannot stand, because he continued to speak in public long after Stanley's death. Leopold's feelings about his public work were summed up in a remark he made at Nottingham on 30 June 1881: 'there is nothing which the Royal Family values more than the goodwill of their fellow countrymen; and there is nothing they will not do to legitimately deserve that goodwill.'[12]

Social issues and health concerned the Prince, but artistic causes involved him too. In June 1879 he was elected to the Council of the Society of Arts. He devoted hours of his time to the Windsor Tapestry Works, and knew the factory well; in March the Finance Committee met at Claremont, and 'we were engaged till luncheon time in discussing about the building of cottages for the workmen'.[13] But 1881 also brought an interesting short-term engagement, when he was invited to chair the committee planning a loan exhibition of Spanish and Portuguese art at the South Kensington Museum. He asked his father's cousin Ferdinand of Saxe-Coburg, the former Regent of Portugal, to lend some items, but the reply was less than generous: 'I feel it would be very painful to me to part even for a short time with some of those old things, I am accustomed to see every day round me.'[14]

Leopold's fascination with the arts began in childhood. As a small boy he sat to Winterhalter, and took lessons in watercolour painting from Corbould and Leitch. When he was nine he told Arthur that Leitch had given him a painting of a Cornish shipwreck.[15] In 1866 Christian Karl Magnussen was teaching him oil painting; they sat together at Osborne that summer, painting portraits of one of the Highland servants. Magnussen was paid £20 for his picture, but Leopold's effort does not seem to have survived; there are only two examples of his work in the Royal Collection, both drawings, dated 24 May 1867 and 1868 – presumably birthday presents for his mother. The first is a pencil sketch of a continental street scene, highlighted in white on buff paper, the second, a watercolour of a castle gateway: both are good, and show that he had talent.[16]

As a teenager Leopold enjoyed sketching, but later his interests turned to collecting – first engravings, then paintings. Emilia Pattison helped him to acquire pictures by struggling French artists, but it was Ruskin who really opened the contemporary art world to him: in an undated copy of a letter to the historian Froude, passed on to the Prince, 'as his attention is at present turned to this subject', Ruskin set out to describe the importance of the Pre-Raphaelites, in demonstrating 'that real Yorkshire rocks, real Dantes & Beatrices, real Christs are better than any of these things & beings constructed by the rules of Idealism'. The letter explained that while Rossetti and Millais had abandoned the early convictions of the movement, Holman Hunt, 'with far inferior intellect than Rossetti, and still more inferior art capacity to Millais, has been intensely, fiercely, patiently and in purity of life faithful to his conviction and his power'.[17]

Leopold had the autographs of many Pre-Raphaelites in his collection, but he probably never knew them. He did know Sir Frederic Leighton, and Gustav Doré became a personal friend after years when the Prince had collected his work. The painter Frank Miles was another friend: in 1874 he and Doré visited Leopold at Windsor, and Lillie Langtry remembered seeing Leopold in Miles's London studio watching the artist draw her portrait, which he later bought. Someone told her that it hung over his bed until the Queen removed it. Miles shared the house with Oscar Wilde, whom Leopold also knew from the Oxford Freemasons. Once, in the late 1870s, Leopold attended a service in Oxford with Mrs

Liddell and her daughters, and heard Wilde shock the congregation by substituting a reading from the Song of Solomon for the expected lesson from Deuteronomy.[18]

The diary confirms Leopold's love for the art world. In March 1881 he saw a Millais exhibition in London and visited Leighton and another artist to view their pictures for the Academy. In May he fell for a painting at the Grosvenor Gallery called *After the Bath*. It cost 30 guineas and Collins, who was with him, did not approve 'on account of the scarcity of clothing', so he went back alone and bought it the next day.[19] A few weeks later he bought a watercolour from an exhibition in Pall Mall; the walls of Claremont must have seen continual changes as his collection grew.

On 24 May 1881, the Queen's birthday, Leopold finally received his peerage. He chose his own title, and ironically for him, it was Scottish; the Stuart dynasty fascinated him, and at his own request he became Duke of Albany, Earl of Clarence, and Baron Arklow, though his mother only allowed this on condition that he would still be known as 'Prince Leopold': anybody who used the new title without the old would receive a very curt telling-off from his sovereign. Nonetheless, Leopold was overjoyed. Even Balmoral could not dampen his spirits, and the presence of his two eldest Hesse nieces made the pleasure complete. On 27 May there was a gillies' ball, and he danced four reels before dinner with Beatrice and his nieces, and afterwards surprised even himself: 'danced again reels with <u>V.R.</u> (with whom I had not danced since the autumn of <u>60</u>! 21 years).'[20]

He stayed at Balmoral for two weeks, walking and playing tennis with his nieces, and once with Ponsonby, who complained that it was 'hard work for he never runs – he cant'.[21] Then, returning to London for the opening of the Spanish and Portuguese Exhibition, he travelled south with the Breadalbanes, who were on their way to a house party given by Arthur at Bagshot Park. After making several visits in London, Leopold joined them, to help with a charity bazaar which lasted three days, and attend the races at Ascot. Lady Breadalbane had a stall at the bazaar; he had seen her several times that spring, and once entertained her and her husband at Claremont. His memories of the previous year were strong, and the very thought of her as he wrote his diary sent him off into adoring rhapsodies in Italian.

From Bagshot he went to London to take his seat in the Lords, then on to Oxford for a ball at Christ Church. He stayed at the Deanery; many old friends were there, and he danced all evening in a magical setting: 'the Hall of Christ Church beautifully arranged – the cloisters & staircase &c lit up with divers coloured lights – quite fairy like.'[22] Then it was back to London to meet Louis of Hesse, and honour several working engagements. At the end of the month, he set off for Nottingham, with Collins, Royle and a small party, to open the new University College.

A detachment of local yeomanry met them at the station and escorted them to Bestwood Park, the home of their host, the Duke of St Albans. During the next two days, Leopold was shown around Newstead and Welbeck Abbeys and the surrounding countryside, receiving enthusiastic welcomes wherever he went. On Thursday 30 June, the day of the ceremony, he gave a major speech on education, and three other speeches during the lunch that followed, which lasted until seven in the evening. The next day he toured Nottingham, and visited the church at Bestwood to see memorials to his father's secretary, General Grey, and the whole party spent their last night at a costume ball at Woollaton Hall. Leopold was dressed as Louis XV, and he revelled in the scene – the costumes, the lit greenhouses and gardens, where the guests wandered and danced into the small hours – 'a charming ball – at 4 a.m. "cotillon" . . . – lasted till after 5 o'clock – we were then photoed in the morn'g dew & then sat down . . . to a last supper & sang "Auld Lang Syne" – separated at 6 a.m.!!!'[23]

The diary illustrates perfectly his reasons for insisting on freedom. When he was well, he could live as others did, with no ill effects, and if he had settled for an invalid lifestyle he would have missed so much. He had only one attack of internal bleeding in 1881, in February, at the end of the long family argument over Calma of Schleswig-Holstein. A severe cold brought on bleeding from the kidneys, and Leopold's pain increased until the doctors tried chloroform, and gave injections of morphine. The attack started just as guests were arriving for a party at Claremont, and his sister-in-law Marie, Duchess of Edinburgh, sat with him and took her meals in his room.

Marie was fond of Leopold. With his intellect and love of music she found him more sympathetic than his brothers, and he was always kind to her children. He looked after the little Edinburghs at Claremont in 1880 when she had to go to Russia to see her dying mother, and in March he was planning to entertain her and her brother Alexei, when news of their father's assassination called them away. Now, finding herself the only woman of the family with Leopold during a haemophilia attack, Marie would not leave him. 'I think, considering all, he is very patient,' she told the Queen, 'only he gets lowspirited. He likes very much to be read to and it is a great pleasure for me, for he takes great interest in books and is very fond of reading, which is rare nowadays amongst young men.'[24]

The attack lasted a little over two weeks, and through the spring and summer Leopold was fine. From Nottingham in July he returned to Windsor, then went to Claremont, where he was joined by Louis and his daughters and a small party of friends, including Duckworth, Yorke, the Royles and the Collinses. The days were hot and easy, with river trips, picnics and music in the evening. 'Yesterday afternoon we went to Hampton Court', Victoria of Hesse told the Queen, 'where we had tea & came back by water, which was very nice & cool & all this morning we spent lying out in the shade or in a punt on the lake.'[25]

One April afternoon that year, Lord Brooke had married Daisy Maynard in Westminster Abbey, and Leopold was the best man. He seemed cheerful; a small bridesmaid caught his attention as she absent-mindedly chewed her bouquet of roses and blew the petals at the congregation, and afterwards he asked her if she had enjoyed her breakfast.[26] Nothing more had been said about his own marriage since the Schleswig-Holstein business. He was probably avoiding the subject to protect himself from another disappointment, but the Queen, frustrated by her daughter and son-in-law over Calma, was keen to push him on, and she had an idea. To the north of Darmstadt, in Arolsen, the Prince and Princess of Waldeck and Pyrmont lived with their family. Their eldest surviving daughters, vague memories from a visit to Buckingham Palace with their mother in the spring of 1860, when she thought them 'enormous, fine children but with . . . literally no noses!', were married, but a younger daughter, Helen, had reached the very suitable age of twenty, and the family's reputation was good.[27] So, when Louis and his daughters returned to Darmstadt, Leopold was to go with them, to call on the Princess of Waldeck on his mother's behalf.

On 13 July the party sailed from Dover to Ostend, then caught the train to Brussels, arriving after seven in the evening to be met by the King and faced with a gala dinner. Hot and exhausted, they would have preferred to rest, but in the early hours Leopold and Louis were still awake, and walking in the Grande Place. When they reached Wolfsgarten, the Hesse hunting lodge outside Darmstadt, the heat was still intense, and they took long outings into the woods, walking late in the evening by glow-worm light. Leopold always said that he felt more at home in Hesse than anywhere. 'He looks very well & does not do anything to fatigue himself', Ella assured the Queen.[28]

At the end of July, Prince August of Saxe-Coburg, a younger brother of the Regent of Portugal, died in Austria, and the Queen asked Leopold to attend the funeral. It took place in Coburg. Louis went with him, and the occasion brought together cousins from across Europe. When the party broke up on 3 August, Leopold and Louis were among thirteen princes and princesses travelling in a single railway carriage, but all Leopold really wanted to do was return to the Hesse children; once back at Wolfsgarten, he read to them each morning, and took them on long afternoon outings, driving, picnicking and catching crayfish. Noticing that twelve-year-old 'Ernie' was continually scolded and criticised by his elder sisters, he persuaded the girls to draw back, knowing only too well how it felt to be under such pressure. He was concerned by the way Irene, at fifteen, was cosseted by an over-cautious nurse who fancied that she was delicate. 'We have begun what Uncle calls Irene's Emancipation', Victoria told the Queen, 'but it is rather difficult, some times.'[29]

Frankfurt provided excitement for them: there was an electric railway on show at the International Exhibition, and once, Leopold went to the zoo. He rode a horse – which was strictly forbidden by his mother – and visited the spa at Homburg. But none of this was what he was supposed to be doing, and when he failed to return for a Volunteer review in Edinburgh the Queen was furious. 'Wrote to V.R. in answer to her violent explosion', he noted on 19 August, though this was the day Princess Louise arrived at Wolfsgarten, so the Queen had no chance of recalling him.[30] He and Louise relaxed with the children; the weather had broken, and indoor badminton was the passion. In the evenings brother and sister sang together to the accompaniment of Christa Schenk, Princess Alice's lady-in-waiting, whom Leopold called 'one of my oldest and greatest friends'.[31]

He was definitely dragging his heels over meeting the Waldecks. At the end of August he took himself off to stay with the Empress Eugénie at Arenenberg, beside Lake Constance, and wrote to Louis: 'Now, dear Mopperl*, what is to be done about the Waldecks? I'm so dreading meeting the Princess. If the Prince doesn't come to Soden, in the end I could go to Soden for a night, staying perhaps in the <u>Hotel Westphalia</u> – <u>without you</u> – then it would be quite natural "to call on the Waldecks". You know, dear Mopperl, I <u>have to</u> see her.'[32] Returning on 1 September he found Herr Sahl waiting for him – sent, perhaps, to boost his will-power – and two days later, he set off for Soden with Louis's aide-de-camp, Major Wehrner. The Princess of Waldeck received him at the Villa Westphalia, with Helen and her eight-year-old sister, for a meeting which lasted an hour. It was quite painless; 'was much pleased with my visit', was Leopold's only comment.

Duty done, he rejoined the Hesses at the Frankfurt Exhibition, where there was 'much pumping, but Wehrner let out nothing', then the whole party went home for a special evening: 'Ernie & Alicky were, at my request, allowed to stay up & dine with us, as it was almost my last evening – & we all played cards. A happy evening with the dear children whom I love so much, if only darling Alice were still with us!'[33] There was time for a little more tennis and singing, another picnic, then came the moment to swallow hard and face 'that gloomy & dismal Balmoral'.[34] Leopold left Wolfsgarten with Wehrner and the Royles, and they found themselves travelling in the same train as Prince Alexander of Hesse and his sons, whom Leopold knew well. Arthur Sullivan joined them at Frankfurt, and Leopold stopped at Koblenz to call on his godmother, the Empress Augusta. He sailed from Flushing on a bright, moonlit night, and landed at Queenborough early the next morning.

The next two months would feel endless: once again, his hopes had been raised, and now all he could do was wait. He told no-one except the Queen – the fewer people knew, the easier it would be to bear disappointment. Balmoral was never his favourite place, and this tension only made things worse. At first his brothers and their wives were in Scotland, but when the men went out shooting and he was left alone, or had to sit with the women, he became very despondent. He thought only Louis understood how he felt: 'Mamma, Arthur & Alfred go on talking all the time about stags & shooting, & I am completely ignored, of course the idea of my having any feelings would be too preposterous, & I am simply here in the position of an unpaid servant.'[35]

The Prince of Wales tried to help by asking if he could take Leopold shooting, but the Queen would not hear of it; instead, she told Ponsonby to give him some work. This was difficult for the secretary, who had some sensitive matters in hand which were outside Leopold's competence and knowledge, and besides, as he told his wife, Leopold, 'when so near to the Prince of Wales – has some delicacy or fear of being the political adviser of the Queen'.[36] So the days dragged by, and Leopold spent much of his time sitting with his youngest sister, who was confined to her room with swollen glands, reading aloud to her and playing the piano. When Beatrice's company was forced on him, he had seemed to resent her, but this autumn marked a change: at heart he must have known her position better than anyone. She lived the life he dreaded, without hope of escape.

All the time, messages were passing to and from Arolsen, and early in October Dr Jenner was asked to prepare medical reports on Leopold's bleeding, and his fits. The weather closed in, and Leopold was laid up for the first time that year with a swollen knee, waiting, and still waiting. To pass the time he embarked on the seven volumes of Richardson's *Clarissa Harlowe*, and played endless piano duets; then, on 15 October, a promising letter came from Germany, which was confirmed two days later. The Waldecks were satisfied; all that remained was for the couple to meet again, and make their decision. He stayed at Balmoral for another week listening to his mother's cautions and advice before returning to London.

The next few days were hectic: Leopold was on edge, and wanted no time to think. He visited friends and family, without telling anyone his secret, attended business meetings, closed up the larger rooms of Claremont for the winter, went riding and shooting, saw five plays and a concert, and dined at various clubs. He consulted Dr Paget, and visited the dentist, Mr Toms, in Cavendish Square, 'where I spent ¾ of an hour, alas!'[37] On 7 November he wrote to Louis to explain his impending trip to Germany; he was concerned that his brother-in-law might not want him to marry, and reassured him that whatever happened, he – Louis – and the children would always be important. A few days later he set off, with Dr Royle and Vic.

They reached Paris, where Collins joined them, early on the morning of 12 November. Leopold was still restless, and he explored the Electrical Exhibition at the Palais d'Industrie, where Gounod's latest opera was being transmitted with the aid of a new invention – the microphone. He was so impressed that he returned the next evening to hear two more pieces. From the Exhibition, he drove to the theatre for a play with a very unsuitable title – *Divorçons*! An invitation from the duc d'Aumale's secretary took him to Chantilly on 13 November, 'one of the most magnificent places I have ever seen, built on a rock quite surrounded by water', and after a three-hour tour it was back to Paris for a Turkish bath and dinner at the Embassy.[38] The next day he explored several artists' studios, before the moment came to catch the night train to Frankfurt – and Helen.

The weather was bright and spring-like, and Leopold and his companions just had time to wash at their hotel before Collins took him for a brief meeting with the Princess of Waldeck and her daughter. More meetings followed in the next few days, at the public garden, the opera and at a gallery, where Leopold was far too nervous to notice the paintings. But things were going well, and on 17 November he was allowed a short time alone with Helen. He sang her one of Tosti's Italian love songs; he had a particularly fine voice and took lessons from a professional, and his unusual approach seems to have worked. The next morning he had a long interview with the Prince of Waldeck and, with his permission, took the final step: 'after luncheon, being alone with Helen, the great question was settled, to my intense happiness.'[39]

Louis was among the first to hear the news, that very evening: 'I <u>am so</u> happy', Leopold told him. 'Now you will know what has happened, without my saying any more; we became engaged this afternoon. . . . Oh my dear brother, I am so overjoyed, and you, who have known this happiness, you will be pleased for me, won't you? . . . You only know Helen a little as yet – when you <u>really</u> know her, then you will understand why I'm mad with joy today.'[40]

The next two days were a whirl of letter writing, and meetings with friends. Leopold arranged for the younger Hesse children to join him and meet their future aunt; Irene had sprained her ankle, but on 21 November Ernie and Alix arrived at the station. They were very shy at first, but after lunch they played cards with Leopold and Helen, and the afternoon passed happily until six, when the children were bundled on to the Darmstadt train. The next day Louis arrived with the two elder girls, and on 23 November the whole party went to Darmstadt, where they visited Alice's tomb at the Rosenhöhe before a large family lunch: Helen was beginning to get to know her future husband through the places and people he cared about.

Next it was his turn. The morning of 25 November was bright but very cold, when Leopold, Collins and Royle left the Hotel d'Angleterre after breakfast and drove straight to the station, where the Waldeck party was waiting. Their train left at nine, and by one o'clock they were in Cassel, where they stopped for lunch with Helen's sixteen-year-old brother Fritz and his governor. Leaving again at three, they had reached Scherfede by five, where the party divided: Leopold rode with Helen and her father 'in an open carriage & 4 through Wrexen, Rhoden, Schwillinghausen, (at each of which places we had speeches & a perfect ovation – every house lit up – by Helsen to <u>Arolsen</u>. We had a torchlight escort on foot from the entrance to A[rolsen] to the Castle – it was a lovely moonlight evening.'[41]

The days that followed were pure celebration. On the first morning the couple went straight to the local photographer. Then, that afternoon, Helen's sister Emma arrived from the Netherlands with her husband, King Willem III – 'he is <u>64</u> – & she (Helen's sister) <u>22</u>!', Leopold noted in amazement.[42] There was a gala dinner, and Leopold had to wear the Trinity House uniform, still the only one he had. This made him feel awkward in settings where uniform mattered, and Royle complained to Ponsonby that it caused endless problems: 'when he explained to Foreign countries that his master was an elder brother of the Trinity – they were horrified at the awful assumption, and wondered why this was expressed in such a uniform.'[43] At least his decorations were real: at the dinner Leopold wore the collar of his new Waldeck 'Ordre de Mérite', and the blue and orange ribbon of the 'Lion of the Netherlands', just presented to him by the King.

The next day was Sunday, spent quietly among the Waldecks, and all the time letters of congratulation were pouring in. Many people had guessed the reason for Leopold's return to Germany, but Helen's name surprised them all. The Duchess of Edinburgh was especially pleased. 'I saw that you were rather mysterious at Balmoral', she wrote, 'but could not imagine whom you intended to propose to! . . . Do you remember, I told you, I would give her a present? And you pretended to choose one? Now, I have had for some time a bracelet ready for your future betrothed, that is not my <u>marriage present</u>, but only a little souvenir. . . . Please give it her from me, with my love.'[44] But Beatrice was the first to write, within hours of the engagement, and though her delight was obvious, she hinted that there were problems: 'Mama is after a momentary agitation quite calm, & I only hope she will remain so.'[45]

It was usual for the Queen to shrink from family weddings, even when she planned them herself, but the emotional complications which had always bedevilled her relationship with Leopold made this reaction more pronounced. Ponsonby told his wife that when the news broke at Balmoral the Household drank Leopold's health and wrote their congratulations to the Queen: 'But in the evg the Duchess told me these were not at all acceptable & read me the Queen's letter lamenting the marriage & thinking it far better he should not marry at all. So we were sorry we spoke.'[46] The Queen did not contact Leopold himself; a day after the news reached her she wrote of her misgivings to Collins, and six days passed before she sent a very kind and welcoming letter for Helen.

By the time it arrived, Leopold must have been on his way home. He left Arolsen on 28 November, 'feeling wretched & miserable', and made his way to Cologne, where he and Collins took a midnight walk by the Cathedral. Then on to Calais, and, crossing the Channel on the *Samphère*, they finally reached Windsor at a quarter to six the next evening. There, to Leopold's obvious relief, 'V.R. & Baby received me . . . <u>all most</u> kind.'[47] At this point the diary ends. He may simply have been too busy to continue, but this was a satisfying conclusion. At last, his life was really about to change.

FIFTEEN

SHORT SUNSHINE

The Queen decided that the wedding would take place in April, because she was haunted by superstitious fear: her uncle Leopold lived at Claremont during his tragic first marriage, which ended with his wife's death in childbirth. She sensed something menacing in the coincidence of name and place, and would not tempt Providence further by allowing her son to marry in May, as her uncle had done. But talk of omens washed over Leopold, and for him the weeks rushed by in a flurry of planning. In December he told his friend Mrs Paget, 'You also say in your letter that my bride is sure to be <u>lovely</u> – that she is not, but <u>very loveable</u>, and I am sure you will like her.'[1]

He was thinking of Helen as his 'darling Nellie', and anticipating the places he would take her, and the friends she must meet. Some friends were already a link between them: one of Dr Acland's brothers was a clergyman, who had lived and worked in Arolsen. He had known Helen almost all her life, and prepared her for confirmation, and he and his wife were quick to recommend Leopold to her. Max Müller praised Leopold to his friend Queen Elisabeth of Romania, Helen's cousin, and these shared acquaintances must have given a feeling of familiarity to a young couple who still knew very little of one another.

The Queen hoped to have Leopold to herself before the wedding, but he had public engagements to fulfil. On 12 December, he went to the Manchester Athenaeum with Prince Alfred and Prince Christian to promote the establishment of a Royal College of Music. Alfred took the chair, but Leopold gave the address and it was a long one, tracing the history of music in England from the medieval period. He spoke with authority and conviction: 'Is it indispensable that the divinest and most impalpable of all arts, capable of affecting and exalting the soul as no other art, not even poetry, can do, should be a thing apart from the mass of our greatest and best men? . . . I think not. I am sure not. I am convinced that the subject only wants to be properly brought before the country.'[2] He felt passionate about this, and when the College was founded he became a hard-working member of its Council, making substantial contributions to the funds.

He was thinking about music for his wedding too, and appealed to his friend Charles Gounod to compose a march for the organ with orchestral accompaniment. Gounod was happy to oblige, but the idea foundered on the Queen's insistence on a simple ceremony – no long march, and certainly no orchestra. The crestfallen composer offered to produce a simpler piece, but someone must have taken pity on him: when Helen walked slowly down the nave of St George's Chapel on the wedding day, with her father holding her left hand and the King of the Netherlands her right, it was Gounod's specially composed wedding march which was played, on the organ alone.

Someone took pity on Leopold too, and at last he would have a real military uniform. In December the Queen told Sir Henry Ponsonby to write to the Commander-in-Chief requesting an honorary colonelcy for him, and, at Leopold's special request, honorary command of the Seaforth Highlanders, 'the Duke of Albany's Own'. The first point was granted easily, but the second met with resistance from the war minister, so a compromise was found, and in March Leopold was gazetted Honorary Colonel of the 3rd Battalion. There was irony in him, of all people, asking to be a 'Highlander', but he seems not to have seen it: the right to wear uniform made him feel at one with his brothers and other men of their class.

Early in January 1882, he returned to Arolsen. He was eager to see the Waldecks again, and delighted by their offer to invite Louis of Hesse and his daughters. 'I do so hope you will come', he wrote from Arolsen, 'Please do.'[3] He looked forward particularly to seeing his nieces, as he did not expect another chance that year, and news of a possible engagement between Ella and Prince Waldemar of Denmark worried him. He thought Denmark dull (that was probably the Prince of Wales's influence), and Waldemar plain, boring and broke. 'Oh! Dear Louis', he wrote in December, '<u>do</u> prevent Ella from being so <u>utterly</u> thrown away – & don't think I want to mix myself up in your affairs; it is only that I love your dear children as if they were my own.'[4]

The Princess of Waldeck gave a dance for the Hesse girls, and Leopold and his brother-in-law planned a sneaky visit to Berlin – a city Leopold had never seen, and never would have seen if his mother had known his plans. 'I . . . would much like to go there', he wrote when it was suggested, 'but Mamma!!!!!!!'[5] On Saturday 28 January, the Waldecks celebrated the forthcoming wedding with a performance of *Sleeping Beauty* in their private theatre. Soldiers from the Arolsen barracks and other local people portrayed the story in four tableaux vivants, with 'appropriate' music, in a fairy-tale setting designed by the painter Carl Sohn and Professor Konitz of Cassel. First came the Bad Fairy's curse, then the hundred years' sleep. Next, the Prince awakened Beauty, at a discreet distance, and in the triumphant conclusion, he showed his new Princess (the part was taken by Miss Brass, 'the beauty of Arolsen') her future home, pointing dramatically at a painted backdrop of Claremont.[6]

Leopold was to have left on 1 February with Helen and her father to join the Queen at Osborne, but a few days before their departure he stumbled over a tree stump and twisted his knee. Hearing the news from Dr Royle, the Queen let Helen know of her concern, and her displeasure: 'I hope the 20<u>th</u> will be the <u>very latest</u> day on w^h you will arrive as I have missed so much of Leopold's company . . . w^h is <u>very</u> hard indeed. You must repay me later.'[7]

They finally arrived at Queenborough on 22 February, after a rough night crossing on the royal yacht *Victoria and Albert*. It was a private visit, so there was no ceremony, but a small crowd had gathered to cheer their new Princess, as she stepped ashore in a silk dress and tight-fitting mantle of dark green velvet. Leopold still found it difficult to walk and he looked ill, but he would have been determined at this moment to make his way without help. General Du Plat met the party, and they left by train for Windsor. The Queen was delighted. 'Helen is tall, & "élancée", with a fine figure, rich colour, very dark hair, dark brown, deep set eyes, & a sweet smile', she wrote after their first meeting. 'She has a charming, friendly manner & is very affectionate & warm hearted.'[8] Ponsonby was impressed too: 'seems a personage or will be one', he commented to his wife after Helen's arrival, and on a later meeting he found her 'full of life and talk and prettier in the day time than at night'.[9]

Arrangements for the wedding had hit problems in Leopold's absence. Parliament was too busy to vote his increased annuity; that would have to wait until the end of March, and Collins and Ponsonby had difficulty sorting out some modernisation work he wanted at Claremont. He planned gas lighting, hot water pipes for heating and washing, a conservatory, and an enclosed entrance portico; the answer to all these was a firm no, though the Queen was prepared to allow some alterations in the drawing-room, and drainage improvements. 'You and I will get our fingers pinched in the collision', Ponsonby warned Collins. 'Her standpoint is that Claremont is her house and her residence.'[10] The Waldecks were rather put out that the wedding must take place in England, and shortly before they left Arolsen, Helen's sister Marie wrote to Queen Emma reminding her not to let their mother kiss the Queen's hand, because she had been generous enough already, and was entitled to stand on her dignity: 'the Queen should be very thankful that Mama allowed Helen to go to England . . .'.[11] Another sensitive point was smoothed over by Prince Arthur: the Queen wanted him to be one of Leopold's supporters, with the Prince of Wales, but he knew that Leopold would want Louis. Gently, he suggested that Louis, as a widower, might find the wedding distressing and would be better occupied as a supporter, while he was happy to sit with his wife; once the situation was explained in this way, the Queen was too kind to object.[12]

On 22 April the Waldecks left Arolsen to a fanfare of trumpets. Helen rode in a carriage with her mother and little sister, and her dog, a small white terrier given by her favourite uncle, Adolf, Duke of Nassau. The family took eighty trunks of luggage and occupied three carriages for their slow progress across Germany, and flowers were presented to Helen at every stop. They met the royal yacht at Flushing, and Prince Christian, an old schoolfriend of

Helen's father, hurried from Windsor to greet them – though he kept them waiting over two hours because their crossing was unexpectedly quick. Leopold could not go because his leg was bad again: holidaying at Mentone with the Queen a few weeks earlier, he slipped on a piece of orange peel, injuring the knee which had barely recovered from the previous accident. But he was waiting on the station platform at Windsor, leaning on a stick, and he claimed the right to help Helen down from the train.

Thursday 27 April started cool and cloudy, but crowds formed early to see the wedding procession. Leopold rode with Louis and the Prince of Wales, whose wedding gift, a Broadwood grand piano, must have been a great delight to him. The reporter from the *Graphic* noticed that Leopold responded to the cheering crowds 'in a pleased, half-nervous fashion', and according to the same reporter, and to the *Illustrated London News*, his lameness was barely noticeable during the ceremony; the writer of the Court Circular had a more dramatic turn of mind, and saw 'the cruel wrench of pain' every time he put his foot to the ground.[13] As the bride's procession formed in the doorway of the chapel, the sun broke through the clouds; the ceremony was conducted in a blaze of light and colour.

Shortly after four that afternoon, Leopold and Helen left the castle and drove down the Long Walk to Old Windsor, where craftsmen of the Tapestry Works had erected a triumphal arch, and a three-year-old child was waiting in the Director's arms to present flowers. It was six by the time they reached Esher, passing through a series of floral arches to a flower-covered pavilion, under which the Rector and a group of local people were waiting to offer their congratulations. Leopold thanked them: 'We both feel the greatest satisfaction in the thought that the first days of our married life will be spent in the parish of Esher', he said, 'for it is here that we shall hope for the future to centre our local cares and interests.'[14]

The sight of the Prince walking with a stick had drawn attention to his health once more, and the Queen was uneasy: it reinforced her instinct that he should never have been allowed to live as a normal, healthy man. 'To me the idea of poor Leopold's marrying . . . not able to walk yet – is terrible', she told her eldest daughter. 'It is a sad exhibition and I fear everyone must be shocked at it and blame me! I pity her but she seems only to think of him with love and affection.'[15] This was an attitude to disability which many of her contemporaries shared. She assumed that the marriage would depend on Helen's ability to support Leopold, but circumstances soon proved her wrong. Helen's sister Marie, Princess Wilhelm of Württemberg, was unable to attend the wedding because she had reached the end of a difficult pregnancy, and the birth was three weeks late. On the wedding day she gave birth to a still-born daughter, and, on 30 April, she died. Suddenly it was Helen who needed the support.

Bereavement was something Leopold understood, and he took control with quiet assurance. He and Helen remained at Claremont, seeing only the family, but his experience of supporting Louis made him conscious of his new brother-in-law's feelings, and some weeks after the funeral he wrote to invite Wilhelm to Claremont. Wilhelm was touched, but did not accept. 'Life lies open to you', he wrote, 'you just start on your happy journey together, so do not look back too much and try to make Helen do the same; a young wife always (always) ought to look forward to the future with thoughts of hope.'[16]

Helen's mourning prevented her from appearing with Leopold that summer, and he undertook a series of public engagements alone. In June, he spoke at the annual dinner of the Newspaper Press Fund, and his words had an almost prophetic ring: 'we feel how intimately the press has entwined itself with our existence', he said, 'till the electric wires seem the very nerves of humanity, carrying in a moment to every corner of the earth the self-same thrill of hope or pain.'[17] Everywhere he went, he apologised for Helen's absence.

Early in July, Louisa, Lady Knightley, and her mother Lady Bowater visited Claremont, and remembering the little boy they looked after at Cannes, they were delighted to see Leopold so happy. 'She is a lively, merry, natural girl of twenty', Louisa wrote in her journal, 'he an extremely pleasant man of the world, and all he said pleased me greatly. There were only us four, no *gêne*, and I really enjoyed it.'[18] During the winter Leopold and the Queen had disagreed over ladies for Helen. Ponsonby thought he wanted only young and pretty ones, but one of his choices was Louisa; she was neither young nor pretty, but had been a good friend for most of his life. It was friends he wanted, to fit into the informality of Claremont, and to stand by Helen if anything should happen to him.

Gradually, he was easing Helen into his world. A few weeks after Louisa's visit, he took her to Boyton for a week, to stay with the tenant, Mrs Fenwick, who had become a good friend. From Boyton the Albanys went on to Osborne; there was an enthusiastic reception waiting for them at East Cowes, but soon after his arrival Leopold became ill and was confined to his room. It was a bleed from the kidneys, lasting a few days at first, and then returning with intense pain; at the end of August he was still unable to stand. Helen was pregnant; Leopold can only have known this for a few weeks, and one evening, watching her go in to dinner, he decided to write an informal will, in case he should die before the baby came.

He wrote with deliberate cheerfulness, but the urgency was there. Estimating that he would leave about £30,000, he suggested things which she might sell if necessary; bequests of £1,000 each were to go to Collins, Royle and Princess Frederica, who had no resources of her own and remained one of his dearest friends. He advised Helen to rely on Collins, who was to be joint guardian if the child was a boy, and to keep the valet Alick Grant in her service. Then he thought of his godchildren, who were each to have a gift – it was quite a list, and all the boys were called 'Leopold', including a Jenner, a Legg, a Royle and a Collins: even remembering them all was an effort. But bequests apart, the thought that he might die suddenly, leaving his papers to be sorted out by other hands, was preying on his mind. 'Darling', he wrote, 'please let Lord Brooke look through all my papers alone – & he may destroy as he likes – you will not, my angel, think this want of confidence – But, darling, I have told you I was not a Saint before we married, though I do not think I ever went far astray – & you will understand that there [are] some things I would sooner you did not see.' He ended, 'Your devoted ever adoring husband. I finish this while you are still at dinner!'[19]

Death did not catch him this time, though, and by early September he was well enough to take Helen on her first visit to Balmoral, cruising around the coast on HMS *Lively*, with a stop at

Wemyss Castle. But the illness had prompted a surprising disclosure. On 2 September *The Lancet* reported that 'Prince Leopold is known to suffer from constitutional weakness with liability to haemorrhage – haematophilia. Of this malady he has recently had an attack.'[20] Leopold's illness must have been an open secret among the medical establishment, but the doctors who treated him would have been trusted to respect his privacy. It seems extraordinary that no-one in the Household picked up on the report, but there is no evidence that they did, no evidence that the Queen ever knew of the betrayal. And Leopold, who read *The Lancet* and had commented on articles in the past, left no reaction on record.

His arrival at Balmoral with Helen was celebrated by pipers and a guard of honour, and toasts were drunk at the doorway of the castle, but the event was eclipsed by news of Arthur's participation in the victorious battle of Tel-el-Kebir in Egypt. The effects of her pregnancy made Helen subdued, and she was not equal to compulsory walks and expeditions in the countryside; the Queen decided that she was delicate, and sent instructions to Collins to allow no heating at Claremont once the Albanys returned – it would be far too unhealthy. There were to be no parties either, and the birth must take place at Windsor. They left Balmoral on 13 October, to visit Leopold's friends at Blythswood; from there, he went to open an exhibition at the Glasgow branch of the Royal School of Art Needlework, and received the freedom of the city before an audience of 5,000 people.

He had no fear of Claremont, and would have preferred the birth to be there, within reach of the London doctors. The Waldecks visited in November, and he assured his mother that they agreed, even knowing the sad history of the house. He did his best to be persuasive: 'If you have now decided on Windsor for Helen's confinement, it is no use my saying anything more about it. Of course at Windsor there will be a great deal of expense, on account of sending for Dr Duncan backwards & forwards. . . . But it is more for you that I dread Windsor. It will be causing you anxiety & worry, when you have so many other things to do & think about – & it makes a fuss in the house . . . & then I am so afraid of my mother-in-law being in your way, with her love of hot rooms & fear of draughts.'[21] It was a good try, but in mid-February, when the birth was imminent, he, Helen and the Princess of Waldeck, settled into Windsor Castle. At half-past six, on the evening of 25 February 1883, Helen gave birth to a healthy baby girl, with thick, dark hair.

Leopold had always loved children, and was the kindest uncle and godfather. Now he was a father himself and his pleasure was boundless, even though he had hoped for a boy; he wrote to everyone, describing 'the young Stranger . . . a <u>very</u> large child, & said to resemble very much the old Royal Family, though it has the dark brown hair, & a <u>great</u> deal of it, of its Mother.'[22] Then there were congratulations to be acknowledged, and one which touched him particularly came from Alice Liddell, now Mrs Hargreaves, who had just given birth herself. She included a special request; 'It is very good of you asking me to be godfather to your boy', Leopold replied, 'and I shall have <u>great</u> pleasure in being so, Please let me know what his names are to be.'[23] The baby was yet another Leopold.

Sometimes the euphoria made Leopold quite wicked. To the Home Secretary, Sir William Harcourt, he wrote, 'I only hope the young lady who you said winked at you on her first appearance, will not do so later in life!'[24] But the person he really wanted to hear from was Louis, for a special reason. He told Queen Emma that the baby reminded him of Princess Alice, and there was no doubt of what her name would be: 'it is so pleasant to think that now there will be an Alice once more in our family', he wrote to his brother-in-law from Windsor, '. . . and, dear Louis, will you associate our child still more with Her dear memory by standing Godfather? It would give us so much pleasure. We hope (we hope still) to have her christening here on Easter Monday; unluckily I have strained the principal muscle in my left thigh, in dragging Helen's sofa about – at least I <u>think</u> that is how I did it – anyhow, I am in bed at the moment, to my great annoyance.'[25]

The christening did take place as planned, in the private chapel at Windsor, though the Queen was in a wheelchair having hurt her leg, and Leopold was on crutches, but Louisa Knightley noticed how happy he looked. It would be the last happy moment at Windsor for some time. On 28 March, two days after the christening, John Brown died, and Leopold had to break the news to his mother. 'I have <u>deep</u> sympathy with her', he told Louis. 'We can feel for her, & her sorrow, without being sorry for the cause. At least <u>I</u> can't be a hypocrite.'[26] Memories of his teenage hatred of the Browns ran deep and he refused to express regret, though he wanted to help Beatrice to reshape their mother's life, which had relied so much on Brown. But he could not stay long at Windsor, because the Princess of Waldeck and the King and Queen of the Netherlands were due at Claremont: 'if you want anything send for me', he told his mother, '& I'll come over <u>at once</u>.'[27]

Ever since the wedding he had continued his secretarial work. From his sofa the previous August he advised the Queen on a very sensitive Cabinet appointment: she was unhappy about Gladstone's choice of the republican MP Sir Charles Dilke, but Leopold was quick to reassure her. Once, Dilke had been his own pet hate, but he had recently met the MP at Boyton and entertained him at Claremont, and had formed a different opinion – even though Dilke abstained from voting for his increased annuity that spring. This was a sign of the growing political maturity Louisa Knightley noticed in Leopold in December 1882: 'he has greatly improved in his politics', she said, 'and takes a thoughtful and intelligent interest in great questions.'[28]

That autumn at Balmoral, a difficult family matter arose which called for his attention: Duke Ernst of Saxe-Coburg was in financial trouble and wanted to sell a collection of engravings valued at £50,000; the money would be invested, providing capital for the Duke and his successors. Legally, the collection was held for the use of the public, and this could not be altered without the consent of all male princes in the Coburg line – including Leopold and his brothers. Alfred, as the future Duke, was in favour, but the Queen was outraged because her husband had set great store by the collection. She turned to Leopold, appealing to him to speak to his cousin Philipp, and to the Prince of Wales: 'It <u>must</u> not be', she said, '. . . Everything must be done to save it.'[29] Leopold agreed that the collection should be kept, but the discussion involved reams of paperwork, and he told the Prince of Wales it was 'a very tiresome business!'[30]

Most of his work now concerned church appointments. When a new Dean of Windsor was needed, it was Leopold who wrote to the successful candidate on the Queen's behalf, ahead of the official notification. When the Archbishop of Canterbury died, it was Leopold who attended the funeral, in a Kent churchyard one snowy December morning. He had immense respect for Archbishop Tait, and became involved in moves to set up a memorial. But the old frustration of being at his mother's beck and call, bound to ask permission for the smallest thing, was never far from the surface. They argued over something in January, and she wrote to Collins in more conciliatory tones than she had ever used about Leopold before, to say that a simple apology was all she required, as 'she <u>really does miss</u> him sadly. Pray say that.'[31]

Leopold still felt the need to prove himself on a wider stage, and seemed unaware of how much he had already achieved. The wedding brought him into the public eye, and even allowing for the obsequious respect paid to Victorian royalty it was clear that he had made an impression. A little book was published that year, which took as its main text six of his speeches, demonstrating his views on a range of educational and cultural issues. It sold well: this work was a relatively new departure for a prince, and people were interested in what he had to say. The editor quoted *The Times*: 'He has made it clear that he is a thinker – a voice, and not merely an echo.'[32] But public engagements were still isolated events, with weeks passing in between, and they did not satisfy his need for regular, demanding work.

Thoughts of the colonies had enticed him for years: perhaps from as early as 1873, when Lord Dufferin, then Canada's Governor-General, wrote to tell him how good the climate would be for his health. Around the end of March, he heard that his brother-in-law Lord Lorne intended to resign the Governor-Generalship of Canada. This was his opportunity, but he saw no point in speaking while the Queen was preoccupied with John Brown's death. At the end of April, he and Helen left for a holiday in France, visiting Fontainebleau and Cannes, and it was from there that he made his move: 'Lorne, as we all know, returns this winter from his post. . . . I come before to implore of you to appoint me as his successor.'

He had obviously discussed his plans with Lorne, Arthur and others, though to admit this would have damned his case without a hearing, but he seemed to have consulted even further – 'I know the Canadians: Government, Opposition, & the <u>people</u>, wish it – & finally people write, ask, talk, till I have felt that I <u>must</u> now speak to you. . . . I feel it is the turning-point in my existence, I feel I could do a <u>great work</u>, at this most important epoch in the History of Canada . . . which may ere long feel that it must choose between becoming a great independent power, or the loyal & devoted ally of England.' He marshalled all his best arguments, saying that the Prince Consort would have approved, and that the dry and bracing air – so like Balmoral – would do him good. 'Will you consider it dear Mamma; it is of such <u>vital</u> importance to me. I have lived in a silent dream for years on the subject.'[33]

His timing was unfortunate. The Queen had already asked the government to recommend someone for the post, and their reply followed close on his letter. They named Lord Lansdowne, and Leopold's unexpected request created a minor storm. His mother was appalled at first, though when he returned from France and put his case in person, she began to waver. He tried writing to his friend Herbert Gladstone, appealing to him 'in memory of our old Oxford days' to speak to the Prime Minister. 'Dear Tuppence,' he said, 'I have written by this post to your Father, on a subject which is to me <u>almost</u> a matter of <u>life & death</u>! At any rate of moral & mental life & death. . . . I fear I have not much chance of getting the appointment, but I am clinging as a drowning man to the least hope.'[34] But the government, guided by their own instincts and their perception of the Queen's wishes, opted for Lord Lansdowne; this came as a shattering blow to Leopold, who had invested so much in his application.

It was not the end. The *Evening News* reported that he had offered to serve as Governor-General and had been refused by the government. Questions were asked in Parliament, and early in June, Gladstone stood up in the House to pronounce that princes should be content 'to perform great decorative offices' – leaving the real jobs to the government and its appointees.[35] This unleashed a furious debate in the press, with some papers taking the same line, and others, the *Daily Telegraph* foremost among them, condemning the jealousy of the politicians. The *Evening News*'s editor, Coleridge Kennard, was a great friend of Leopold's from the committee of the Windsor Tapestry Works, and Ponsonby was suspicious, believing that Leopold had planted the story. If he had, it did him no favours. He was too depressed to be comforted by the positive comments, and some of the others were vicious. The scurrilous *Reynolds' Newspaper* described him as a feeble-minded invalid, covered in sores, who would not even be able to find Canada on a map.

Leopold escaped to Oxford, taking Helen to her first Commemoration. They stayed at the Deanery, and attended a flower festival and a concert with Mrs Liddell and her daughters. On Tuesday 14 June they visited the High School where, three years earlier, Leopold had laid the foundation stone and spoken of his lasting debt: 'the city and university of Oxford have always a first claim upon my time and services, for it was here that I first became acquainted, so to speak, with the outer world, and it was here that I found displayed before me those educational advantages which I am now so anxious should be placed, in some degree at least, within reach of all.'[36] Oxford returned his affection. On 13 June he took Helen to the Encaenia in the Sheldonian Theatre, and an already lively assembly exploded into 'such a thunder of cheers . . . as actually drowned the organ music, rendering inaudible two or three bars at a time. It has been customary on former occasions to sing the National Anthem', the local paper reported, 'but singing yesterday was quite put out of all thoughts by the spontaneous and irrepressible salvoes of cheering as the Duke and Duchess of Albany walked up the middle of the Theatre to the dais.'[37] Afterwards, the Albanys attended a lunch at All Souls, a Masonic fete and the University ball, and following their visit to the High School the Liddells took them on a river trip on the houseboat *British Queen* to Nuneham, where they took their leave.

Helen was beginning to accept engagements of her own, and on 16 June she presented prizes at the National Orphan Home at Ham Common, with Leopold's help. But the excitement of Oxford, following the tension of the previous weeks, took its toll, and a few days later she suffered a miscarriage. Once again, Leopold appeared in public alone, until July, when she was well enough to resume her programme. In August they travelled to Germany, though baby Alice had to remain with the Queen; their first stop was Arolsen, and September found them in Frankfurt, preparing to visit Wolfsgarten for Louis of Hesse's birthday. Next came Ludwigsburg, and a visit to Helen's widowed brother-in-law.

The days rushed past. 'Our stay in Hohenburg was <u>charming</u>!' Leopold told Louis. 'Uncle Adolf nice and friendly as ever – & the surroundings <u>delightful</u>. I rode with him up a high mountain, from which I could see <u>Tegernsee</u>. In Munich we met Amélie (formerly Coburg, now married to Mapperl in Bavaria) – and old Buff too, who has become very deaf.'[38] Their last destination was The Hague, where they stayed with King Willem and Queen Emma and their little daughter, and before September was over they were on their way home, bound ultimately for Balmoral, and eagerly anticipating the reunion with little Alice.

Leaving Balmoral in October, Leopold and Helen attended the Leeds Festival and made an important visit to Huddersfield, where the Prince opened an art exhibition and a new public park. He took the opportunity while in Yorkshire to visit Farnley Hall, where Turner stayed more than half a century before, and this brought Ruskin to his mind; he wrote from the artist's room at Farnley to thank his old friend for opening his eyes to Turner's painting, and to invite him to Claremont. Ruskin was one of several friends who stayed with the Albanys that autumn and winter, and all were touched by the warmth and friendliness of their home. 'I wish you could have a photograph of the scene in the hall after tea, yesterday', Ruskin told his cousin, 'they have a lovely piano organ for baby. . . the duke ground it – mama sat on the stairs with baby on her lap – and I danced to it.'[39]

Life at Claremont revolved around the baby, who sat in a high chair during adult mealtimes, playing with her wooden bricks, and rolled about on the carpet afterwards, amusing everyone; she reached for her parents instinctively, and the nurse was seldom in evidence. People in Esher became used to seeing Leopold driving the baby about in a small dog-cart. She had lost her first mass of dark hair, and Dr Poore, who stayed at Claremont in November, noticed something disturbingly familiar about her: 'The baby is most advanced & sits up in a chair to eat toast & Jam!' he told his mother. '. . . It is the very image of the Queen & to me this likeness was startling – in fact I felt quite afraid of the imp.'[40] Ella Taylor, who visited the house with Princess Frederica in January, made a series of rapid sketches of the baby on Claremont notepaper. One showed Leopold holding Alice upright between his knees, with Helen sitting on the floor a little way off, encouraging her to walk.

Leopold had put a lot of work into the house, and Poore remarked that it was 'much beautified since I saw it last'.[41] New textiles had been commissioned from the Windsor Tapestry Works, and from further afield; on her first evening Ella Taylor was shown into the Grand Drawing Room: 'such a beautiful room; the walls hung with silk of a most lovely indescribable colour, neither orange, nor amber nor strawberry nor terra cotta, the curtains which were drawn hung in rich folds are of the same colour. The effect of this drapery by the soft light of watt candles was so magical that I could not help exclaiming "Oh how beautiful"! The Duke was pleased for he had chosen the colour & had had the silk Damask woven at Lyons.'[42] But there was simplicity as well as splendour: among Leopold's wedding gifts was a cushion embroidered by Dr Poore's elderly mother, and the doctor was pleased to tell her that he saw it on the fireside chair in the Prince's study, 'with the Royal impress upon it'.[43]

In the evenings, Helen liked nothing better than to stand by the piano, turning the music while Leopold played. They were happy, and in this one area of his life, Leopold could not have been luckier – he had, after all, proposed to someone he hardly knew. But he had found a woman generous enough to enter into his world, and intelligent enough to share it, and the relationship showed every sign of lasting and growing. Helen could be shy with new people, but she was determined: during an argument with the Queen in her first summer in England she astonished Ponsonby by confronting her mother-in-law directly, instead of writing notes.[44] 'The more I see of the Duchess of Albany', wrote Ella Taylor, 'the more I like & admire her, so simple, so unaffected & good. She is clever too & full of humour & fun.'[45] Helen was also coming to understand Leopold very well, and knew that, however warm and loving their domestic setting was, it could not satisfy his need for work. His campaign for an appointment in the colonies was a cause she had come to share.

SIXTEEN

THE VILLA NEVADA

Leopold gave careful thought to the government's reasons for refusing the Canadian post, which the Colonial Secretary, Lord Derby, spelt out for him in May. Setting aside their worries about his health and their preference for political appointees, he focused on the comment that he lacked experience for such a senior post, particularly in Canada, where the nearness of the United States would create extra difficulties for a royal governor. It was a fair point, and recognising this helped him to see a way forward. Lord Normanby's term as Governor of Victoria in Australia was due to end in late 1884 or early 1885. A governorship was a lesser position, and Australia had no sensitive land borders. During the autumn and winter he discussed the idea with Prince Arthur, before waving him off to India to command a division at Meerut for two years, with Princess Louise and Lord Lorne, who stayed at Claremont in November on their return from Canada, and with the Prince of Wales, who had already approached Gladstone to find out about his brother's prospects. The biggest problem was how to approach the Queen.

There was no right way to tell Queen Victoria something she didn't want to hear. Leopold prepared the ground by asking Lord Derby if he stood a chance of the post – if not, there was no point in raising the subject. The answer sounded promising, but his plans were thrown into confusion by the discovery that Lord Normanby wanted to bring the retirement forward because his wife was in poor health. Suddenly, the room for manoeuvre was gone.

Over Christmas and the New Year, Leopold tried to find his

moment – and failed. The Queen was niggled because her children, with the exception of Arthur, had not given her new collection of extracts from her Highland journal as much praise as she thought it deserved. She told Leopold off for this by letter, though they were both under the same roof at Osborne, and his reply was evasive: 'I am sure I appreciate your book <u>quite</u> as much as anyone who may have told you how much they liked it.'[1] But he tried to soothe her by praising the way she had controlled her emotions over Christmas, and he wished consolation for her sorrows in the year to come. It was no use: in return she sent Arthur's letter from India, to show what he should have said, and complained that his new-found happiness had made him more selfish than ever. He left Osborne without mentioning Australia.

He and Helen went on to Eastwell to stay with the Duke and Duchess of Edinburgh. On their way through London, Leopold had hoped to call on Sir Charles Dilke, but having no opportunity he wrote from Eastwell, 'to tell you that a matter in which I am vitally interested will be brought before the next Cabinet meeting (I ought to say <u>probably</u>) – & as you are sure to be consulted therefore, I write to express a hope that your opinion will coincide with the request which I have made to Lord Derby . . . to succeed Lord Normanby as Governor of Victoria – you will remember that I told you last year at Claremont of my hopes of going to Canada, wh were not realized.' As a known republican, Dilke's voice would be a powerful one to have to his side, and Leopold explained that he had received encouraging letters from Gladstone and Lord Granville as well as Derby, and had consulted the war minister, Mr Childers. He had not yet told the Queen, he said, 'as I thought it wd be useless to trouble Her, if the Ministers had someone else already in view for the App^t'.[2]

Tensions permeated the visit to Eastwell. Leopold was glum and tetchy, Helen chattered to cover his silences, and Marie, who was normally so fond of them, was driven nearly to distraction: 'I am exhausted and stupified', she told a friend, 'he is always grumbling and she very nearly silly with her stupid small talk and infantine remarks.'[3] On 14 January Leopold took his nephew Alfred on an outing to Canterbury Cathedral; he put off the inevitable for two more days, then wrote to the Queen.

He knew his letter would provoke a storm. 'I do not for a moment conceal from myself that I am asking you for something, which it is more or less repugnant to you to grant', he said, 'and I earnestly appeal to your motherly affection for me . . . . <u>At first</u> my desire must appear to you to a certain extent selfish, but when you think over it you will see that it is not a "bed of roses", or a life of idleness, that I look forward to.'[4] He had no idea that on that very day Ponsonby was writing to the Queen and to Collins to say that Lord Derby had told him of Leopold's application. To the Queen, the secretary remarked that Leopold should certainly have asked her first; it was about the most damaging thing he could have said.

The next day, 17 January, the Albanys arrived at Claremont and Collins told them what had happened. The news sent Leopold reeling. He wrote a desperate letter to his mother explaining why he had spoken to Derby first, with no hope at all that his action would be forgiven. It would have been better not to write, because he lost control completely, and all the old resentments came out: 'My brothers have been given appointment after appointment, & though the many sad disappointments of my life have not led me to expect much, it w^d indeed be bitter to lose this, the last thing I shall ever beg of you.'[5]

It was a terrible moment, and Helen was so worried that she wrote herself to the Queen in secret: '<u>Please</u>, dear Mamma, dont be angry with him!! & <u>do</u> remember how <u>very much</u> he wishes for that post! – The idea of having a chance of going to Australia, & working <u>there</u> for the welfare of your colony was, what helped him last year over his disappointment about Cannada. – He feels more & more the necessity to have a decided work, which he can carry through.'[6] But the Queen was very angry indeed, and declined to answer either of them directly, writing instead to Princess Frederica, who was about to visit Claremont and could pass on her decision: 'Leopold <u>cannot</u> go to a <u>distant Colony while Arthur is away</u>. <u>When</u> Arthur <u>returns</u> . . . <u>I will let him go</u> – but it <u>cannot</u> be for <u>very long</u>. His <u>1</u>^st duty is <u>to me</u>, but this he has <u>never understood</u>. . . . <u>You</u> can tell him what deep pain he has caused me, & that sad & suffering as I am, I was made quite ill by this new & totally unexpected shock!'[7]

Ironically, this time the Cabinet wanted to appoint Leopold, and only the Queen stood in his way. Gladstone and Derby both tried to soften the blow, holding out the hope that he might be appointed somewhere, in a year, or maybe two. It would not have helped. Leopold's temper had burned itself out, leaving only resignation among the ashes. On 19 January Frederica arrived at Claremont with Ella Taylor, and he seemed his normal self, but he and Helen were glad of the company and clung to Frederica, persuading her to stay several days longer than she intended.

Pressure was being brought on the Queen to make a definite promise to Leopold. She complained bitterly to Arthur of the selfishness of his brother's action, but by the end of January was asking the government if appointments in Australia could not be rearranged to make Victoria fall vacant again in 1885. Ponsonby told Derby that 'the Leopoldian advocates' were behind this; almost certainly he meant the Prince of Wales and Lord Lorne, since no-one else would have been able to push the point when the Queen had spoken so decisively.[8] Arthur added his voice to the campaign: 'I so well understand your feelings', he told his mother, '& yet you must not forget that Leopold, like all men, is anxious to have some fixed employment where he can feel that he may use his talents & energies in the service of the Country. – He, not unnaturally feels jealous of Affie & I. . . . He frets at being kept at home & I am afraid that nothing you will do or say will make him feel otherwise.'[9] Coming from Meerut, though, his letter did not arrive until 18 March, when it was too late to make a difference.

Leopold was suffering badly from painful swelling of the smaller joints, and Helen was pregnant again. He planned a trip to Cannes for them both, but first had several public engagements in the north; then, at the last moment, Helen was taken ill, and it looked as if she was about to have another miscarriage. For her, Cannes would be out of the question. The doctor ordered her to lie down for several weeks, and afterwards to take extreme care. The baby was due in August, and after the end of May she was not even to leave Claremont. Leopold had to go north on his own. He distributed certificates to children from the elementary schools of Liverpool, and took advantage of the occasion to plead for the general teaching of cookery: 'I should like to see a rapid lift given to the standard of cleanliness, and care in the poorest of homes', he said. 'I should like to see meals, which are now mere scrambles, becoming points of real family union, and occasions for showing forethought, and kindliness, and self-respect.' But he was not the sort of reformer who stopped short at improving the poor – he wanted them to have fun as well. He left Liverpool with the question: 'How could a man feel himself so separate from his fellow-creatures as to think that the pleasures which were worth his own attention were quite superfluous trivialities in the case of poor men and women?'[10]

From Liverpool he went on to Stockton-on-Tees, to stay with the Marquess of Londonderry and visit Seaham Harbour and Durham. There was a Grand Masonic Lodge in Durham Castle, and he was awarded the degree of DCL at the university, and received an address from the city corporation. Wherever he went he apologised for Helen's absence, and, as soon as possible, he returned to Claremont. On 5 February he attended the Bachelors' Hunt Ball in Dorking, still alone, entering the town under a triumphal arch made from the illuminated escape ladders of the Volunteer Fire Brigade. Ten days later, he went to an amateur concert in Esher, held to raise funds for the village national schools. He sang *The Sands of Dee*, and it was so well received that he gave an encore. But the pains in his joints never ceased to plague him, and in the end he gave in and accepted the advice that he must go to Cannes on his own. He was not in the best of moods about this, but Helen and the baby were in no more danger, and she would certainly have urged him to go.

Leopold was to leave on 21 February, but continued working to the last moment. The Windsor Tapestry Works had financial problems, so that morning he sat down and drafted a letter to be sent to the mayors and corporations of the principal towns in the British Isles, to the City Guilds, and to the heads of the Oxford and Cambridge Colleges, explaining the aims of the factory, reminding the country at large that its craftsmen could repair ancient tapestries as well as creating new ones, and appealing for orders. That done, he prepared to leave, pausing only to hear the tune of a much-loved old musical clock which had once belonged to King Leopold's wife, Princess Charlotte. In later years the clock was treasured at Claremont in his memory. In London he met the Duke of Cambridge, and had lunch with the Prince of Wales. He saw Louise too, and pleaded with her to go to Claremont if Helen needed anything. Then he caught the train.

The journey would have taken about two days, and Leopold, travelling incognito as 'Baron Arklow', was accompanied by Royle and Alick Grant. They were to stay in Cannes with the Prince's friend and former equerry Captain Perceval and his aunt Marie at the Villa Nevada, to the west of the town, on a hill overlooking the sea and the distant Esterel mountains. Leopold loved Cannes, remembering the five months he had spent there in childhood – months which marked the transition between the happy childhood he idealised and the long difficult years of his growing up. If he had been older in 1861, he might have associated Cannes with his father's death and Sir Edward's, but he had been so young, and remembered only sunlit outings, endless croquet, and friends around him.

The Percevals gave him a room on the first floor with its own small balcony, and one day, looking out at the sea and the southern flowers, he remarked, 'Perceval, I would rather die here than anywhere else in the world.'[11] It was one of those lines which mean very little, when we say them, but later seem heavy with meaning. Every day he drove out or took longer expeditions into the mountains, and often he and Perceval went yachting. He attended a church with a comfortingly familiar name, Christ Church, and the Reverend Smith later recalled his hearty manner; everyone in Cannes agreed that he was well, full of life, and had a friendly word for each person he met – everyone, that is, except Perceval, who knew him better than most and sensed that behind the charm, Leopold was not at ease. They had an accident in the yacht one day, and Perceval heard him mutter, 'My usual fate. Disaster to friends as well as to myself.'[12]

But as the days passed, Cannes worked its magic, and Leopold decided to keep a permanent foothold in the south. He contracted to buy a plot of land at Golfe Juan, to the west of Cannes along the coast. Every day he wrote to Helen, and was pleased to hear that Louisa Knightley was staying with her; his letters began to include messages to his old friend and Helen told her 'that I was the first person outside his own family of whom he spoke to her, even before their engagement'.[13] The Queen sent continual letters and telegrams, urging his return.

Leopold was longing to see Helen again, but his feelings about his mother were more mixed, because he was still brooding over Australia. In a few weeks one of his favourite nieces, Victoria of Hesse, was to marry; he wanted to attend the wedding and had already bought his present, a handsome pearl and diamond bracelet. He heard from Louis, and on 15 March he wrote to arrange his accommodation in Darmstadt; he asked not to be put in the same building as his mother, because they had not spoken for three months. Then, not wishing to say more about this in a letter, he added, 'Don't say anything when you write to Windsor about the squabbles between myself and the Queen – I'll tell you about it when I come to Darmstadt. But it is <u>very</u> serious this time, and no joke.'[14]

On Monday 24 March, Leopold attended the Bachelors' Ball at the Club Méditerranée in Nice, where he told the Count of Paris and Lord Colquhoun that he kept dreaming of Princess Alice. His mind always turned to Alice when there was trouble in the family; this, and plans for the wedding were enough to explain the dreams, but after his death they would be given quite another meaning. He was planning to leave for home on Friday, and on the Wednesday evening he went to a ball at Mont Fleuri, which lasted until 4 a.m. After a few hours sleep, he took a warm sea bath and wrote letters in his room at the Cercle Nautique, the yacht club, before going out for lunch with the Percevals and other friends.

That afternoon there was to be a 'Battle of the Flowers' procession along the Promenade and Leopold was keen to join in, but first, needing a shave, he went back to the Cercle Nautique, and was hurrying to his room when he slipped on the tiled floor at the foot of the staircase and hit his right knee hard against the bottom step; '<u>such</u> pain it was!', he said, in a letter to Helen. 'I at once thought – as I lay on the ground – of my sweet Nellie, & the idea of your making yourself unhappy made me burst into tears!!!'[15] It was about 3.30 p.m. Dr Royle had already taken his place in the procession, so the manager sent someone to find him while he and one of the waiters, with Perceval and his friend Ussher, carried Leopold into the games room. When the doctor arrived he applied arnica and bandaged the knee, but there was no panic; before leaving the club, Leopold sent a telegram to Collins and signed a petition to protect the Île Sainte-Marguerite, once the prison of the Man in the Iron Mask, from development. He arranged for Perceval to attend a dinner that evening in his place, and only then was carefully manoeuvred into a carriage and taken back to the Villa Nevada.

It was about 5 o'clock by the time they had settled him into bed. He was in considerable pain, so Royle injected morphine, and through the evening, Miss Perceval kept him company. He had dinner, and Alick Grant sat and rubbed his leg, the usual treatment but perhaps not the most helpful, as the knee became painful and more morphine had to be given. During the evening Leopold, fighting hard against sleep, wrote to Helen, his 'dear Guardian angel':

Darling, you shall know the whole truth every day – I do not mind the pain (I have very little this moment) but the idea of you unhappy – perhaps crying – at Claremont joined to my horrible disappointment at not coming home – makes me howl. Oh! death w^d be preferable to this – Darling, we must not shut our eyes – I may be 3 or 4 weeks or longer without being able to move – You see I tell you all the worst (& shall do so on my honour always) – Could you come? by going by sea to Bordeaux, & then by canals to Marseilles? Oh! w^d it be possible? You see up comes my vile selfishness. You would have no rail then. Oh! if it were possible!!

Thanks [for] your letter, arrived only 2 hours ago – Darling the morphia is struggling so with me – that I can not possibly write more.

> Good night,
> God bless you
> Your ever
> devoted
> Leo[16]

Later it would be said that Leopold died from a slow but fatal haemorrhage. 'The Doctors think that in falling (he never hit his head) he must have burst some small blood vessel in his brain,' Princess Helena told the Duchess of Teck. She was adamant that her brother had not had a fit: 'it produced a convulsion at the last', she said, 'but was not one of his old attacks.'[17] But the French staff at the Cercle Nautique were convinced that the fall itself was caused by a lapse in consciousness, and early sources gave epilepsy as the cause of death. Only *The Weekly Scotsman* picked up on *The Lancet* of September 1882, and reported that Leopold had died of haemophilia. Really, nobody knew why it happened, and nobody ever would. Even official certificates from Cannes and London give no cause of death. In the uncertainty legends flourished, and it was said that Leopold's conversation on the last evening was full of death and tombs: his dreams of Alice were transformed into a touching premonition. There was comfort, maybe, in stories like this, but this last letter, which no-one but Helen saw, demonstrates that he did not expect to die.

Royle read Leopold to sleep, but found it difficult to sleep himself that night: Perceval had persuaded him to stay in the adjoining room with the door open, and the light was left on. At about 3 a.m., Royle said, 'my attention was aroused by seeing the Prince in a convulsion'.[18] He rushed to the bed, undid Leopold's collar and threw cold water on his face, shouting for help. Soon Perceval and Grant were in the room; they tried smelling salts and brandy, but it was hopeless. They could only stand and watch while the Prince's life slipped away. When it was over, Royle sent his first message to Windsor, a telegram to the Queen's doctor: 'Fits quite sudden, probably unconnected with fall. Results sinking pulse. We are brokenhearted.'[19] He sent for a Dr Frank, who came in immediately, and Dr Russell Reynolds; both agreed that nothing more could have been done.[20] Death was confirmed by Professor Spinabelli, presumably acting for the French authorities, and it was he who went later in the day to register the death, with the royal courier Leonard Riebold, who had arranged many of Leopold's journeys; Riebold signed himself simply as a 'friend' of the Prince.[21] In the early hours somebody, probably Perceval and the valet, dressed the body in the violet satin frock coat, decorated with ribbons and lace, which Leopold would have worn to the 'Battle of Flowers': it was a last, flamboyant gesture against the darkness.

The Prince of Wales was at Aintree race course when the news reached him, and he hurried to London by special train. From Marlborough House he wrote to the Queen, appealing for permission to go to Cannes to bring his brother home. At

Claremont, early in the afternoon of 28 March, Helen was sitting in an armchair by the fire, talking and laughing with Princess Helena and a group of ladies. She knew about the accident and was trying to arrange for baby Alice to be taken to Cannes to keep her father company. The telegram was handed to Helena, who hid her feelings and said nothing, waiting for the first opportunity to leave the room and speak to Collins; only then did she break the news.

From Windsor, Alick Yorke and Sir John Cowell were sent to Cannes, and they stopped at Claremont on their way to collect a small cross of garden flowers which Helen had made. The air of unreality was strong in these first days, because Leopold had cheated death so many times that no-one could quite believe what had happened. The Prince of Wales arrived in Cannes on 31 March, and he, Yorke and Cowell brought the body home, by train to Cherbourg and then by sea to Portsmouth on the royal yacht *Osborne*, with the *Alberta* and the Admiralty yacht *Enchantress*, draped in black, as an escort. Once, Leopold had told Helen that he wanted to be buried in St George's Chapel where they were married, 'beneath the place where the beautiful music & singing was going on'.[22] The Queen would have preferred the Mausoleum at Frogmore, but respected his wish – almost. She decided to place him in the adjacent memorial chapel, dedicated to her husband, because the vault of St George's was too difficult to visit. In a final irony, she insisted that Archie Brown must be present when the sarcophagus was moved to the chapel, because he had served Leopold with such devotion. It showed how little she really knew her son.

Perhaps it no longer mattered. Helen did know Leopold, and she was always loving and tolerant to his mother. In July 1884 she gave birth to the son Leopold had longed for. The baby inherited his father's name and title, and at first he was known as Leopold, officially at least, but later the names 'Charles Edward' – a mark of his father's enthusiasm for the Stuarts – took over. He was healthy, and in time became heir to his uncle Alfred, who was then Duke of Saxe-Coburg-Gotha and had lost his only son. Arthur was the true heir, then his son, but they refused the position, and Helen was forced to bow to family pressure; having become an English princess by marriage, she saw her son transformed, rather reluctantly, into a German prince. He went on to marry the eldest daughter of Calma of Schleswig-Holstein.

Baby Alice was bound to be a carrier because her father had haemophilia; this is in the nature of the condition. She married Prince Alexander of Teck, whose elder brother had been her father's first godchild, and her son Rupert was haemophilic; no-one will ever know if her other son, Maurice, was affected as he died in infancy. Her only daughter escaped the defective gene, which appeared again among the children and grandchildren of Princess Beatrice, and the children of Irene of Hesse and her sister Alix; little Alix, who learned her first card trick from her uncle Leopold, became the last Tsaritsa of Russia. When she was murdered in Ekaterinburg in 1918, she was still wearing two bracelets he had given her, which her Bolshevik captors could not remove.

In widowhood Helen gravitated naturally towards Leopold's real friends, to Ruskin, and Princess Frederica, and Captain Perceval, whose aunt became one of her ladies. Perceval died in Cannes in 1892, and on his aunt's death two years later, the Villa Nevada passed to Helen: she always sensed that Leopold was closer to her there than elsewhere. She turned also to his Oxford friends, the Liddells, Max Müller, Sidney Owen, Mandell Creighton and others, and always, always to Collins. To Collins, who entered the Household in 1867, expecting to be dismissed for speaking too plainly, and found a career for life. He knew the worst of Leopold as well as the best, yet the Prince's death left a lasting emptiness in his life, and he dedicated himself consciously to Helen and the children. On 31 March 1884 he wrote to Max Müller from Claremont, expressing his bewilderment at the news from Cannes: 'I have you & several other Oxford friends down in my Diary to come here this summer. But his life had been hurried & feverish of late, & he never seemed able to do half he wished to do, or see half the people he desired to see – But his heart went out to them just the same – amid all the hustle & unrest of the world. He is at peace now. May we meet that gentle, loving boy again! I can wish nothing more joyful in the hereafter –'[23]

NOTES

MANUSCRIPT SOURCES

Royal Archives, Windsor Castle: abbreviated in notes as RA. QVJ references are taken from Queen Victoria's Journal. RL refers to the Royal Library, Windsor
Hessisches Staatsarchiv Darmstadt, Großherzogliches Familenarchiv: abbreviated as HSD GF
Bodleian Library
British Library: abbreviated as BL
Hampshire County Record Office, Poore Collection: abbreviated as Hampshire CRO
Royal College of Physicians Library

Queen Victoria's family were prolific letter writers, and they appear to have written quickly, using abbreviations for common words like 'would', 'should' and 'very'. The Queen made a great point of underlining words, sometimes two or three times, and Leopold followed her example – to preserve the flavour of the original letters, I have tried to reproduce these features, and the writers' own spelling, as closely as possible.

All quotations are acknowledged: if a quotation is not followed directly by a note, the next note gives the correct reference. Information in the text which is not directly acknowledged comes from the manuscript collections listed above, or from printed sources in the bibliography.

PUBLISHED SOURCES

Full details of books appear at the first reference only, afterwards short titles are used.

Vague references to 'Contemporary newspaper report', or in one case 'Central News interview' come from the large bound volumes of press cuttings kept in the Royal Archives, referred to as Court Circulars, though other material is included.

Publishers' location is London, unless stated otherwise.

Notes

CHAPTER ONE

1 A.G.W. Whitfield, 'The Scholar Prince', *Journal of the Royal College of Physicians of London*, vol. 18 no. 3 (July 1984), 195
2 RA Z294/9 April 1853
3 Christopher Hibbert (ed.), *Queen Victoria in Her Letters and Journals* [John Murray, 1984], p. 97
4 RA Y78/62; King Leopold to Queen Victoria, 1 July 1853
5 RA QVJ, 23 April 1853
6 Cecil Woodham-Smith *Queen Victoria* [Book Club Associates edn, 1973], pp. 389–90; RA QVJ, 7 May 1853
7 RA QVJ, 24 May 1853
8 RA PP2/2/3593; 18 July 1853
9 RA Add A17/487; Leopold to Princess Louise, 4 June 1871
10 RA QVJ, 28 June 1853
11 RA M19/68; Leopold to Prince Albert, 22 August 1858
12 RA M16/56; Lady Caroline Barrington to QV, 17 September 1853
13 Mary Howard McClintock, *The Queen Thanks Sir Howard* [John Murray, 1945], p. 25
14 RA Y40/64, 134; Princess Feodora to QV, 21 January 1854, 15 June 1855
15 RA Y101/35; QV to King Leopold, 26 August 1856
16 RA Y125/12; Princess Augusta to QV, 2 August 1859; original in German
17 RA QVJ, 5 November 1853; RA Y79/17; King Leopold to QV, 23 December 1853
18 RA Z294, 2 July 1855; RA QVJ, 8 July 1855
19 RA Add A24/51; QV to the Duchess of Sutherland, 14 July 1855
20 RA M16/67; RA Add. C26/140; this account of Leopold's illness is based on Lady Caroline's letters in RA M16 and the Queen's Journal
21 RA Z130/205; Duchess of Kent to QV, 2 August 1855
22 RA M16/72, 73; Mrs Thurston to QV, 3 & 4 August 1855
23 *Letters of Lady Augusta Stanley* (ed.), The Dean of Windsor and Hector Bolitho [Gerald Howe, 1927], pp. 79–80, 85
24 RA M16/87; Lady Caroline to QV, 11 October 1856
25 RA QVJ, 17 October 1856
26 RA M16/86; Lady Caroline to QV, 10 September 1856
27 RA QVJ, 24 December 1856
28 RA QVJ, 7 April 1857, 8 May 1857
29 RA M19/66; Leopold to his parents, 18 September 1857
30 RA M19/41; Princess Helena to Prince Albert, 3 June 1858
31 Delia Millar, *The Victorian Watercolours and Drawings in the Collection of Her Majesty The Queen* [Philip Wilson, 1995], vol. 2, p. 588

32 RA M19/38, 54; Princess Alice to Prince Albert, 19 August 1858; Princess Louise to Prince Albert, 3 June [1858?]

33 RA M19/67, 68; Leopold to Prince Albert, 3 June & 22 August 1858

34 It is often said that Queen Victoria's family spoke German among themselves, but this is untrue. The children's letters demonstrate that their first language, the language of home and family, was English

35 RA QVJ, 20 January 1859; RA M16/93; QV to Lady Caroline, 25 July 1858; RA M18/34; QV to Lady Caroline, 22 September 1858

36 Roger Fulford (ed.), *Dearest Child* [Evans, 1964], p. 146

37 Ibid., p. 164

38 RA Add U303/8; QV to Leopold, 22 September 1858; *Dearest Child*, p. 154

39 Ibid., p. 208

40 RA Add U32/224; QV to the Princess Royal, 24 November 1858

41 RA Add A8/22; Leopold to Princess Mary Adelaide, 26 November 1859; original in French

42 *Lady Augusta Stanley*, p. 131

43 RA Z283/54; Leopold to Mme Rollande, 20? August 1859; original in French

44 RA Add C26/71; Alice to Lady Caroline, 18 September 1857

45 Sophie Dupré, Catalogue No. 40, April 1996, p. 39

46 RA QVJ, 4 March 1858

47 RA Add U303/6; Prince Albert to Leopold, 27 August 1861

CHAPTER TWO

 1 RA M16/86; Lady Caroline to QV, 10 September 1856

 2 RA QVJ, 16 October 1857

 3 RA Add A8/1257; Leopold to Princess Mary Adelaide, 2 November 1858

 4 RA QVJ, 18 April 1858

 5 Dr J. Wickham Legg, M.D., *A Treatise on Haemophilia* [H.K. Lewis, 1872], p. 17

 6 Royal College of Physicians of London, MS 715/96; Elizabeth Baly to her sister Fanny, 3? April [1859]

 7 Hampshire CRO 39M85/PCF27/19; G.V. Poore to his mother, 7 April 1870

 8 Some women who carry the disease show slight symptoms, as their clotting factor is lower than normal. This is interesting in relation to the known carriers within the royal family, who seemed to suffer from such problems as rheumatism and sciatica at an unusually early age

 9 Roger Fulford (ed.), *Darling Child* [Evans, 1976], pp. 75–6

10 RA M29/24; original in German

11 RA M29/30; original in German

12 SOA Plzen, pobocka Klatovy, Czech Republic: fond Mensdorff-Pouilly, denky Sophie, 3–8 May 1821; original in German: I am indebted to Miss Radmila Slabakova for this reference from the diary of Countess Sophie Mensdorff-Pouilly

13 His mother mentions his having had a shivering fever – 'Fieber-Frost' – some time before, but gives no clue to how long. Clearly, it did not worry her at the time, or put the child off his games

14 RA QVJ, 7 April 1859; the Journal as it exists today was heavily edited by Princess Beatrice, after the Queen's death

15 *Dearest Child*, p. 175

16 Millar, *The Victorian Watercolours*, vol. I, pp. 62–3

17 RA Add U303/38; Alfred to Leopold, 22 March 1859

18 RA Add U303/40; Helena to Leopold, 15 May 1859

19 RA Y104/26; QV to King Leopold, 26 August 1856

20 *Dearest Child*, p. 208

21 RA Add U303/9; QV to Leopold, 9 September 1859

22 RA Add A15/65; Leopold to Arthur, 13 September 1859; original in French; RA Add U303/55; Louise to Leopold, 22 September 1859

23 RA M16/99, 102; Lady Caroline to QV, 13 & 23 September 1859

24 RA QVJ, 25 September 1859, RA Add U303/43; Helena to Leopold, 28 September 1859

25 McLintock, *Sir Howard*, p. 31

26 Woodham-Smith, *Victoria*, p. 390

27 RA Y199/334; QV to King Leopold, 3 January 1860

28 RA Z4/20; Princess Royal to Prince Albert, 31 May 1861; *Lady Augusta Stanley*, p. 212

29 RA Y43/6; Princess Feodora to QV, 22 November 1861

30 RA QVJ, 7 April 1860

31 RA Add U303/25; Princess Royal to Leopold, 7 April 1860

32 RA Add U303/39; Alfred to Leopold, 8 May 1860

33 RA QVJ, 23 August 1860

34 RA M18/47; 24 January 1861

35 RA M18/48; 29 January 1861

36 *Dearest Child*, p. 336

37 RA QVJ, 1 June 1861

38 RA M18/50; Lady Caroline to QV, 5 June 1861

39 RA M18/54, 55; the same, 5 June 1861

40 RA M16/115; the same, 8 June 1861

41 RA M16/120; the same, undated

42 RA M16/119; the same, 12 June 1861

43 RA Add U303/32, 44, 56; Alice to Leopold, 11 June 1861, Helena to Leopold, 16 June 1861, Louise to Leopold, 8 June 1861

44 RA M16/126; Lady Caroline to QV, 8 July 1861

CHAPTER THREE

1 RA Add A30/545; Charles Ruland to Dr Günther, 16 July 1861; original in German
2 RA M16/131; Lady Caroline to QV, 25 August 1861
3 RA Z283/52; Leopold to Mme Rollande, 25 September 1861
4 Julia Cartwright (ed.), *The Journals of Lady Knightley of Fawsley* [John Murray, 1915], p. 25
5 *Dearest Child*, p. 362
6 *Lady Knightley*, p. 371
7 RA Add A17/464; Leopold to Louise, 5 April 1871
8 RA Add A30/548; 2 November 1861
9 RA Add A30/549; Elphinstone to Günther, 8 November 1861
10 RA Add U303/16; QV to Leopold, 5 November 1861
11 *Lady Knightley*, p. 27
12 Ibid., pp. 27–8
13 Ibid., p. 28
14 Ibid., p. 29. The Château Leader was built in 1843 in the west of Cannes for Sir John Temple Leader, an Englishman and friend of Lord Brougham, who discovered Cannes as a resort. Part of the house has since been destroyed; the remainder, presumed to be the service wing, still stands on the Avenue W. Weym
15 RA Add A30/550; Prince Albert to Günther, 14 November 1861; original in German
16 RA Add U303/17; QV to Leopold, 15 November 1861. In fact, the Portuguese King and his brothers were cousins to the Queen and Prince Albert – first cousins, once removed. Victoria probably used 'nephews' in recognition of the difference in their ages
17 RA Add A17/45; Leopold to Louise, 18 November 1861
18 RA Add U303/57; Louise to Leopold, 28 November 1861; RA Add A30 /555; RA Add U303/18; QV to Leopold, 29 November 1861
19 RA Add A30/552; Prince Albert to Günther, 21 November 1861; original in German
20 RA Add A30/553; Elphinstone to Günther, 23 November 1861
21 RA Add A30/554; the same, 27 November 1861
22 RA Add A30/555; the same, 29 November 1861
23 *Lady Knightley*, p. 30
24 RA Add U303/7; Prince Albert to Leopold, 2 December 1861; nap:^{n} = napoléon, a French coin
25 RA Add U303/58; Louise to Leopold, 8 December 1861
26 RA Add A30/558, 559; Elphinstone to Günther, 7 & 9 December 1861
27 *Lady Knightley*, p. 30
28 RA R1/77; Günther to QV, 16 December 1861; original in German

Notes

29 RA Add A30/560; Elphinstone to Günther, 15 December 1861
30 *Lady Knightley*, p. 31
31 RA Add A15/115; Leopold to Arthur, 18 December 1861
32 RA Add A17/48; Leopold to Louise, 20 December 1861
33 RA Add A15/116; Leopold to Arthur, 22 December 1861
34 RA Add A17/49; Leopold to Louise, 26 December 1861
35 RA Add U303/19; QV to Leopold, 16 January 1862
36 RA Add A15/119; Leopold to Arthur, 31 January and 1 February 1862
37 RA Add U303/20; QV to Leopold, 15 February 1862
38 RA Add U303/21; QV to Leopold, 11 March 1862
39 RA Add U303/60; Louise to Leopold, 30 January 1862
40 RA Add A30/563; Jenner to Günther, 15 March 1862
41 *Lady Knightley*, p. 32
42 McLintock, *Sir Howard*, p. 49
43 RA Add A15/162; Elphinstone to QV, 3 April 1862
44 *Lady Knightley*, pp. 34–5
45 RA Add U303/48; Helena to Leopold, 3 May 1862
46 BL Add MS 46361 f.1–3; Louise to Louisa Bowater, 11 April 1862
47 RA Add A15/172; Leopold to Arthur, 7 May 1862
48 BL Add MS 46360 f.28–29; Leopold to Louisa Bowater, 11 May 1862
49 RA Add A30/569, 570; Louisa Bowater to Günther, 12 & 14 May [1862]; originals in German
50 RA Add A15/183; Leopold to Arthur, nd [?spring 1862]; the spelling is Leopold's own
51 RA PP1 52/3; Elphinstone to Sir Charles Phipps, 5 June 1862
52 RA PP Minute Book 1 1851–1876/p. 100: Buff was recommended to the Queen by his uncle Professor Hofmann, a noted German chemist who knew the Prince Consort. A letter written by Dr Ernst Becker in June 1862 [RA Add U105] refers to Buff as Leopold's tutor, but this record of his engagement and salary refers specifically to both princes

CHAPTER FOUR

1 RA Add U143/Reel 1; QV to Alice, 2 October 1862
2 Roger Fulford (ed.), *Dearest Mama* [Evans, 1968], p. 125
3 *Lady Augusta Stanley*, pp. 271–2
4 McClintock, *Sir Howard*, p. 48
5 *Dearest Mama*, p. 108
6 RA Add U143/Reel 1; 2 October 1862
7 RA Add A25/95; QV to Elphinstone, 7 December 1862
8 RA Add U303/61; Louise to Leopold, 29 April 1862
9 Hope Dyson and Charles Tennyson, *Dear and Honoured Lady* [Macmillan, 1969], pp. 77–8

10 *Lady Knightley*, p. 47
11 According to most accounts, but the story has been told a great many times and the details do vary. Some say it was Arthur he bit, and some Alfred: perhaps the future Kaiser was just prone to biting knees
12 *Dearest Mama*, p. 234
13 Ibid., p. 239
14 RA M18/69; Lady Caroline to Mrs Robert Bruce, 18 July [1863]; RA Add C26/130; Leopold to Lady Caroline, 21 July 1863
15 *Lady Knightley*, p. 69
16 RA Add A15/336; Leopold to Arthur, 28 July 1863
17 RA Add A15/349; the same, 16 August 1863
18 RA Add A15/578; the same, 22 July 1864
19 RA Add A15/349; the same, 16 August 1863
20 Elizabeth Longford (ed.), *Darling Loosy* [Weidenfeld & Nicolson, 1991], p. 91
21 RA Add A15/502; Leopold to Arthur, ?8 July 1864
22 RA Add A15/546, 539; the same, 16 August & 10 August 1864
23 RA Add A15/808; the same, 4 Feb 1866
24 *Dearest Mama*, p. 321; 'the Queen' was Queen, later Empress, Augusta, Leopold's godmother
25 RA Add A15/546; Leopold to Arthur, 16 August 1864
26 RA Add A15/453; Elphinstone to QV, 17 April 1864
27 RA S16/67; Sir Charles Phipps to Alfred
28 RA Y112/6; QV to King Leopold, 16 June 1864
29 RA Add A25/138; August 1864
30 Bodleian Library MS Eng d.2349, f.7–8. Undated note in a volume of letters to Max Müller from royal secretaries and members of the Household, which is written on Windsor crested paper and headed 'Tutor for Prince Leopold'. The hand appears to be that of Lady Katherine M. Bruce, one of the Queen's ladies
31 RA Add A25/138; August 1864
32 There were people outside the family who knew – Theodore Martin, for example, who was commissioned to write a biography of the Prince Consort, regularly received letters from the Queen about Leopold's bleeding attacks, and in 1877, Lord Beaconsfield was told the full truth – but in general the rule now was secrecy: as far as the outside world was concerned, Leopold was 'delicate', and suffered from chronic rheumatism
33 Alick Grant did become Leopold's valet in 1870, and stayed with him until his death
34 RA Add A25/168; QV to Elphinstone, 19 March 1866
35 *Darling Loosy*, p. 92
36 BL Add MS 46360 f.67–68; Leopold to Louisa Bowater, 9 September 1865: RA Add C26/131; Leopold to Lady Caroline, 11 September 1865

37 RA Add C18/93; Diary entry, 10 November 1864
38 RA Add U303/23; QV to Leopold, 6 February 1866
39 BL Add MS 46360 f.69–70; Leopold to Louisa Bowater, 6 March 1866
40 RA Add A25/168; QV to Elphinstone, 19 March 1866
41 RA Add A15/835; Elphinstone to QV, 21 March 1866; RA Add A25/171; QV to Elphinstone, 22 March 1866
42 RA Add A25/168; QV to Elphinstone, 19 March 1866
43 RA Add A30 /315; 4 April 1866
44 *Lady Knightley*, p. 96
45 BL Add MS 46360 f. 69–70
46 RA Add A17/146; Leopold to Louise, 30 April 1866
47 *Lady Knightley*, p. 117
48 RA QVJ, 15 April 1866
49 RA Add A30/357; Leopold to Stirling, 14 January 1871
50 *Lady Knightley*, p. 117
51 RA Add A15/864; Leopold to Arthur, 22 May 1866
52 McLintock, *Sir Howard*, p. 84
53 RA Add A25/176; QV to Elphinstone, 28 May 1866
54 *Lady Knightley*, p. 120
55 RA Add A15/884; Elphinstone to QV, 10 July 1866
56 RA Z266/3; Jenner to QV, 6 October 1881
57 RA Add A25/179; QV to Elphinstone, 8 July 1866

CHAPTER FIVE

1 RA Add A25/180; QV to Elphinstone, 12 July 1866
2 Ibid.
3 RA Add A25/181; QV to Elphinstone, 26 July 1866
4 RA Add A22/106; QV to Lady Biddulph, 27 July 1866
5 RA Add A30/317; Leopold and Louise to Stirling, 6 August 1866
6 RA Add A25/185; QV to Elphinstone, 10 September 1866
7 RA Add A22/108; QV to Lady Biddulph, 1 August 1866
8 He kept the letters to himself, and in the 1960s his grandson gave them to the Royal Archives
9 RA Add A30/316; Leopold to Stirling, 5 August 1866
10 RA Add A30/319; the same, 19 August 1866
11 RA Add A30/320; the same, 27 August 1866
12 BL Add MS 46361 f.58–61; Louise to Louisa Bowater, 22 December 1866
13 RA Add A30/318; Leopold to Stirling, 12 August 1866
14 RA Add A30/319; Leopold to Stirling, 19 August 1866
15 RA Add A17/157; Leopold to Louise, 4 October 1866
16 RA Y44/78; Princess Feodora to QV, 11 February 1867
17 RA Add U303/26; Crown Princess Victoria to Leopold, 5 April 1866

18 RA T4/67; Leopold to the Prince of Wales, 8 November 1865
19 RA Add U303/37; Alice to Leopold, 29 April 1867
20 This album, together with the two later albums which made up the Prince's collection, were presented to the Bodleian Library by the Duchess of Albany after his death
21 Bodleian Library MS Autogr. b.3, f.104; all other references also from MS Autogr. b.3, the Prince's first album
22 Roger Fulford (ed.), *Your Dear Letter* [Evans, 1971], p. 141
23 RA Add A30/328; Leopold to Stirling, 4 August 1867
24 HSD GF Abt D24 Nr.24/3; 27 December 1867
25 RA Add A30/329; Leopold to Stirling, 28 December 1867
26 RA QVJ, 21 January 1868
27 RA QVJ, 29 January 1868
28 RA Add C26/106; Louise to Lady Caroline, 29 January 1868
29 RA Y44/119; Princess Feodora to QV, 9 February 1868
30 The Dean of Windsor and Hector Bolitho (eds), *Later Letters of Lady Augusta Stanley, 1864–1876* [Jonathan Cape, 1929], p. 74
31 RA QVJ, 4 February 1868
32 *Your Dear Letter*, p. 184
33 RA Y44/127; Princess Feodora to QV, 19 April 1868
34 RA Add A17/254; 18 March 1868
35 RA Add A30/330; Leopold to Stirling, 24 April 1868
36 QV to Crown Princess Victoria, quoted in Peter Arengo-Jones, *Queen Victoria in Switzerland* [Robert Hale, 1995], p. 41
37 RA Add A30/332, 333; Leopold to Stirling, 28 July & 4 August, 1868
38 RA Add A30/335, 338, 334; Leopold to Stirling, 31 August, 17 November, 10 August 1868
39 *Queen Victoria in Switzerland*, p. 98
40 RA Add A30/336; Leopold to Stirling, 3 September 1868
41 Ibid.
42 RA Add A30/341; Leopold to Stirling, 14 January 1869

CHAPTER SIX

1 *Your Dear Letter*, p. 225
2 RA Y167/42; QV to Sir Theodore Martin, 9 April 1869
3 RA Add X/138; Leopold to Sir James Paget, 14 May 1869
4 RA Add A15/1383; QV to Gladstone, 9 April 1869
5 *Your Dear Letter*, p. 259
6 RA Add A30/343; Leopold to Stirling, 8 August 1869
7 RA Add A17/321; Leopold to Louise, nd [November 1869]
8 RA Add A30/347; Leopold to Stirling, 9 February 1870
9 RA Add A30/348; the same, 11 March 1870

10 RA Add A30/349; the same, 3 April 1870
11 Hampshire CRO 39M85/PCF27/19; Poore to his mother, 7 April 1870
12 RA Add A30/350; Leopold to Stirling, 17 April 1870
13 HSD GF Abt D24 Nr.24/3; 21 April 1870
14 Jehanne Wake, *Princess Louise* [Collins, 1998], p. 117
15 RA Add A30/349; Leopold to Stirling, 3 April 1870
16 RA Add C26/135; Leopold to Lady Caroline, 8 April 1870
17 RA Add A17/366; Leopold to Louise, 27 May 1870
18 RA Add A17/367; the same, 28 May 1870
19 RA Add A30/6, 9, 14; Leopold to Collins, 9 June 1870, nd [June 1870], 2 July 1870
20 RA Add A17/371; RA Add A30/14; Leopold to Louise, 10 June 1870; to Collins, 2 July 1870
21 RA R13/102; Alick Yorke to Miss Stopford, 31 March 1884
22 RA Add A30/11; Leopold to Collins, 20 June 1870
23 RA Add A30/10, 12; the same, 18 & 22 June 1870
24 RA Add A30/15; the same, 4 July 1870
25 RA Add A30/14; the same, 2 July 1870
26 Hampshire CRO 39M85/PCF30; Poore to his mother, 10 July 1870
27 RA Add A30/17; QV to Collins, 12 July 1870
28 Hampshire CRO 39M85/PCF27/22; Poore to his mother, 18 August 1870
29 Ibid.
30 Hampshire CRO 39M85/PCF27/27; Poore to his mother, 26 October 1870
31 Hampshire CRO 39M85/PCF27/26, 25, PCF/30; the same, 11 October, 28 September, 5 September 1870
32 RA Add A30/353; Leopold to Stirling, 11 August 1870
33 HSD GF Abt D24 Nr.24/3; 3 August 1870
34 RA Add A30/356; Leopold to Stirling, 21 December 1870
35 Hampshire CRO 39M85/PCF27/25; Poore to his mother, 28 September 1870
36 RA Add A30/354; Leopold to Stirling, 5 October 1870
37 Hampshire CRO 39M85/PCF30; Poore to Marcus Beck, 9 November 1870
38 RA Add A30/356; Leopold to Stirling, 21 December 1870
39 Ibid.
40 *Lady Knightley*, p. 212
41 RA Add A30/357; Leopold to Stirling, 14 January 1871
42 Hampshire CRO 39M85/PCF32/2; Leopold to Poore, 25 May 1871; the word 'cabinet' refers to a particular size of photograph, roughly equivalent to a modern 6 × 4 inch print
43 RA Add A30/357, 359; Leopold to Stirling, 14 January & 5 March 1871

44 RA Add A17/460; Leopold to Louise, 5 March 1871
45 RA Add A17/478; the same, 4 May 1871; in the original, Leopold started to write 'love', then crossed it out, so that his meaning would still be obvious
46 RA Add A36/291; Sir Henry Ponsonby to Lady Ponsonby, 3 June 1871
47 RA Add A30/20; QV to Collins, 28 May 1871; RA Add A36/283; Sir Henry Ponsonby to Lady Ponsonby, 26 May 1871
48 RA Add A17/481; Leopold to Louise, 15 May 1871
49 RA Add A30/357; Leopold to Stirling, 14 January 1871
50 Hampshire CRO 39M85/PCF27/33; Poore to his mother, 25 May 1871
51 Hampshire CRO 39M85/PCF32/24; Leopold to Poore, 31 May 1871
52 RA Add A1/16
53 HSD GF Abt D24 Nr.15/6; 7 March 1861 – original in French
54 HRH Princess Alice, *Letters to Her Majesty The Queen* [John Murray, 1897], p. 199; the baby's full name was 'Friedrich Wilhelm August Victor Leopold Ludwig'; his mother called him 'Frittie' but others, including Leopold, used the diminutive 'Fritzie'
55 RA Add A30/364; Leopold to Stirling, 21 November 1871
56 RA Add A30/24, QV to Collins, 22 December 1871
57 RA Add A30/366; Leopold to Stirling, 16 January 1872

CHAPTER SEVEN

1 RA R16: F.W.H. Myers 'Personal Recollections of Leopold, Duke of Albany' *The Fortnightly Review*, p. 621; the poet and academic Frederic Myers was a close friend of Robert Collins, and knew Leopold well
2 RA Add A30/30; Leopold to Collins, 10 January 1872
3 RA R16: Myers 'Recollections', p. 613
4 RA Add A30/19; Myers to Collins, 27 December 1870
5 RA Add A17/532; Leopold to Louise, 21 February 1872
6 RA Add A30/32; Leopold to QV, 6 March 1872
7 RA Add A30/33; QV to Leopold, 6 March 1872
8 RA Add A30/34; Leopold to QV, 6 March 1872
9 RA Y45/113, 119; Princess Feodora to QV, 11 April & 21 May 1872
10 HSD GF Abt D24 Nr.24/3; 18 April 1872
11 RA Add A30/28; Leopold to Collins, nd [April 1872]
12 RA Add A30/38; QV to Collins, 14 April 1872
13 The character of 'Arthur' in *Tom Brown's Schooldays* was based on Stanley, who attended Rugby under Dr Arnold
14 Nirad C. Chaudhuri, *Scholar Extraordinary: The Life of Professor the Rt Hon. Friedrich Max Müller, P.C.* [Chatto & Windus, 1974], p. 294

15 RA Add A30/35

16 RA Add A30/48; QV to Leopold, 21 November 1872

17 RA Add A30/41; QV to Collins, 11 May 1872

18 *Darling Child*, pp. 42, 44

19 RA Add A17/535, Leopold to Louise, 21 May 1872

20 Hampshire CRO 39M85/PCF32/7; Leopold to Poore, 17 June 1872; RA Add A30/42; QV to Collins, 30 May 1872

21 RA Add U303/75; 10 August 1872, original in French

22 RA Add A30/46; QV to Collins, 20 August 1872

23 RA Add A17/539; Leopold to Louise, 22 August 1872

24 RA Add A30/44; Dean of Windsor to Collins, 19 July 1872

25 RA PP Vic 13600; Collins to Sir Thomas Biddulph, 14 & 19 November 1872

26 RA Add A17/548; Leopold to Louise, 6 November 1872

27 RA Add A30/48, 49; QV to Leopold, 21 November 1872

28 RA Add A17/550; Leopold to Louise, 2 December 1872. Wykeham House is still standing, with later additions, and is now the headquarters of the Oxford University Careers Service

29 Ibid.

30 RA Add A30/50, 51; QV to Collins, 30 November & 5 December 1872

31 RA Add A7/306; Leopold to Jenner, nd [November 1872]

32 RA Add A17/550; Leopold to Louise, 2 December 1872

33 HSD GF Abt D24 Nr.24/3; 16 December 1872

34 RA Add A17/550; Leopold to Louise, 2 December 1872

35 RA Add A17/552; the same, 16 December 1872

36 RA Add A36/470; Ponsonby to Lady Ponsonby, 17 December 1872

37 RA Add A25/350; QV to Leopold, 23 December 1872

38 RA Add A30/53, 54; QV to Gladstone, 23 December 1872; Biddulph to Gladstone, 27 December 1872

CHAPTER EIGHT

1 RA Add A30/52; Ruskin to Leopold, 21 December 1872

2 Bodleian Library MS Eng d.2350, f.50–53; Leopold to Max Müller, 29 December 1878: Professor Müller's name is confusing. Müller was his family name, and he was christened Friedrich Max; 'Max' was the Christian name he used from childhood. But he gave his children, including daughters, 'Max Müller' as a surname, and later generations added a hyphen; now he is often referred to as if his own surname was 'Max Müller'

3 J.B. Atlay, *Sir Henry Wentworth Acland, Bart.* [Smith, Elder & Co., 1903], pp. 377ff

4 RA Add A17/564; Leopold to Louise, 27 February 1873

5 Bodleian Library MS Acland d.2, f.81–82; Leopold to Acland, 14 April 1873

6 RA Add U303/170; Gladstone to Leopold, 10 April 1873

7 BL Loan 73/28; Leopold to Gladstone, 14 April 1873

8 RA Add A30/373; Leopold to Stirling, 11 May 1873

9 HSD GF Abt D24 Nr.24/3; 22 April 1873

10 RA Add A36/548; Ponsonby to Lady Ponsonby, 20 May 1873

11 RA Add A30/373; Leopold to Stirling, 11 May 1873

12 Hampshire CRO 39M85/PCF32/10, 11; Leopold to Poore, 12 April & 6 August 1873

13 RA Add A30/82; Leopold to Collins, 2 January 1874

14 The full text of *Cakeless* is printed in Anne Clark, *The Real Alice* [Michael Joseph, 1981]

15 John Ruskin, *Praeterita*, Vol III, quoted in Clark, *Alice*, p. 121

16 Chaudhuri, *Scholar Extraordinary*, p. 272

17 RA Add A30/99; Leopold to Collins, 8 September 1874

18 Surviving grandchildren of Alice Liddell and her brother were told by their parents that Alice was the object of the Prince's love. It may be so: he was deeply fond of Alice, but the parents who passed on the story were themselves far removed from the event, and the evidence of his own papers points to Edith. Perhaps his reference to 'the two loveliest females I know' in Poore's picture frame suggests that even he was unsure for a time

19 HSD GF Abt D24 Nr.24/3; 11 May 1873

20 HSD GF Abt D24 Nr.24/3; 30 May 1873

21 HSD GF Abt D24 Nr.24/3; 30 Dec 1873

22 RA Add A30/419, 419a &b

23 RA Add A30/68; QV to Collins, 19 June 1873

24 RA Add A17/573; Leopold to Louise, 27 August 1873

25 RA Add A17/581, 592; the same, 5 October & 18 December 1873

26 RA Z264/1; Leopold to QV, 16 October 1873

27 RA Z264/2; QV to Leopold, 19 October 1873

28 RA Add A17/586; QV to Louise, 9 November 1873

29 RA Add A30/71; QV to Collins, 3 November 1873

30 *Darling Child*, p. 116

31 BL Loan 73/28; Gladstone to Leopold, 9 September 1873; Leopold to Gladstone, 12 September 1873

32 RA Z264/6; Collins to QV, 8 December 1873

33 RA Z264/10; the same, 11 December 1873

34 RA Z264/12; Leopold to QV, 12 December 1873

35 RA Z264/13; QV to Leopold, 13 December 1873

CHAPTER NINE

1 RA Add A30/374; Leopold to Stirling, 31 December 1873
2 RA Add A30/82; Leopold to Collins, 2 January 1874
3 RA Add A17/595; Leopold to Louise, 23 December 1873
4 RA Add A30/82; Leopold to Collins, 2 January 1874
5 HSD GF Abt D24 Nr.24/3; 30 December 1873
6 Bodleian Library MS Acland d.2, f.83–84; Leopold to the Prince of
   Wales, 22 December 1873
7 RA Add A30/83; Leopold to Collins, 2 January 1874
8 RA Add A30/79; Ruskin to Collins, nd
9 RA Z264/16; Duckworth to QV, 7 January 1874
10 RA Z264/21; QV to Leopold, 13 January 1874
11 Quoted in *The Graphic*, 5 April 1884, p. 318
12 RA Add A17/610; Leopold to Louise, 13 February 1874
13 Ibid.
14 RA Add A30/88; Ruskin to Collins, 20 February 1874
15 RA Add U303/129; Myers to Collins, 27 January 1875
16 Bodleian Library MS Eng d.2349, f.90; Collins to Müller, 20 February
   1900
17 RA Add A17/613; Leopold to Louise, 15 February 1874
18 Wake, *Princess Louise*, pp. 95–6
19 RA Add A17/613; Leopold to Louise, 15 February 1874
20 RA Add A30/375; Leopold to Stirling, 3 March 1874
21 HSD GF Abt D24 Nr.24/3; 15 April 1874
22 *Darling Loosy*, p. 183
23 HSD GF Abt D24 Nr.24/3; 15 April 1874
24 RA Add A36/726; Ponsonby to Lady Ponsonby, 7 April 1874
25 RA Add A30/95; Leopold to Collins, 12 April 1874; the new man's
   name was Edney
26 RA Z264/23; QV to Collins, 3 May 1874
27 RA Z264/33; Collins to QV, 5 May 1874
28 RA Z264/34, 35; Elphinstone to QV, 6 & 7 May 1874
29 RA Z264/36; Leopold to QV, 7 May 1874
30 RA Add A30/98; QV to Collins, 4 June 1874
31 RA J86/11, RA D5/2; Disraeli to QV, 16 June 1874, QV to Disraeli,
   10 July 1874
32 Hampshire CRO 39M85/PCF28/11; Poore to Marcus Beck, 21 June
   1874
33 Bodleian Library MS Acland d.2, f.87–88; Leopold to Acland, 24
   June 1874
34 HSD GF Abt D24 Nr.24/3; 29 June 1874
35 RA L18/124; QV to Ponsonby, nd [August 1874]
36 BL Add MS 43907 f.4–5; Collins to Mrs Pattison, 29 August 1874

37 RA Add A30/86; Leopold to Collins, nd; 'old B' was Collins, whom Leopold always called 'Bob'

38 RA Add A30/100; Leopold to Collins, 11 September 1874

39 RA Add A30/101; Leopold to Collins, 19 September 1874

40 RA Add A17/643; QV to Louise, 7 October 1874

41 RA Add A30/107; QV to Collins, 27 November 1874

42 RA Add A30/381; Leopold to Stirling, 23 November 1874

43 Hampshire CRO 39M85/PCF30; Poore to his mother, 29 November 1874

44 RA Add C26/139; Leopold to Lady Caroline, 8 December 1874

45 RA Add A36/861; Ponsonby to Lady Ponsonby, 19 December 1874; 'Old Car' was Lady Caroline

46 *Darling Loosy*, p. 188

47 RA Add A30/383; Collins to Stirling, 20 January 1875

48 Louise expressed misgivings about her brother's treatment to Lady Caroline in July 1874: 'The poor Boy had been badly managed as usual, you know what I mean' RA Add C26/125. 'I am a good deal...', quoted in Wake, *Princess Louise*, p. 189

49 Bodleian Library MS Acland d.2, f.110; Louise to Acland, 31 January 1875

50 Wake, *Princess Louise*, p. 189

CHAPTER TEN

1 RA Add U303/114; Reverend Dalton to Collins, 20 January 1875

2 RA Add A30/19; Myers to Collins, 27 December 1870

3 RA Add U303/118, 119; Bonamy Price, Sidney Owen to Collins, 22 January 1875

4 RA Add U303/106; Revd M. Creighton to Collins, nd

5 Bodleian Library MS Acland d.2, f.89–90; Leopold to Acland, 20 February 1875

6 *Darling Loosy*, p. 192

7 RA Add A36/876; Ponsonby to Lady Ponsonby, 18 March 1875

8 RA Add A30/112, 113; QV to Leopold, 23 March 1875; Leopold to QV, 24 March 1875

9 RA Add A30/109; Ruskin to Collins, nd

10 *Lady Knightley*, p. 278

11 Colin Gordon, *Beyond the Looking Glass* [Hodder and Stoughton, 1982], p. 172

12 Morton N. Cohen, *Lewis Carroll* [Macmillan, 1995], p. 515

13 Quoted in *The Graphic*, 5 April 1884, p. 318

14 RA Z264/43; QV to Jenner, 4 June 1875

15 RA Z264/44; Jenner to Lady Ely, 6 June 1875

16 RA Add A36/927; Ponsonby to Lady Ponsonby, 12 June 1875; RA

Z264/45, 46; QV to Louise, 11 June 1875; Louise to QV, 13 June 1875

17 RA Add A36/934; Ponsonby to Lady Ponsonby, 16 June 1875
18 RA Add A30/123; QV to Collins, 27 June 1875
19 RA Z265/6; QV to Leopold, 16 August 1875
20 RA Add A36/939, 940; Ponsonby to Lady Ponsonby, 20 & 21 August 1875
21 RA Add A36/964; the same, 17 September 1875
22 RA Z265/9; Leopold to QV, 20 September 1875
23 RA Z265/12; QV to Leopold, 24 September 1875
24 RA Z265/13; Collins to QV, 26 September 1875
25 RA Add A30/387; Leopold to Stirling, 1 October 1875
26 RA Z265/16; Dean Liddell to Dean of Windsor, 19 October 1875
27 RA Z265/19; Collins to QV, 23 October 1875
28 RA Add A30/147; QV to Collins, 16 November 1875
29 RA Add A30/131; QV to Collins, 9 December 1875
30 RA Add U303/124; Max Müller to Leopold, 13 December 1875
31 RA Z265/21; Collins to QV, 3 November 1875
32 RA Z265/23; QV to Leopold, 31 January 1876
33 RA Z265/26; Collins to QV, 15 February 1876; RA Add A30/135; QV to Leopold, 29 February 1876
34 RA Add U165; Tuesday 29 February 1876
35 RA Add A30/420; Queen Sophie to Leopold, nd [?March 1876]
36 RA Add A30/141; Ruskin to Leopold, 19 June 1876
37 RA Add A30/137; Ruskin to Leopold, 4 March 1876; the papers contain no clue about the fate of this collection
38 Clark, *Alice*, pp. 161–2
39 Gordon, *Looking Glass*, p. 128
40 RA Add A30/409; Leopold to Creighton, 9 July 1876
41 McLintock, *Sir Howard*, p. 176
42 RA Z265/27; QV to Leopold, 7 July 1876
43 RA Add A30/139; QV to Collins, 25 May 1876
44 RA Z265/29; QV to Leopold, 19 July 1876
45 Ibid.
46 RA Z265/30; Collins to QV, 21 July 1876
47 RA Z265/31; Duckworth to QV, 23 July 1876
48 RA Z265/32; Duckworth to Leopold, 23 July 1876

CHAPTER ELEVEN

1 RA Add U303/134; Beaconsfield to Leopold, 25 August 1876
2 RA S31/49; Leopold to Beaconsfield, 27 August 1876
3 RA Z265/38; QV to Leopold, 19 September 1876
4 RA Add A36/1136; Ponsonby to Lady Ponsonby, 24 September 1876

5 RA Add A30/581; 22 May 1881

6 RA Z265/41, 42; QV to Leopold, 15 November 1876; Leopold to QV, 18 November 1876

7 RA Add A30/145; QV to Collins, 9 November 1876

8 RA Z265/39; Lord Hertford to Lady Ely, 10 November 1876

9 RA Z265/43; Collins to QV, 19 November 1876

10 RA Add A17/1976; William Gillett to Lady Sophia Macnamara, 17 April [?1884, or later]

11 RA Z265/45; Dean of Windsor to QV, 26 November 1876

12 RA Z265/47; Royle to Marshall, 3 December 1876

13 RA Z265/54; Duckworth to QV, 12 February 1877

14 RA Z265/50; QV to Leopold, 7 December 1876

15 RA Add A36/1177; Ponsonby to Lady Ponsonby, 26 January 1877

16 Quotation from RA Z265/52; Duckworth to QV, 9 December 1876

17 RA Add A36/1339; Ponsonby to Lady Ponsonby [? 23 October 1877]

18 RA Add A36/1176; 25 January 1877

19 RA Z265/54; Duckworth to QV, 12 February 1877

20 RA A51/32, 33; Beaconsfield to QV, 13 April 1877; RA U303/92; Queen Victoria to Leopold, 18 April 1877

21 Bodleian Library MS Acland d.176, f.14–15; Leopold to Acland, 17 April 1877

22 RA Z265/61; the letter is dated Friday 18 May 1877, but 10/11 May seems more likely because this appears to be Leopold's first mention of the peerage, and of his brothers; Z265/58, dated 11 May, is the Queen's reply, then in Z265/57, which Leopold dated 'Friday evening, 11 May', he picks up various points in his mother's letter. He was very excited, and angry, when Z265/61 was written, and this may explain a mistaken date

23 RA Z265/56; QV to Leopold, nd [May 1877]

24 RA Z265/66; Collins to QV, 18 June 1877

25 RA Z265/67; Collins to QV, 22 June 1877

26 RA Z265/68; Leopold to QV, 4 July 1877; 'Bertie' refers to the Prince of Wales

27 RA Add A30/28; Leopold to Collins [April 1872]

28 RA Z265/69; Collins to QV, 14 July 1877

29 RA O12/224; Leopold to QV, 24 July 1877

30 RA S31/58; Leopold to Corry, 31 July 1877

31 HSD GF Abt D24 Nr.15/6; 16 December 1881

32 RA Add A36/1295; Ponsonby to Lady Ponsonby, 19 August 1877; Ponsonby and the Court Circular refer to 'Miss Liddell': this is likely to have been Alice as she was the oldest daughter still unmarried

33 RA Add A36/1320; the same, 13 September 1877

34 Bodleian Library Dep Hughenden 94/3, f. 91–4; Corry to Beaconsfield, 27 August 1879

35 RA Z265/78; Helena to QV, 30 December 1877
36 Mrs J. Comyns Carr, *Reminiscences* [Hutchinson, *c.*1925], pp. 241–2; RA Add A36/1339; Ponsonby to Lady Ponsonby [? 23 October 1877]
37 RA Add A36; Ponsonby to Lady Ponsonby, 26 October 1877
38 RA Z265/70; Leopold to QV, 14 October 1877
39 RA Z265/77; Helena to QV, 13 December 1877

CHAPTER TWELVE

 1 RA Add A36; Ponsonby to Lady Ponsonby, 5 & 10 November 1877
 2 RA Add A30/127; Ruskin to Collins, 4 November [?1877]
 3 RA Z265/77; Helena to QV, 28 December 1877
 4 RA Z265/79; QV to Helena, 5 January 1878
 5 RA Add C12/98; Leopold to Doyne C. Bell, 26 October 1877
 6 RA Z265/78; Helena to QV, 30 December 1877
 7 John Dixon Hunt, *The Wider Sea: A Life of John Ruskin* [J.M. Dent, 1982], p. 369
 8 Bodleian Library MS Eng Lett c.42/f.10; Ruskin to Allen, 4 January 1878
 9 *Darling Child*, p. 276
10 RA H21/6; Leopold to QV, 3 March 1878
11 RA Z265/92; Collins to QV, 2 April 1878
12 RA R16/*The Times*, 2 April 1884
13 RA Z265/92; Collins to QV, 2 April 1878
14 RA Add A15/2793; Leopold to QV, 11 May 1878
15 RA S31/66; QV to Beaconsfield, 19 May 1878; *Darling Child*, pp. 288–9
16 RA Add A36; Ponsonby to Lady Ponsonby, 24 May 1878
17 RA S22/12; Leopold to QV, 12 June 1878
18 RA Add A36; Ponsonby to Lady Ponsonby, 20 July 1878
19 Lillie Langtry (Lady de Bathe), *The Days I Knew* [Hutchinson, 1925], p. 70
20 RA Add A36; Ponsonby to Lady Ponsonby, 22 August 1878
21 RA Add A36; the same, 24 August 1878
22 RA Add A15/6846; Arthur to Princess Luise Margarete of Prussia, 7 November 1878
23 Queen Victoria put the idea of a long voyage to the Prime Minister in May 1878; in November 1878 a letter from Sir Michael Hicks Beach to the Queen suggests that the destination was to be Australia, RA S31/66; RA P25/86
24 Bodleian Library MS Acland d.2/f. 98–9; Leopold to Acland, 29 October 1878
25 Bodleian Library MS Eng d.2350/ f.50–3; Leopold to Max Müller, 29 December 1878

26 RA Z86/25, 26; Elisabeth of Hesse to QV, 2 March 1879; Irene of Hesse to QV, 3 March 1879
27 RA Z86/27; Elisabeth of Hesse to QV, 7 March 1879
28 RA Z86/30; the same, 11 March 1879
29 RA Z86/35; Victoria of Hesse to QV, 4 April 1879
30 RA Z86/40; Elisabeth of Hesse to QV, 19 April 1879
31 HSD GF Abt D24 Nr.15/6; 10 April 1879; original in German
32 HRH Princess Alice, Countess of Athlone, *For My Grandchildren* [Evans, 1966], p. 21
33 Revd Charles Bullock (ed.), *Talks with the People by Men of Mark: HRH Prince Leopold* [Home Words Publishing Office, 1882], p. 41
34 *For My Grandchildren*, p. 21
35 *Talks with the People*, p. 51
36 *The Wider Sea*, p. 378
37 RA S31/78; Leopold to Beaconsfield, 31 October 1879
38 RA Add A15/6927; Arthur to Luise Margarete, 14 February 1879
39 RA H25/62; QV to Beaconsfield, 26 June 1879
40 RA R12/87; Revd Teignmouth Shore to Lady Ely, 29 March 1884

CHAPTER THIRTEEN

1 RA Add A30/12; Leopold to Collins, 22 June 1870
2 RA Z266/3; Jenner to QV, 6 October 1881
3 RA Z266/1; QV to Leopold, 14 February 1879
4 Roger Fulford (ed.), *Beloved Mama* [Evans, 1981], p. 71
5 HSD GF Abt D24 Nr.15/6; 10 December 1879
6 Ibid., New Year's Eve, 1879
7 Ibid., 16 March 1880
8 Margaret Blunden, *The Countess of Warwick* [Cassell, 1967], p. 30
9 RA Z34/13; Crown Princess Victoria to QV, 21 March 1880
10 HSD GF Abt D24 Nr.15/6; 24 March 1880; in the original, 'with the old life' is in German, presumably as a quotation from the Crown Prince's letter
11 RA Add U30/3; Beaconsfield to Corry, 21 March 1880
12 RA Add U30/8; Leopold to Corry, 31 March 1880
13 HSD GF Abt D24 Nr.15/6; 29 April 1880
14 RA Add U30/12; Mary Baring to Corry, 27 April 1880
15 RA Add U30/19; Lady Ashburton to Corry, nd
16 RA Add A30/581; 11 March 1881; the original remark is in Italian
17 Contemporary newspaper report, Thursday 13 May 1880
18 RA Add A17/1878; Eva Langham to QV, 28 May 1880
19 RA FF3/4/17; memo to Collins, nd [April/May 1880]
20 All quotations from RA Add A30/411 (cuttings from contemporary US and Canadian newspapers)

21 Gordon, *Looking Glass*, p. 173–4
22 RA Add A30/375; Leopold to Stirling, 3 March 1874
23 RA C34/33, 43; Leopold to QV, 3 & 7 April 1880
24 Frank Hardie, *The Political Influence of Queen Victoria 1861–1901* [Oxford University Press, 1935], p. 193; present author was unable to find this quotation in Fitzroy's memoirs
25 RA Add A36; Ponsonby to Lady Ponsonby, 19 September 1881
26 RA Add A36; Ponsonby to Lady Ponsonby, 25 October 1880
27 HSD GF Abt D24 Nr.15/6; 24 October 1880: original in German
28 HSD GF Abt D24 Nr.15/6; 12 December 1880
29 Ibid.
30 RA Add U32; QV to Crown Princess Victoria, 31 January 1881
31 RA Add U32; the same, 13 January 1881; 'Lenchen' was the family's nickname for Princess Helena

CHAPTER FOURTEEN

1 HSD GF Abt D24 Nr.15/6; 30 December 1880
2 RA Add A30/581; 5 January 1881
3 Ibid., 26 January 1881
4 Ibid., 17 June 1881
5 Ibid., 12 July 1881; this must have happened during Lillie's affair with Prince Louis of Battenberg
6 Ibid., 18 January 1881
7 Ibid., 19 January 1881
8 RA Add U303/220; Lord Beaconsfield to Leopold, March 1881
9 RA Add A30/581; 21 April 1881
10 Contemporary newspaper report, Thursday 5 May 1881
11 RA R16; *The Fortnightly Review* – Myers 'Recollections', pp. 615, 617
12 Frank Prochaska, *Royal Bounty: The Making of a Welfare Monarchy* [Yale University Press, 1995], p. 119
13 RA Add A30/581; 9 March 1881
14 RA Add U303/79; Ferdinand of Saxe-Coburg to Leopold, 22 April 1881
15 RA Add A15/183; Leopold to Arthur, nd [May 1862]
16 RA Add A30/318; Oliver Millar, *The Pictures in the Collection of Her Majesty The Queen: The Victorian Pictures* [Cambridge University Press, 1992], p. 182; RL K1004, K1007
17 RA Add A30/63, 62; the letter was copied by Collins on Wykeham House paper: the date must have been 1873–5
18 Richard Ellmann, *Oscar Wilde* [Hamish Hamilton, 1987], p. 66
19 RA Add A30/581; 4 May 1881
20 Ibid., 27 May 1881

21 RA Add A36; Ponsonby to Lady Ponsonby, 1 June 1881
22 RA Add A30/581; 20 June 1881
23 Ibid., 1 July 1881
24 RA Add A20/1599; Marie, Duchess of Edinburgh to QV, 22 February 1881
25 RA Z87/39; Victoria of Hesse to QV, 5 July 1881
26 Blunden, *Countess of Warwick*, p. 36
27 Quotation from *Dearest Child*, pp. 254–5. In her own home, the name of Leopold's future wife was Helene, spelt with a final 'e' which would have been pronounced, but in England she was almost always 'Helen', and I have used that spelling throughout
28 RA Z87/46; Elisabeth of Hesse to QV, 22 July 1881
29 RA Z87/49; Victoria of Hesse to QV, 3 August 1881
30 RA Add A30/581; 19 August 1881
31 Ibid., 15 August 1881
32 HSD GF Abt D24 Nr.15/6; 29 August 1881: the original is in German, except the phrase 'to call on the Waldecks'
33 RA Add A30/581; 3 September 1881
34 Ibid., 4 September 1881
35 HSD GF Abt D24 Nr.15/6; Leopold to Louis, 9 September 1881
36 RA Add A36; Ponsonby to Lady Ponsonby, 10 September 1881
37 RA Add A30/581; 27 October 1881
38 Ibid., 13 November 1881
39 Ibid., 18 November 1881
40 HSD GF Abt D24 Nr.15/6; 18 November 1881: the original is in German
41 RA Add A30/581; 25 November 1881
42 Ibid., 26 November 1881
43 RA Add A36; Ponsonby to Lady Ponsonby, 11 September 1881
44 RA Add A30/429; Marie, Duchess of Edinburgh to Leopold, 21 November 1881
45 RA Add A30/432; Beatrice to Leopold, 18 November 1881
46 RA Add A36; Ponsonby to Lady Ponsonby, 21 November 1881
47 'feeling wretched & miserable' – RA Add A30/581; 28 November 1881: 'V.R. & Baby' – Ibid., 29 November 1881

CHAPTER FIFTEEN

1 Lt Colonel J.P.C. Sewell (ed.), *Personal Letters of King Edward VII* [Hutchinson, 1931], p. 60
2 *Illustrated London News*, 2 May 1882, p. 11
3 HSD GF Abt D24 Nr.15/6; 16 January 1882
4 HSD GF Abt D24 Nr.15/6; 16 December 1881
5 HSD GF Abt D24 Nr.15/6; 16 January 1882; the exclamation marks are his own

6 *The Graphic Royal Wedding Number*, 6 May 1882, p. 25
7 RA Add A30/475; QV to Helen, 6 February 1882
8 RA QVJ, 21 Feb 1882
9 RA Add A36; Ponsonby to Lady Ponsonby 21, 22 February 1882
10 RA Add A30/188; Ponsonby to Collins, 22 January 1882
11 Koninklijk Huisarchief, Netherlands: Marie, Princess Wilhelm of Württemberg to Queen Emma of the Netherlands, 18 April 1882; original in German
12 RA Add A15/3503; Arthur to QV, 27 January 1882
13 *The Graphic Royal Wedding Number*, p. 21
14 *Illustrated London News Royal Wedding Number*, 2 May 1882, p. 23
15 *Beloved Mama*, p. 117
16 RA Add U303/85; Prince Wilhelm of Württemberg to Leopold, 25 May 1882
17 Contemporary newspaper report, Saturday, 24 June 1882
18 *Lady Knightley*, p. 355; *gêne* = embarrassment
19 RA Add A30/413; Leopold to Helen, 30 August 1882
20 *The Lancet*, 2 September 1882; 'haematophilia' was one of the early names for the condition
21 RA Z266/4; Leopold to QV, 5 November 1882
22 Bodleian Library MS North c.18/f.193–4; Leopold to Sir Hastings & Percy Doyle, 2 March 1883
23 Clark, *Alice*, p. 193; in later years, Leopold Reginald Hargreaves came to be known as 'Rex'
24 Bodleian Library MS Harcourt dep.7/f. 34–5; Leopold to Sir William Harcourt, 5 March 1883
25 HSD GF Abt D24 Nr.15/6; 14 March 1883
26 HSD GF Abt D24 Nr.15/6; 28 March 1883
27 RA Z210/91; Leopold to QV, 31 March 1883
28 *Lady Knightley*, p. 361
29 RA S17/82; QV to Leopold, 27 September 1882
30 RA S17/80; Leopold to the Prince of Wales, 28 September 1882
31 RA Add A30/195; QV to Collins, 20 January 1883
32 *Talks With the People*, p. xii
33 RA Z266/6; Leopold to QV, date missing [May 1882]
34 RA GV PS 50837; Leopold to Herbert Gladstone, 14 May 1883
35 RA Add A12/821; newspaper cuttings, June 1883
36 Contemporary newspaper report, Tuesday 13 April 1880
37 *Jackson's Oxford Journal*, Saturday 16 June 1883
38 HSD GF Abt D24 Nr.15/6; 23[?] September 1883. 'Uncle Adolf' was Helen's uncle the Duke of Nassau, later Grand Duke Adolf of Luxembourg; 'Amélie' a sister of Philipp of Saxe-Coburg, married to Duke Max Emanuel in Bavaria (Crown Prince Rudolf's uncle); and 'old Buff' Leopold's former tutor

39 J.S. Dearden (ed.), *The Professor: Arthur Severn's Memoir of John Ruskin* [Allen & Unwin 1967], p. 109

40 Hampshire CRO 39M85/PCF30; Poore to his mother, 19 November 1883

41 Ibid.

42 RA Add A8/395; Ella Taylor, 20 January 1884

43 Hampshire CRO 39M85/PCF30; Poore to his mother, 19 November 1883

44 RA Add A36; Ponsonby to Lady Ponsonby, 23 August 1882

45 RA Add A8/395; Ella Taylor, 23 January 1884

CHAPTER SIXTEEN

1 RA Z266/13; Leopold to QV, 2 January 1884

2 BL Add MS 43874 f.109–11; Leopold to Sir Charles Dilke, 7 January 1884

3 RA Add A20/1081; Marie, Duchess of Edinburgh to General Wolseley, 11 January 1884

4 RA Z266/15; Leopold to QV, 16 January 1884

5 RA Z266/18; Leopold to QV, 17 January 1884

6 RA Z266/17; Helen to QV, 17 January 1884

7 RA L1/119; QV to Princess Frederica, 18 January 1884

8 RA L1/129; Ponsonby to Derby, 29 January 1884

9 RA Z266/29; Arthur to QV, 15 February 1884

10 RA R16; *The Weekly Scotsman*, 5 April 1884; *The Graphic*, 5 April 1884, p. 318

11 *Central News* interview with Captain Perceval, Cannes, 30 March 1884

12 Ibid.

13 *Lady Knightley*, p. 371

14 HSD GF Abt D24 Nr.15/6; 15 March 1884; original in German

15 RA Add A30/418; Leopold to Helen, 27 March 1884: the letter was headed 'no.36'. Sadly, the other thirty-five do not seem to have survived

16 Ibid.

17 RA Add A8/51; Helena to the Duchess of Teck, 10 April 1884

18 RA Add A8/52; Royle to QV, 28 March 1884: this copy of Royle's letter to the Queen, describing her son's last hours, was sent to the Cambridge family. Another copy of the same letter is preserved in the Family Archives in Darmstadt

19 Michaela Reid, *Ask Sir James* [Viking, 1987], p. 59; Royle, who actually witnessed the death, seems to have favoured the idea of epilepsy, but there may have been an element of wishful thinking in this. In his letter to the Queen he did not make it clear that he

was in the carnival procession, and not with Leopold when he fell. He may have felt easier in his own mind to think that the fall was not the cause of death.

A fit might have been involved: modern medical opinion suggests that death happened too rapidly for a slow bleed into the brain to have been the cause. If there had been a head injury, it would be a different matter, but we know that there was not. There is another, horribly simple possibility: the combined effect of too much morphine with the claret Leopold was given during the evening. Morphine had often made him sick before, even without alcohol. If he had vomited while he was asleep, lying on his back because of the bandaged knee, it would probably have killed him. The convulsion that roused the doctor from the next room might in fact have been his patient choking

20 RA Add A8/52; Royle to QV, 28 March 1884
21 Curiously, the two men gave the wrong age for Leopold when they registered the death, so official records still state that he was twenty-nine when he died; in fact, he was ten days short of his thirty-first birthday
22 Bodleian Library MS Eng c.2805, f.17; Collins to Max Müller, 31 March 1884
23 Ibid.

The Villa Nevada is now a private house, close to a memorial fountain erected by the French people of Cannes and the surrounding area, who felt closely involved in the tragedy because Leopold died on French soil. The English also put up a memorial, St George's Church in Cannes. In Oxford, the Christ Church Society honoured the Prince with a relief portrait in the Military Chapel of the Cathedral, with the simple inscription, 'In Affectionate Remembrance'

NOTE ON THE FAMILY TREES

1: QUEEN VICTORIA'S ANCESTRY IN THE FEMALE LINE (p. 268)

Family trees always focus on the male line, because it is men who pass on names and titles to their children, giving the family its identity and continuity. Here the focus is on women; it is women, not men, who pass on haemophilia to their sons. To find out whether Queen Victoria inherited the haemophilia gene, it is among her female ancestors – mother, maternal grandmother, maternal great-grandmother, and their sisters and daughters, that you need to look, and you look for sons and grandsons who died in childhood. Finding them, of course, cannot be seen as proof. At best, it is an indication, and only clear evidence that one of these boys suffered unusual bruising and joint problems, or died of bleeding, could prove the case. But *if* there was haemophilia in the family before the Queen was born, it must have affected someone on this table – for that reason alone, the table is important.

There do appear to be a number of possibilities, and to highlight this, boys who died young for no known reason, or for a reason which seems unusual, or insufficient to cause death, are highlighted with a single border. Potential carriers – their mothers – are highlighted with a lighter single border. This can only be speculative, but it makes a point: Queen Victoria's maternal ancestors were very unlucky with their sons.

Only one adult is highlighted as a potential sufferer. Heinrich LI Reuss-Ebersdorf died in a convulsive fit, like Prince Leopold. There is no evidence that he had haemophilia, but if he did, his daughters would have been carriers. One of his daughters had a family, and of her five sons, four died in childhood – two were said to have died of apoplexy (a stroke). Once again it is not proof, but it is interesting.

2: HAEMOPHILIA IN THE QUEEN'S FAMILY (p. 269)

The second tree develops the story further, by tracing the known course of the haemophilia gene through the Queen's family. For interest, the children and grandchildren of the Queen's half-sister Princess Feodora are also shown, because the two women shared a mother: if Victoria did inherit the gene, Feodora had a 50 per cent chance of inheriting it too. Her sons were healthy, but both her daughters had sons who died at a very early age, and, as on the first tree, the possibilities are marked. In this instance, however, haemophilia seems less likely because there is no sign of a problem in the families of Princess Feodora's granddaughters.

In Queen Victoria's own family, boys known to be haemophilic are indicated by a double border or underline, and known carriers by a lighter double border. Even here there are problems. It is sometimes said that the Queen's eldest daughter, Crown Princess Victoria, carried the gene because two of her sons died in childhood, but if either boy had shown signs of the bruising and other symptoms suffered by his uncle Leopold, this would surely have been mentioned in his mother's letters to the Queen: it never was. Prince Sigismund died of meningitis and Prince Waldemar of diphtheria, diseases which can still kill healthy children, and there is no sign of bleeding in their sisters' sons.

Princess Helena, on the other hand, could have been a carrier. Her elder sons were healthy, but the third died a week after his birth, and her daughters had no children. Similarly, Princess Louise, who had no children of her own, may have carried the gene. The Queen's youngest grandchild, Prince Maurice of Battenberg, is always said to have had haemophilia, but the evidence suggests overwhelmingly that he was a fit, strong boy who grew up without health problems and joined the army. Like so many of his generation, it was war, not haemophilia, which killed him.

This underlines the problem. If it is difficult to decide which of the Queen's descendants was affected by haemophilia, how much more so to make pronouncements about minor princes in the first half of the nineteenth century, or in the eighteenth century, when the condition was not even recognised by doctors? The door to inheritance may not be so closed as has been thought.

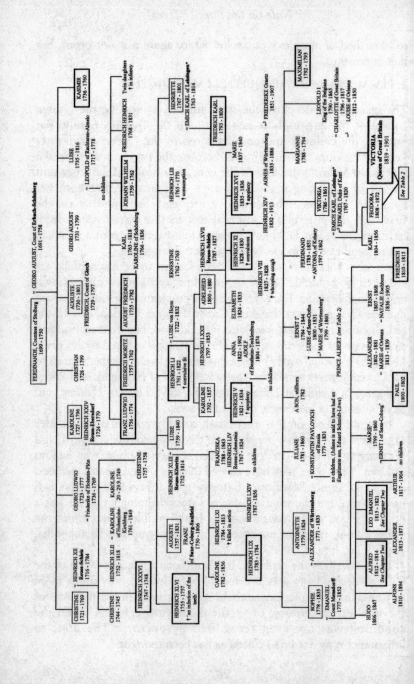

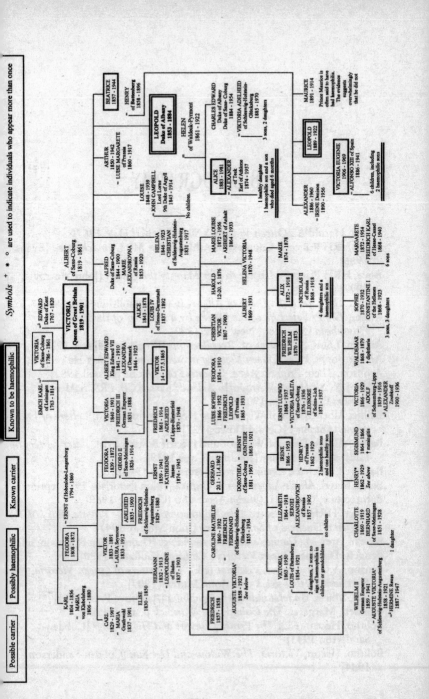

Possible carrier   Possibly haemophilic   Known carrier   Known to be haemophilic

VICTORIA of Saxe-Coburg 1786 - 1861
EDWARD Duke of Kent 1767 - 1820

EMICH KARL of Leiningen 1763 - 1814
= ERNST of Hohenlohe-Langenburg 1794 - 1860

VICTORIA Queen of Great Britain 1819 - 1901
= ALBERT of Saxe-Coburg 1819 - 1861

Symbols + * ° are used to indicate individuals who appear more than once

BEATRICE 1857 - 1944
= HENRY of Battenberg 1858 - 1896

ARTHUR 1850 - 1942
= LUISE MARGARETE of Prussia 1860 - 1917

LEOPOLD Duke of Albany 1853 - 1884
= HELEN of Waldeck-Pyrmont 1861 - 1922

CHARLES EDWARD Duke of Saxe-Coburg 1884 - 1954
= VIKTORIA ADELHEID of Schleswig-Holstein-Glücksburg 1885 - 1970
3 sons, 2 daughters

MAURICE 1891 - 1914
Prince Maurice is often said to have had haemophilia. The evidence suggests overwhelmingly that he did not

LEOPOLD 1889 - 1922

LOUISE 1848 - 1939
= JOHN CAMPBELL Lord Lorne 9th Duke of Argyll 1845 - 1914
No children.

ALICE 1883 - 1981
= ALEXANDER Earl of Athlone 1874 - 1957
1 healthy daughter 1 haemophilic son and a son who died aged 6 months

VICTORIA EUGENIE of Spain 1886 - 1941
= ALFONSO XIII of Spain 1886 - 1941
6 children, including 2 haemophilic sons

ALEXANDER 1886 - 1960
= IRENE Denison 1890 - 1956

KARL 1804 - 1856
= MARIA von Klebelsberg 1806 - 1880

FEODORA 1808 - 1872
= ERNST of Hohenlohe-Langenburg 1794 - 1860

VICTORIA 1840 - 1901
= FRIEDRICH III German Emperor 1831 - 1888

ALBERT EDWARD King Edward VII 1841 - 1910
= ALEXANDRA of Denmark 1844 - 1925

ALFRED Duke of Saxe-Coburg 1844 - 1900
= MARIE ALEXANDROVNA of Russia 1853 - 1920

HELENA 1846 - 1923
= CHRISTIAN of Schleswig-Holstein-Augustenburg 1831 - 1917

MARIE LOUISE 1872 - 1956
= ARIBERT of Anhalt 1864 - 1933

ALICE 1843 - 1878
= LOUIS IV of Hesse-Darmstadt 1837 - 1892

VIKTOR 14 - 17.5.1865

CAI 1859 - 1907
= MARIA Gruthwol 1837 - 1891

ELSE 1830 - 1850

FEODORA 1839 - 1872
= GEORG II of Saxe-Meiningen 1826 - 1914

ADELHEID 1835 - 1900
= FRIEDRICH of Schleswig-Holstein-Augustenburg 1829 - 1880

ERNST 1859 - 1941
= KATHERINE Jenssen 1874 - 1945

FRIEDRICH 1861 - 1914
= ADELHEID of Lippe-Biesterfeld 1870 - 1948

CHRISTIAN VICTOR 1867 - 1900

HAROLD 12 - 20. 5. 1876

HELENA VICTORIA 1870 - 1948

MARIE 1874 - 1878

ALBERT 1869 - 1931

VIKTOR 1833 - 1891
= LAURA Seymour 1833 - 1912

HERMANN 1832 - 1913
= LEOPOLDINE of Baden 1837 - 1903

VICTORIA 1863 - 1950
= FRIEDRICH III German Emperor 1831 - 1888

FRIEDRICH 1870 - 1873

LUISE SOPHIE 1866 - 1952
= FRIEDRICH LEOPOLD 1865 - 1931

FEODORA 1874 - 1910

ALIX 1872 - 1918
= NICHOLAS II of Russia 1868 - 1918
4 daughters and a haemophilic son

SOPHIE 1870 - 1932
= CONSTANTINE I of the Hellenes 1868 - 1923
3 sons, 3 daughters

MARGARETE 1872 - 1954
= FRIEDRICH KARL of the Hessen 1868 - 1940
6 sons

CAROLINE MATHILDE 1860 - 1932
= FRIEDRICH LEOPOLD of Schleswig-Holstein-Glücksburg 1855 - 1934

ERNST LUDWIG 1868 - 1937
= VICTORIA MELITA of Saxe-Coburg 1876 - 1936
= ELEONORE of Solms-Lich 1871 - 1937

VICTORIA 1866 - 1929
= ADOLF of Schaumburg-Lippe 1859 - 1916
= ¹ ALEXANDER Zoubkoff 1900 - 1936

FRIEDRICH 1857 - 1858

AUGUSTE VIKTORIA° 1858 - 1921
See below

ELIZABETH 1864 - 1918
= SERGEI ALEXANDROVICH of Russia 1857 - 1905
no children

GERHARD 20.1 - 11.4.1862

DOROTHEA 1881 - 1967
= ERNST GÜNTHER of Saxe-Coburg 1863 - 1921

IRENE 1866 - 1953
= HENRY* of Prussia 1862 - 1929
2 haemophilic sons and one healthy son

WALDEMAR 1868 - 1879
† diphtheria

VICTORIA 1863 - 1950
= LOUIS of Battenberg 1854 - 1921
2 daughters, 2 sons: no sign of haemophilia in children or grandchildren

WILHELM II German Emperor 1859 - 1941
= ¹ AUGUSTE VIKTORIA° of Schleswig-Holstein-Augustenburg 1858 - 1921
= ² HERMINE Reuss 1887 - 1947

CHARLOTTE 1860 - 1919
= BERNHARD of Saxe-Meiningen 1851 - 1928
1 daughter

HENRY* 1862 - 1929
See above

SIGISMUND 1864 - 1866
† meningitis

BIBLIOGRAPHY

Albert, Harold A., *Queen Victoria's Sister* [Robert Hale 1967]

Alice, HRH Princess, Countess of Athlone, *For My Grandchildren* [Evans 1966]

Alice, HRH Princess, *Letters to Her Majesty the Queen* [John Murray 1897]

Anon., *The Life of the Duke of Albany* [Crown Publishing Co. 1884]

Anon., *The Private Life of the Queen by a Member of the Royal Household* [Appleton, New York 1897]

Antrim, Louisa, Countess of, *Recollections* [King's Stone Press 1937]

Arengo-Jones, Peter, *Queen Victoria in Switzerland* [Robert Hale 1995]

Aronson, Theo, *Princess Alice, Countess of Athlone* [Cassell 1981]

Atlay, J.B., *Sir Henry Wentworth Acland, Bart. KCB, FRS, A Memoir* [Smith, Elder & Co. 1903]

Baillie, Albert, Dean of Windsor and Hector Bolitho (eds), *Letters of Lady Augusta Stanley* [Gerald Howe 1927]

Baillie, Albert, Dean of Windsor and Hector Bolitho (eds), *Later Letters of Lady Augusta Stanley* [Jonathan Cape 1929]

Bakewell, Michael, *Lewis Carroll* [Heinemann 1996]

Batey, Mavis, *Alice's Adventures in Oxford* [Pitkin Pictorials, 1994 reprint]

Battiscombe, Georgina, *Queen Alexandra* [Constable 1969]

Beatrice, HRH Princess (ed.), *In Napoleonic Days; the Private Diary of Augusta, Duchess of Saxe Coburg* [John Murray 1941]

Beneke, Amy M., *Cannes and its Surroundings* [George Allen & Unwin, nd]

Bennett, Daphne, *Queen Victoria's Children* [Gollancz 1980]

Benson, A.C. and Esher, Viscount (ed.), *The Letters of Queen Victoria; First Series, 1837–61* 3 vols [John Murray 1907]

Berger, Marie, *Understanding Haemophilia* [Ashgrove Press 1989]

Blunden, Margaret, *The Countess of Warwick* [Cassell 1967]

Bolitho, Hector (ed.), *The Prince Consort and His Brother* [Cobden-Sanderson 1933]

Bolitho, Hector, *Victoria, The Widow and Her Son* [Cobden-Sanderson 1934]

Bibliography

Bolitho, Hector (ed.), *Further Letters of Queen Victoria* [Thornton Butterworth 1938]

Bristowe, John Syer, M.D., *A Treatise on the Theory and Practice of Medicine* [Smith, Elder 1882]

Buckle, G.E. (ed.), *The Letters of Queen Victoria; Second Series 1862–85* 3 vols [John Murray 1926]

Buckle, G.E. (ed.), *The Letters of Queen Victoria; Third Series 1866–1901* 3 vols [John Murray 1930]

Bullock, Reverend Charles (ed.), *Talks with the People by Men of Mark: H.R.H. Prince Leopold, Duke of Albany* [Home Words Publishing Office, 1882]

Cartwright, Julia (ed.), *The Journals of Lady Knightley of Fawsley* [John Murray 1915]

Chaudhuri, Nirad C., *Scholar Extraordinary; the Life of Professor the Rt. Hon. Friedrich Max Müller, P.C.* [Chatto & Windus 1974]

Clark, Anne, *Lewis Carroll* [Dent 1979]

Clark, Anne, *The Real Alice* [Michael Joseph 1981]

Cohen, Morton N., *The Letters of Lewis Carroll* [Macmillan 1979]

Cohen, Morton N., *Lewis Carroll* [Macmillan 1995]

Collingwood, Stuart Dodgson, *The Life and Letters of Lewis Carroll* [T. Fisher Unwin 1898]

Cullen, Tom, *The Empress Brown; The Story of a Fatal Friendship* [Bodley Head 1969]

Dearden, James S., *The Professor: Arthur Severn's Memoir of John Ruskin* [Allen & Unwin 1967]

Dixon Hunt, John, *The Wider Sea; A Life of John Ruskin* [J.M. Dent & Sons, 1982]

Duff, David, *The Shy Princess* [Evans 1958]

Duff, David (ed.), *Victoria in the Highlands* [Frederick Muller 1968]

Dyson, Hope and Tennyson, Charles, *Dear and Honoured Lady* [Macmillan 1969]

Ellmann, Richard, *Oscar Wilde* [Hamish Hamilton 1987]

Evans, J. and Whitehouse, J.H. (eds), *The Diaries of John Ruskin* [Oxford 1959]

Fitzroy, Sir Almeric, *Memoirs* [Hutchinson 1925]

Frankland, Noble, *Witness of a Century* [Shepheard Walwyn 1993]

Fulford, Roger (ed.), *Dearest Child* [Evans 1964]

Fulford, Roger (ed.), *Dearest Mama* [Evans 1968]

Fulford, Roger (ed.), *Your Dear Letter* [Evans 1971]

Fulford, Roger (ed.), *Darling Child* [Evans 1976]

Fulford, Roger (ed.), *Beloved Mama* [Evans 1981]

Gernsheim, Helmut, *Lewis Carroll Photographer* [London, Max Parrish & Co Ltd 1949]

Gordon, Colin, *Beyond the Looking Glass; Reflections of Alice and her Family* [Hodder & Stoughton 1982]

Gower, Lord Ronald Sutherland Leveson, *My Reminiscences* 2 vols [Kegan, Paul, Tench & Co. 1883]

Gower, Lord Ronald Sutherland Leveson, *Old Diaries 1881–1901* [John Murray 1902]

Guedalla, Philip, *The Queen and Mr. Gladstone* [Hodder & Stoughton 1933]

Guedalla, Philip, *Idylls of the Queen* [Hodder & Stoughton 1937]

Hardie, Frank, *The Political Influence of Queen Victoria* [Oxford University Press 1935]

Hewison, Robert, *Ruskin and Oxford; The Art of Education* [Oxford, Clarendon Press 1996]

Hibbert, Christopher (ed.), *Queen Victoria in her Letters & Journals* [John Murray 1984]

Hobhouse, Hermione, *Prince Albert; His Life and Work* [Hamish Hamilton 1983]

Hopkins, Anthony, *Epilepsy: the Facts* [Oxford 1984]

Iltis, Hugo, 'Haemophilia: The Royal Disease and the British Royal Family' *The Journal of Heredity*, vol. 39, no. 4, pp. 113–16 [April 1948]

Jagow, Dr. Kurt (ed.), *Letters of the Prince Consort: 1831–1861* [John Murray 1938]

Jones, Steve, *In the Blood* [Harper Collins 1996]

Juta, René, *Cannes and the Hills* [Martin Secker 1924]

Lancelyn Green, Roger (ed.), *The Diaries of Lewis Carroll* 2 vols [Cassell 1953]

Langtry, Lillie (Lady de Bathe), *The Days I Knew* [Hutchinson 1925]

Lee, Sir Sydney, *King Edward VII: A Biography* [Macmillan 1925]

Legg, Dr. J. Wickham, *A Treatise on Haemophilia* [H.K. Lewis 1872]

Legge, Edward, *King George and the Royal Family* 2 vols [Grant Richards 1918]

Longford, Elizabeth, *Victoria R.I.* [Weidenfeld & Nicolson 1964]

Longford, Elizabeth, *Darling Loosy* [Weidenfeld & Nicolson 1991]

MacGeorge, A., *William Leighton Leitch* [Blackie & Son 1884]

Marie, Queen of Roumania, *The Story of My Life; vol. I* [Cassell 1934]

McClintock, Mary Howard, *The Queen Thanks Sir Howard* [John Murray 1945]

Millar, Delia, *The Victorian Watercolours and Drawings in the Collection of Her Majesty The Queen* 2 vols [Philip Wilson 1995]

Millar, Oliver, *The Victorian Pictures in the Collection of Her Majesty The Queen* 2 vols [Cambridge University Press 1992]

Milnes, Richard Monkton, *HRH Prince Leopold, Duke of Albany. In Memoriam: reprinted in Some Writings and Speeches of Richard Monkton Milnes, Lord Houghton* [Privately printed 1888]

Bibliography

Nicholls, David, *The Lost Prime Minister: A Life of Sir Charles Dilke* [The Hambledon Press 1995]

Noel, Gerard, *Princess Alice* [Constable, 1974]

Paget, Lady Walburga, *The Linings of Life* [Hurst & Blackett nd]

Ponsonby, Sir Frederick, *Sidelights on Queen Victoria* [Macmillan 1930]

Ponsonby, Sir Frederick, *Henry Ponsonby* [Macmillan 1942]

Ponsonby, Magdalen, *Mary Ponsonby: A Memoir, Some Letters and a Journal* [John Murray 1927]

Potts, D.M. and Potts, W.T.W., *Queen Victoria's Gene: Haemophilia and the Royal Family* [Stroud, Alan Sutton 1995]

Prochaska, Frank, *Royal Bounty; The Making of a Welfare Monarchy* [Yale University Press 1995]

Reid, Michaela, *Ask Sir James* [Viking 1987]

Ruskin, John, *Praeterita* 3 vols [G. Allen 1885–1900]

Sewell, Lieut. Col. J.P.C. (ed.), *Personal Letters of King Edward VII* [Hutchinson 1931]

Stamp, Robert M., *Royal Rebels* [Toronto & Oxford: Canada 1988]

Stirling, A.M.W. (ed.), *The Richmond Papers* [Heinemann 1926]

Stueart Erskine, Mrs (ed.), *20 Years at Court 1842–1862, from the writings of Lady Eleanor Stanley* [Nisbet & Co. 1916]

Thompson, H.L., *A Memoir of Henry George Liddell, DD* [Christ Church, 1900]

Tisdall, E.E.P., *Queen Victoria's John Brown* [Stanley Paul 1938]

Van der Kiste, John, *Queen Victoria's Children* [Gloucester, Alan Sutton 1986]

Wake, Jehanne, *Princess Louise* [Collins 1988]

Ware, J. Redding (ed.), *The Life and Speeches of His Royal Highness Prince Leopold* [Diprose & Bateman 1884]

Warner, Marina, *Queen Victoria's Sketchbook* [Macmillan 1979]

Whittle, Tyler, *Victoria and Albert at Home* [Routledge & Kegan Paul 1980]

Wilhelm II, Ex-Emperor of Germany, *My Early Life* [Methuen 1926]

Wilhelmina, HRH Princess of the Netherlands, *Lonely But Not Alone* [Hutchinson 1960]

Woodham-Smith, Cecil, *Queen Victoria* [Hamish Hamilton 1972]

York, HRH The Duchess of, with Benita Stoney, *Victoria and Albert: Life at Osborne House* [Weidenfeld & Nicolson 1991]

INDEX

L = Leopold, QV = Queen Victoria

Index

Index

Index